# The Social Control
# of Mental Illness

# STUDIES ON LAW AND SOCIAL CONTROL

DONALD BLACK *Series Editor*

Center for Criminal Justice
Harvard Law School
Cambridge, Massachusetts 02138

**P. H. Gulliver.** Disputes and Negotiations:
A Cross-Cultural Perspective

**Sandra B. Burman and Barbara E. Harrell-Bond**
(Editors). The Imposition of Law

**Cathie J. Witty.** Mediation and Society:
Conflict Management in Lebanon

**Francis G. Snyder.** Capitalism and Legal Change:
An African Transformation

**Allan V. Horwitz.** The Social Control of Mental Illness

**Richard L. Abel** (Editor). The Politics of Informal Justice, Vol. 1:
The American Experience; Vol. 2: Comparative Studies

In preparation

**William M. O'Barr,** Language Strategy in the Courtroom

# The Social Control of Mental Illness

ALLAN V. HORWITZ
Department of Sociology
Rutgers University
New Brunswick, New Jersey

**ACADEMIC PRESS**
*A Subsidiary of Harcourt Brace Jovanovich, Publishers*
New York   London   Toronto   Sydney   San Francisco

ACADEMIC PRESS, INC.
111 Fifth Avenue, New York, New York 10003

*United Kingdom Edition published by*
ACADEMIC PRESS, INC. (LONDON) LTD.
24/28 Oval Road, London NW1 7DX

Library of Congress Cataloging in Publication Data

Horwitz, Allan V.
    The social control of mental illness.

    (Studies on law and social control)
    Bibliography: p.
    Includes index.
    1. Psychology, Pathological--Social aspects.
2. Social psychiatry.  I. Title.  II. Series.
RC455.H67        362.2'042        81-20664
ISBN 0-12-356180-9                AACR2

PRINTED IN THE UNITED STATES OF AMERICA

82 83 84 85     9 8 7 6 5 4 3 2 1

*To my parents*

# Contents

PREFACE    ix
ACKNOWLEDGMENTS    xi

## 1

## Introduction    1

*The Sociological Study of Mental Illness    1*
*The Plan of the Book    10*

## 2

## The Meaning of Mental Illness    13

*Mental Illness as Incomprehensibility    14*
*Mental Illness as Culturally Relative or Universal    21*
*✹ Mental Illness, Disease, and Deviance    25*
*Conclusion    29*

## 3

## The Recognition of Mental Illness    31

*Relational Distance and the Recognition of Mental Illness    35*
*Cultural Distance and the Recognition of Mental Illness    47*
*Psychiatric Professionals and the Recognition of Mental Illness    52*
*Conclusion    57*

# Contents

## 4

## The Labelers of Mental Illness    61

Social Class and the Labeling of Mental Illness    63
Culture and the Labeling of Mental Illness    70
Gender and the Labeling of Mental Illness    75
Social Evolution and the Labeling of Mental Illness    78
Conclusion    83

## 5

## The Reaction to Mental Illness    85

Social Variation in the Reaction to Mental Illness    89
Individual Variation in the Reaction to Mental Illness    109
Conclusion    118

## 6

## The Nature of Therapeutic Social Control    121

The Elements of Therapeutic Social Control    121
The Application of Therapeutic Social Control    128
Mental Illness and Therapeutic Social Control    138
Conclusion    140

## 7

## Communal Styles of Therapeutic Social Control    143

Types of Societies and Types of Therapies    146
Therapeutic Social Control in Tribal Groups    148
Therapeutic Social Control in Other Communal Groups    158
Conclusion    165

## 8

## Individualistic Styles of Therapeutic Social Control    167

The Development of Individualistic Psychotherapy    168
Psychotherapy after Psychoanalysis    176
Modern Communal Therapies    180
Conclusion    182

REFERENCES    187
SUBJECT INDEX    205

# Preface

Every society, regardless of time or place, has considered some of its members to be mentally ill. These people, who behave in ways that often seem incomprehensible to others, are found in all social groups. More striking than the universal presence of individuals who are labeled mentally ill is the great diversity in the social response to mental illness. Depending on the cultural and historical setting, symptoms of mental illness have been interpreted as signs of prophetic insight, sin, or disease. The recognition that people are mentally ill varies by the cultural characteristics and social roles of both the affected individuals and those who label the behavior. Once labeled as mentally ill, individuals may receive sympathy, be ignored, or enter institutions that isolate them from society. Their treatment may explore the depths of their personalities, mobilize the entire community to participate in healing ceremonies, or consist solely of the injection of powerful drugs.

The great variation in the societal reaction to mental illness presents a challenge to the sociologist. From the multitude of varying interpretations of mental illness, range of measures used to restrain the mentally ill, and variety of treatments aimed at normalizing mental symptoms, are any socially structured patterns discernible? The goal of a theory of the social control of mental illness is to seek the patterned variation in the social response to mental illness, order this variation, and explain why it occurs. Why, for example, are unusual behaviors interpreted as signs of mental illness in certain settings but as indications of sin, laziness, or divine inspiration in other settings? Under what circumstances are the mentally ill expelled from the community or included within it? Why are some patients provided with long, elaborate, and expensive treatments for mental distress that explore the depths of their personalities, whereas others are kept in custodial care or provided only with medication? The core concern of a theory of social control is to detect the patterns that underlie the processes of recognition, response, and treatment of mental illness.

This book synthesizes a number of disparate works that have examined various aspects of the social response to the mentally ill. Numerous scholars—including sociologists, anthropologists, and historians—have explored how different social groups respond to mental illness. Studies of the societal reaction to mental illness have been made in contexts as diverse as the highlands of New Guinea, medieval Great Britain, East African tribal societies, or contemporary China. Yet no work has attempted to examine the range of social reactions to mental illness, to detect the similarities and differences in response styles in various social settings, and to uncover the factors that predict the variation in the social control of mental illness. In this book, I attempt to systematize various pieces of research about the social control of mental illness in a wide variety of times and places, and begin to provide a theoretical ordering of research about this topic.

# Acknowledgments

Many people have contributed in various ways to this book. I am especially grateful to Donald Black for first stimulating my interest in the study of social control, for suggesting that I undertake this project, and for encouraging and assisting me in every stage of writing. A number of colleagues also read earlier drafts of the manuscript. In particular, I thank Paul Cleary, Peter Conrad, Gerald Grob, David Mechanic, Michael Radelet, Robert Scott, and Carol Warren for their comments on various chapters. All have suggested numerous revisions, and I am sure that all would suggest many more in the completed version. I am also indebted as well to all the researchers who carried out the studies on which this book draws. In addition, my editors at Academic Press have provided invaluable support throughout the writing and production of this book. I also thank Joy Nakashima for typing the manuscript. Finally, my wife, Colleen, helped me in ways too numerous to acknowledge.

# 1

## Introduction

### The Sociological Study of Mental Illness

The study of social control has long been a central part of sociological research. Social control was one of the major concepts in the work of early American sociologists such as Ross (1901), Cooley (1909), and Thomas (1923). For them, social control had a broad meaning that referred to all processes social groups use to foster and maintain order and consensus. This definition encompassed all phenomena that serve to secure conformity to the normative order of society, including socialization, education, and media exposure.

More recent work has taken a narrower view of the appropriate subject matter for the field of social control. The concept of social control has come to refer to the response made to deviant behavior (Parsons, 1951; Gibbs, 1972a). Only processes that specifically respond to norm violations—not any process that maintains social conformity—are considered to be instances of social control. From this viewpoint, the study of social control encompasses both formal institutions and agents of control such as courts, judges, police, mental hospitals, and psychiatrists, and informal reactors to deviants such as their family and friends and community members. In addition, social control refers not only to negative sanctions against deviants such as coercion or isolation but also to positive attempts to promote conformity such as rehabilitation or conciliation

(Black, 1976:5). Hence, a voluntary entry into outpatient psychotherapy is as much one style of social control as an involuntary commitment to a mental hospital is another style. As the term is used in this work, *social control* encompasses the entire range of reactions to behavior that is defined as mental illness and to people who are defined as mentally ill.

The study of the social control of mental illness has attracted the attention of many sociologists. Research about the societal reaction to mental illness in the United States especially flourished during the 1950s and early 1960s. During this period, researchers examined many aspects of the societal reaction to the mentally ill, including the recognition and definition of mentally ill individuals (Clausen and Yarrow, 1955); the reaction of families to their mentally ill members (Sampson *et al.*, 1964); the influence of social class on the recognition and treatment of the mentally ill (Hollingshead and Redlich, 1958; Myers and Roberts, 1959); the community response to the mentally ill (Cumming and Cumming, 1957; Mechanic, 1962); and the treatment of the mentally ill within formal institutions (Stanton and Schwartz, 1954; Goffman, 1961). While there was little concern with developing any general theory of social control at this time, the quality of the empirical data generated by these studies has not been surpassed.

The kinds of questions raised in the studies just mentioned are central to the study of the social control of mental illness. These include:

1. Under what conditions is mental illness, rather than some other label, used to categorize behavior?
2. When will observers label or deny that someone is mentally ill?
3. How does the attribution of mental illness vary by the social class, ethnic identification, gender, and other characteristics of the labeler and labelee?
4. After people have been labeled mentally ill, what factors predict the type of social response accorded them?
5. What circumstances are associated with the variation in the amount and type of psychotherapy provided to the mentally ill?

Adequate answers to these questions cannot be obtained solely through contemporary studies conducted in the United States but also require an examination of the response to the mentally ill in a variety of cultural contexts and historical periods. In addition, a theory of the social control of mental illness cannot be developed in isolation from studies of other types of social control but must take into account the similarities and differences in the response to mental illness and the response to other types of undesirable behaviors. How the recognition of, response to, and treatment of the mentally ill varies across different individuals, groups, and societies, and how this variation is related to the social response to other types of deviation are the core questions in the study of the social control of mental illness.

The concerns of research about the social control of mental illness contrast with the great bulk of studies of mental illness carried out by sociologists and other researchers. Over the past 15 years, most of this work has not dealt with the societal reaction to mental illness but with the etiology and development of mental symptoms. Two major perspectives, the psychiatric perspective and the labeling perspective, have dominated theory and research in the sociology of mental illness. I will briefly review the major tenets of each of these viewpoints and show how the concerns of the social control perspective taken here diverge from both the psychiatric and the labeling perspectives.

### THE PSYCHIATRIC PERSPECTIVE

Most students of mental illness have been interested in why some individuals but not others develop symptoms of mental illness. This question has preoccupied most researchers who have studied mental illness. Adherents of the psychiatric perspective believe that the question can best be answered by regarding mental illness as a disease manifesting the same properties as most physical illnesses (R. L. Spitzer, 1976; Wing, 1978). In their view, the concept of mental illness refers to various pathological symptoms displayed by the affected individuals. This concept is used for three major purposes: to order the symptoms subsumed in the category of mental illness, to develop laws that explain and predict the occurrence of symptoms, and to control these symptoms.

The ordering function of the concept of mental illness found in the psychiatric perspective groups various symptoms into underlying entities such as schizophrenia, affective disorders, or hysteria. Once symptoms have been organized into various diagnostic categories, explanatory and predictive laws can be developed that state the conditions under which past instances of symptoms in these categories developed and future cases will emerge. The classification of individuals in a particular diagnostic category leads to a search for common background factors associated with the development of their symptoms. These factors need not stem from any particular source, whether intraindividual or environmental. Rather, causal factors may be sought in the genetic, biochemical, psychological, or social environments. Finally, practitioners who use the psychiatric perspective strive to control the symptoms of the affected individual through treatments such as medication or psychotherapy, or an alteration in the social environment. In each of these aspects, the focus of concern is on the individual who is afflicted with the mental illness, not on the persons who respond to the affected individual's condition.

Many sociologists have adopted the psychiatric perspective toward mental illness. They have contributed to the ordering of the concept of mental illness by developing instruments that detect psychopathology in community populations (e.g., Langner, 1962); to the explanatory and predictive functions by relating factors such as social class (e.g., Kessler and Cleary, 1980), race (e.g., Warheit *et al.*, 1975), marital status (e.g., Pearlin and Johnson, 1977), and sex (e.g., Gove and Tudor, 1973) to the development of mental symptoms; and to the control function by examining how social resources can be mobilized to alleviate mental symptoms (e.g., Mechanic, 1980).

The social control approach to mental illness found in this book does not conflict with a psychiatric approach but addresses different types of questions. It is concerned with explaining the reaction of observers to symptoms of mental illness, not with understanding why these symptoms develop. The concept of mental illness for the study of social control has a different referent than for the study of the etiology of mental symptoms. For a social control perspective, *mental illness* refers to a category that observers use to classify particular individuals, not to the symptoms these individuals display. The concept of mental illness is located in observers' categories rather than in actors' symptoms. For example, Scheff (1966a:33–34) conceptualizes mental illness as "residual rule-breaking":

> The culture of the group provides a vocabulary of terms for categorizing many norm violations: crime, perversion, drunkenness and bad manners are familiar examples. Each of these terms is derived from the type of norm broken, and ultimately from the type of behavior involved. After exhausting these categories, however, there is always a residue of the most diverse kinds of violations, for which the culture provides no explicit label. . . . These violations may be lumped together into a residual category: witchcraft, spirit possession, or, in our own society, mental illness. In this discussion, the diverse kinds of rule-breaking for which our society provides no explicit label, and which, therefore, sometimes lead to the labeling of the violator as mentally ill, will be considered to be technically *residual rule-breaking*. [This quotation and following quotations from Scheff (1966a) are reprinted by permission. Copyright © 1966 by Thomas J. Scheff. Reprinted with permission from *Being Mentally Ill: A Sociological Theory* (New York: Aldine Publishing Company).]

Here, residual rule-breaking refers to a category observers use to identify rule-violating behavior when they are unable to explain this behavior through other culturally recognizable labels. Mental illness is a social label observers attach to certain behaviors, not the symptoms that individuals display.

## 1. Introduction

The purpose of a concept of mental illness located in the rules, conventions, and understandings that are employed by labelers is different from one that refers to individuals' symptoms. The phenomena that are ordered are the different types of conceptualizations observers use to interpret mental illness. The kinds of laws developed explain and predict the conditions under which observers label and respond to individuals as mentally ill. Finally, because a theory of social control is not concerned with symptoms of individuals, the control or treatment purpose is largely irrelevant, although it is possible that someone might want to change the behavior of the labelers of mental illness. A theory of social control predicts the variation in the societal reaction to mental illness, not in the development of mental symptoms.

Answers to the questions critical to a theory of social control about the recognition of, response to, and treatment of mental illness do not require that any assumptions be made regarding the nature of mental illness as a condition of individuals. A social control perspective predicts the behavior of the labelers of mental illness, not of the individuals who are labeled mentally ill. Hence, it is not contradictory to or mutually exclusive with the psychiatric perspective but addresses a different set of questions. When the study of social control is regarded as a process distinct from the study of mental symptoms, many of the controversies and confusions generated by the development of the labeling theory of mental illness can be avoided.

### THE LABELING PERSPECTIVE

The second major paradigm of mental illness that has guided theory and research in sociological studies over the past 15 years is the labeling perspective. The major presentation of labeling theory is found in Thomas Scheff's *Being Mentally Ill* (1966a). Scheff developed this theory as an explicit contrast to the psychiatric perspective. According to Scheff, mental symptoms, which he calls residual rule-breaking, are extremely widespread in the population; most persons who display these symptoms are never categorized and treated as mentally ill. Because psychiatric symptoms are presumed to be so widespread, labeling theorists are unconcerned with why some persons develop them in the first place, and they assume that a variety of genetic, family, or situational factors may account for their emergence. Instead, they focus on why certain individuals but not others are selected to take on the social role of the mental patient.

Labeling theory predicts that the social response to individuals, and not their psychiatric conditions, is the major determinant of whether they

5

will be socially identified as mentally ill. It posits that once persons are officially recognized and labeled mentally ill by psychiatric personnel, they are likely to assume the mentally ill role, which becomes the basis for other persons' response to them. Individuals are likely to take on the mentally sick role to conform to the stereotyped expectations that treatment personnel and family members have of how a mentally disturbed person is supposed to behave. The factors that the psychiatric perspective stresses as leading to the development of primary symptoms of illness are presumed to be relatively unimportant determinants of who assumes the mentally ill role. Instead, the social response to individuals, shaped by the official labeling of them as mentally ill, is the major reason why they take on the role of chronic mental patients.

The controversy between advocates of the labeling and of the psychiatric perspectives has generated more attention than any other issue in the sociology of mental illness over the past 15 years (Gove, 1970; Scheff, 1974; Gove, 1975). There have been a number of central issues in this controversy. The first is whether mental illness is best conceptualized as a type of illness or as a label applied to certain types of deviant behavior. Upholders of the psychiatric perspective claim that mental illness is a genuine type of illness (e.g., Ausebel, 1961; R. L. Spitzer, 1976; Wing, 1978). In their view, the symptoms of mental illness are manifestations of an underlying disease process. They advocate that the mentally ill, like the physically ill, should be treated by medically informed personnel and not held accountable for their illnesses.

In contrast, labeling theorists argue that mental illness is not an objective disease process but a subjective label applied to certain kinds of deviant behavior (Szasz, 1961; Scheff, 1966a; 1975). In their view, people who are labeled mentally ill violate cultural standards of appropriate behavior, which vary from time to time and from place to place, unlike the physically ill, who depart from universal standards of appropriate organic functioning. Mental illness is a negative social evaluation of certain types of norm-violating behavior rather than a value-free disease process.

Unlike the labeling theorists, I do not contrast a view of mental illness as social deviance with a view of mental illness as a genuine type of illness. The psychiatric and labeling perspectives present concepts of mental illness that are neither true nor false but only more or less useful for different purposes. If the conception of mental illness as an illness allows for the successful ordering, explanation, and control of symptoms, the psychiatric perspective is a useful one; if not, it should be modified or replaced. Whatever the usefulness of a psychiatric conceptualization of mental illness may be, however, the notion of mental illness as a cultural label neither conflicts with nor provides an alternative to the illness concept, but is posed at a different level of analysis. A social control perspective explains the variation in observers' categorizations of mental illness, not the variation in actors' symptoms. For this purpose, viewing mental illness as social deviance or as residual rule-breaking is valuable but does not compete with a psychiatric view of mental illness. While this work adopts a concept of mental illness grounded in observers' categorizations that is congruent with labeling theory, this concept does not vie with a psychiatric concept but is appropriate for addressing a different set of issues than those that concern users of the psychiatric perspective.

A second issue in the controversy between adherents of the psychiatric and labeling perspectives has been whether psychiatric symptoms or social contingencies best can predict who will take on the mentally ill role. In his initial formulation of labeling theory, Scheff (1966a) considered that the presence of mental symptoms provided explanations competing with the presence of social contingencies in predicting the application of social control:

> Other things being equal, the severity of the societal reaction is a function of, first, the degree, amount and visibility of the rule-breaking; second, the power of the rule-breaker and the social distance between him and the agents of social control; and finally, the tolerance level of the community, and the availability in the culture of the community of alternative nondeviant roles. Particularly crucial for future research is the importance of the first two contingencies (the amount and degree of rule-breaking), which are characteristic of the rule-breaker, relative to the remaining five contingencies, which are characteristics of the social system [Scheff, 1966a: 96–97].

In this view, a theory of social control is only viable as long as social factors independent of psychiatric symptoms predict the labeling of mental illness. Similarly, Gove (1975), a proponent of the psychiatric perspective, asserts that the central research question in the study of the societal reaction to mental illness is whether the psychiatric condition of the individual or various social factors best predict the application of mental illness labels. When observers' labeling practices are reflective of actors' behavior, the psychiatric perspective is supported. When, on the other hand, social contingencies best predict the labeling of mental illness, the labeling view is upheld.

If the question of interest is whether people who are labeled mentally ill also display symptoms subsumed in the psychiatric concept of mental illness, or whether the presence of these symptoms or other contingencies best predict the entry into psychiatric treatment, viewing mental symptoms and social contingencies as competing independent variables may be appropriate. If, however, the goal of research is to predict variation in the societal reaction to the mentally ill, it is more fruitful to hold constant the psychiatric conditions of individuals than to use their conditions as independent variables. Indeed, when mental illness is conceptualized as a label observers apply to behavior, rather than as a condition of individuals, those who are labeled mentally ill must in every case have been perceived as mentally ill. The relevant research question is how the responses of labelers to these conditions vary by their own and by the labeled individuals' social characteristics, not whether symptoms or social factors best predict their reaction. This work examines the variation in the social response to mental illness as a topic in its own right, not as a competing perspective to the psychiatric study of mental illness.

A third issue of controversy between users of the labeling and the psychiatric perspectives centers around the determinants of decision-making processes in psychiatric control agencies (see the summaries in Scheff, 1974; Krohn and Akers, 1977). The central question in this research has been whether psychiatric professionals base their diagnostic and treatment decisions on the psychiatric condition of the individual, as the psychiatric perspective claims, or on extrapsychiatric variables such as social characteristics of patients, as the labeling perspective asserts. For example, a number of labeling studies demonstrate that the commitment of the mentally ill is often carried out in a routine fashion with little detailed examination of patients' mental conditions (Scheff, 1964; Miller and Schwartz, 1966; Wenger and Fletcher, 1969). Or, Rosenhan (1973) demonstrates that psychiatrists easily can be induced to diagnose "sane" persons as "insane." When patient characteristics actually provide the basis for diagnostic and treatment decisions, labels of mental illness have been appropriately applied and the psychiatric perspective supported; when they do not, psychiatric decision making is deficient and the labeling perspective upheld.

The major value of this type of research is to evaluate the effectiveness of psychiatric decision making. It can help answer the important social policy question of whether psychiatric professionals take appropriate care in their response to the mentally ill or make mistaken diagnoses and treatment decisions. The concern for the effectiveness of social control agents, however, is not a substitute for a theory of social control. A theory of social control does not assess the accuracy of labeling practices, but examines the actual application of mental illness labels to individuals. The concern here will not be with the appropriateness or effectiveness of social control practices but with explaining and predicting these practices.

A related controversy between advocates of the psychiatric and labeling perspectives concerns the consequences of being labeled mentally ill. The psychiatric view assumes that labels of mental illness can be helpful because they provide names for individuals' problems, enable them to receive appropriate medical attention and care, and release them from responsibility for their condition (e.g., Siegler and Osmund, 1974; R. L. Spitzer, 1976; Wing, 1978). Labeling theorists, on the other hand, view the labeling of mental illness as a stigmatizing and degrading process that leads to the isolation and rejection of the labeled individual and to the exacerbation of the original symptoms (e.g., Scheff, 1966a; Rosenhan, 1973). In this book, by contrast, I am not concerned with whether the consequences of being labeled mentally ill are helpful or harmful, but only with the factors that evoke these labels.

The final difference between the social control perspective taken here and both the psychiatric and labeling perspectives is in the use of social control as a dependent variable. The psychiatric perspective is relatively unconcerned with social control processes and neither uses these processes to explain the development and course of mental symptoms nor makes them problematic in their own right. By contrast, labeling theory uses social control as an independent variable that predicts the stabilization of psychiatric symptoms. It considers the societal reaction to mental illness as the major factor producing the stabilization of symptoms in a mentally ill role. Whatever the validity of this view, it is one concerned with the etiology of mental illness, not with the application of social control. What is explained by labeling theory is the variation in the assumption of the role of a mentally ill person, not the variation in the societal reaction to the individual. By contrast, I will not discuss the effect of social control on labeled individuals but only the type of social response accorded them.

This work does not deal with the controversies that have dominated the sociology of mental illness for many years; it presents the study of social control as a topic in its own right. A social control perspective grounds mental illness in the categorizations of observers rather than in the personalities of actors. What is explained is the variation in the labels observers apply to rule-breaking behavior and in the social response to individuals who have been labeled for such behavior. The contribution such a view makes is not to a theory of mental illness but to a theory of social control. While this type of study does not resolve any of the controversies between the psychiatric and labeling perspectives, it does allow for the examination of social control unencumbered by the disputes that have plagued much recent work in the sociology of mental illness.

## The Plan of the Book

The chapters that follow examine selected aspects of the societal reaction to mental illness. They are based upon data gathered from a variety of sociological, anthropological, and historical sources. The bulk of empirical studies concerning the social control of mental illness have been conducted by sociologists in the contemporary United States. These studies examine both formal agents and agencies of social control such as psychiatrists, outpatient clinics, and mental hospitals, and informal responders to the mentally ill such as family, friends, and community members. In addition to sociological studies, a number of anthropological works view the response to the mentally ill in a variety of cross-cultural settings. Typically, anthropological studies focus on the social control of mental illness within one tribal group, and present detailed descriptive material from the particular context. While the quality of the empirical material in these studies is generally very high, they usually contain little theoretical or comparative analysis of the data that is generated. Finally, a number of historical works present detailed and carefully documented analyses of the response to the mentally ill in prior eras. Because of the limits of data sources, these studies usually examine the response of official agencies of social control, especially mental hospitals, and rarely provide information about the community response to mental illness. Like most anthropological writings, the work of historians is usually more descriptive than theoretical or comparative.

Attempts to generalize from this disparate collection of material are perilous. Sociologists, anthropologists, and historians generally have conducted their research in isolation from each other and each discipline shows little awareness of the findings of other disciplines. Different studies use different research techniques, analytic frameworks, and methods of analysis. The settings and types of research are highly diverse and the quality of data generated is widely variable. For some topics the available evidence is often limited to contemporary Western societies and, in particular, to the contemporary United States. For all these reasons, it is difficult to incorporate these diverse studies into the same framework of analysis. Despite these difficulties, however, it is possible to make a number of generalizations from the available material.

In this book, I attempt to provide some theoretical ordering to the various case studies about the social control of mental illness. The model for my approach is found in Donald Black's *The Behavior of Law* (1976). Black takes a number of selected aspects of society—stratification, morphology, culture, organization, and informal social control—and uses them to predict variation in the quantity of legal social control found in any setting. He constructs a number of two-variable propositions that relate each aspect of social life to the presence of law. These propositions predict and explain the variation in the quantity of law in a wide variety of social and cultural settings.

I follow Black in constructing several highly abstract two-variable propositions that order the empirical material regarding the social control of mental illness. The independent variables are several social and cultural characteristics of individuals and of groups. The dependent variables are selected processes associated with the recognition of, response to, and treatment of mental illness. Any theory must limit the number of variables it contains to those relevant to the purpose at hand. The aim here is to use social and cultural factors to predict variation in the response to mental illness. Therefore, variables that may have predictive power, but are not relevant to my theoretical purpose, such as the personalities of observers and actors or the nature of mental symptoms, are rarely discussed.

The study of the social control of mental illness is one part of the examination of how societies respond to undesirable behaviors of all types. Eventually, the kinds of propositions that order the response to the mentally ill should be deducible from propositions about the operation of social control systems in general. While the development of such a general theory of social control is unrealistic at this time, the construction of even the simplest two-variable propositions is a necessary first step toward this end. While the approach taken in this book considerably oversimplifies the actual complexities in the reaction to the mentally ill, it is a starting point for the eventual development of more complex theoretical systems.

The chapters that follow examine selected aspects of the societal reaction to mental illness. Chapter 2 considers the nature of the cultural label of mental illness and the kinds of perceptions that evoke the use of this label. In particular, it examines the similarities in the categorizations of mental illness in a wide variety of times and places and the differences of mental illness labels from labels of physical illness and of deviant and criminal behavior. Chapters 3 and 4 deal with the conditions under which people are labeled mentally ill. The first of these chapters considers how the social and cultural distance between labelers and persons who are labeled mentally ill predicts whether or not someone will be

11

recognized as mentally ill, and how the lay labeling of mental illness differs from professional labeling. Chapter 4 examines how individuals with varying social and cultural characteristics are more or less likely to apply labels of mental illness. Chapter 5 looks at the social response to individuals after they have been labeled mentally ill. In particular, it addresses the question of whether labeled individuals will be excluded from or maintained within social groups. The next three chapters are concerned with the nature of psychotherapeutic social control. Chapter 6 outlines the nature of psychotherapy as a system of social control and the conditions under which a psychotherapeutic response is made to distressed individuals. Chapters 7 and 8 examine how the major styles of psychotherapeutic systems reflect the nature of the society and culture in which they arise. Chapter 7 shows how psychotherapy in tightly knit communal groups denigrates individual identity and reinforces community solidarity. Chapter 8, the final chapter, examines the emergence of individualistic psychotherapies in modern Western societies and shows how the major elements of these therapies reflect the social and cultural matrix of certain groups in these societies. Together, these chapters provide a beginning for a theory of the social control of mental illness.

# 2

## The Meaning of Mental Illness

In every society, certain people are considered "mad," "crazy," or "insane." Their behavior has been so unusual that observers believe it lies beyond the boundaries of sanity. One task of a theory of social control is to predict and explain the conditions under which people apply labels of mental illness and their response to those who are labeled mentally ill. Before examining these conditions, however, it is helpful to understand what sorts of behaviors people see when they use the label of "mental illness." I approach mental illness as it appears to persons who respond to the affected individual. My concern is with the indigenous labeling practices of ordinary men and women, not with the clinical conditions psychiatric professionals might consider as mentally ill. Hence, this chapter is not a contribution to the clinical study of mental illness but to the study of lay perceptions of mental illness.

Several issues regarding the lay response to mental illness are discussed in this chapter. What perceived features of behavior lead observers to apply labels of mental illness? How do these features differ from phenomena that are considered to indicate signs of physical disease or of criminal behavior? Is there any common referent to the label of mental illness out of the wide variety of particular behaviors that are considered instances of mental illness in various times and places? Answers to these questions are preliminary to the examination of the social variation in the recognition of mental illness and the treatment of individuals who are labeled mentally ill.

A label as diffuse as mental illness is impossible to define with precision. In various times and places an extremely diverse range of symptoms have been judged indicative of mental illness. Nevertheless, there are some common elements in observers' perceptions of what constitutes mental illness. Regardless of the particular cultural or historical setting, when observers perceive that behaviors lack purpose, intent, or reason, they are likely to apply labels of "madness," "craziness," or "insanity." I call this the *incomprehensible* aspect of mental illness labels. While the boundaries of this core category are vague and there are many borderline cases, there does seem to be something central to the mental illness label in all societies.

To establish that there are certain universal elements in perceptions of mental illness does not imply that other kinds of judgments do not also enter the labeling process or that there is not a tremendous diversity in the application of mental illness labels. That certain perceptions of incomprehensible behavior always lead to labels of mental illness does not imply the converse, that labels of mental illness are only applied when behavior appears incomprehensible. For example, in certain cultures psychosomatic disturbances, depression, or anxiety may lack the appearance of incomprehensibility yet still be labeled mental illness. While incomprehensible behaviors may be universally judged as signs of mental illness, other behaviors may be labeled mentally ill by some groups but not others. While the core meaning of the label of mental illness seems universal, the boundaries of this label are culturally specific. It is helpful, however, to first establish the invariant features of mental illness labels in a wide range of times and places, before examining the variability in the labeling of mental illness.

The recognition of mental illness by ordinary men and women is a central part in the study of the social control of mental illness. The initial recognition that someone is mentally ill is usually made by community members, not by psychiatric professionals. An examination of what laypersons perceive when they apply labels of mental illness is the first stage in the social response to the mentally ill.

## Mental Illness as Incomprehensibility

The anthropological and historical literatures indicate that a wide variety of particular behaviors have been considered at some point in time as indicative of mental illness. In medieval England, for example, symptoms associated with *wood*, or madness, included: "staring, crying and roaring, prancing about, flight, depression, extreme dejection from love, and raving like a wild beast or a mad dog [Clarke, 1975:73]." Or, among the Australian aborigines:

> The Pela word *wambaba* and the pidgin word 'crank' are used to mean mad or crazy. The Kalumburu idea of 'crank' is an excited or assaultive individual who talks strangely, swears a lot, forgets his manners, opens his bowels where people live, knocks over his water holder, or runs off in fright to the bush. He behaves in a highly disturbed and incomprehensible way [Cawte, 1974:56–57].

Similarly, among the Eskimo, *nuthkavihak* means "crazy" and refers to

> a complex pattern of behavioral processes of which the hallmark is conceived to be that something inside the person—the soul, the spirit, the mind—is out of order. Descriptions of how *nuthkavihak* is manifested include such phenomena as talking to oneself, screaming at someone who does not exist, believing that a child or husband was murdered by witchcraft when nobody else believes it, believing oneself to be an animal, refusing to eat for fear eating will kill one, refusing to talk, running away, getting lost, hiding in strange places, making strange grimaces, drinking urine, becoming strong and violent, killing dogs, and threatening people [Murphy, 1976:1022].

What unites all of these various manifestations of behavior is that they seem to fall outside the boundaries of comprehensible social action.

The essential quality of lay perceptions of mental illness is succinctly stated in a study of mental illness labeling among East African tribesmen:

> There is one essential feature of African psychosis. Respondent after respondent qualifies his description of a psychotic behavior by saying "without reason." That is, murder as such is not psychotic—only murder *without some good reason is psychotic.* The same thing is true of every other behavior cited [Edgerton, 1966:419; italics in original].

The distinctive quality of perceptions of mental illness is that some behavior appears to be "without reason," that is, it seems to lack any comprehensible motivation. For example, murders that seem to stem from recognizable motives such as jealousy, quarrels, or blood feuds typically are not viewed as signs of mental illness. On the other hand, someone who randomly kills strangers usually does not fit within any socially recognizable category of murder. Because his or her intentions cannot be comprehended, the individual is likely to be viewed as mad.

The special feature of mental illness labels is tried to the essential qualities of social action in general. The comprehension of social action

15

involves understanding the motives, intentions, and thoughts of the actors, or the customs or rules that their behavior follows (Weber, 1922/ 1964). Any piece of behavior is made intelligible either by attributing a socially recognizable motivation to the behavior (e.g., he murdered his wife out of jealousy) or by locating the action as an instance of a typical social category (e.g., that man is chopping wood). When observers assume that actors know what they are doing and are guided by rules in their behavior, social behavior appears to be meaningful (Blum and McHugh, 1971). It is when observers cannot find meaning or comprehensibility in behavior that they are likely to apply labels of mental illness.

Because the attribution of meaning to social action is a fundamental requirement of any social interaction, it is not surprising that there is a universal aspect to the labeling of mental illness. No interaction can occur unless each participant can understand what the other is doing. Therefore, all societies need some category to designate behaviors that fall outside the boundaries of comprehensibility. The notion of mental illness is rooted in the basic requisites of social interaction: that persons be able to find each other's behavior mutually comprehensible. Labels of mental illness are applied to behavior when the *categories observers use to comprehend behavior do not yield any socially understandable reasons for the behavior.*

I call the failure of observers to find any meaningful purpose in behavior *incomprehensibility* and consider it the essential quality of the core behaviors that are labeled mentally ill (see also Scheff, 1966a:33–34; Coulter, 1973). To say that incomprehensibility is the major criterion observers use to label mental illness is not merely to say that they cannot understand or empathize with the motives of the mentally ill or that they cannot "take the role of the other." Observers may not understand the work of a nuclear physicist or empathize with the political terrorist. Similarly, a visitor to a foreign country may not comprehend much of the social action that occurs there. In these cases, however, observers assume that the actors have some purpose in mind. In contrast, behaviors that appear to them to be mentally disordered seem beyond the possibility of understanding and the actors themselves seem incapable of providing a socially plausible reason for the behavior. Observers are unable to attribute any motive whatever to the behavior.

The mad not only depart from reasonable behavior but do not seem to know that they are acting in a socially unrecognizable manner. This aspect of incomprehensibility seems implied in the definition of mental illness found in the *Encyclopedie* compiled by the Enlightenment philosophers: "To depart from reason with confidence and in the firm conviction that one is following it—that, it seems to me is what is called mad [quoted in Foucault, 1965:104]." Because mentally ill actors do not appear to know what they are doing, there are no socially recognizable motivations that observers can grasp in their behavior. Indeed, if observers could infer a plausible motive for the behavior, they would no longer have common sense grounds for considering the behavior to be an instance of mental illness (Coulter, 1973). Observers attribute labels of mental illness when the rules, conventions, and understandings they use to interpret behavior fail to find any intelligible motivation behind an action.

The recognition of mental illness is grounded in the common-sense knowledge shared by the members of any society. The rules, conventions, and understandings that provide comprehensibility to social action are not an aspect of specialized professional knowledge, but are contained in lay knowledge of social interaction. Socrates, for example, noted that the Greeks of his time

> do not call those mad who err in matters that lie outside the knowledge of ordinary people: madness is the name they give to errors in matters of common knowledge. For instance, if a man imagines himself to be so tall as to stoop when he goes through the gateways in the Wall, or so strong as to try to lift houses or to perform any other feat that everybody knows to be impossible, they say he's mad. They don't think a slight error implies madness, but just as they call strong desire love, so they name a great delusion madness [quoted in Rosen, 1968:94].

Because the knowledge involved in the recognition of mental illness stems from the knowledge of ordinary people that is taken for granted, the core cases of mental illness are easily recognizable from grossly inappropriate behaviors. The recognition of the *loco*, or insane person, among slum dwellers in Puerto Rico, illustrates this quality of mental illness labeling:

> [*Locos*] meander without purpose, sometimes quickening their pace as if a tormenting spirit were pursuing them. In convivial groups of persons who are joking light heartedly, the *loco* may appear to be in deep introspective thought. At other times, he may laugh hilariously when nothing funny has occurred. *Locos* respond to the "ant hill in their minds" or the "roller skate in their brains" rather than to the surroundings. [Rogler and Hollingshead, 1965:217. This quotation and following quotations from Rogler and Hollingshead (1965) are from *Trapped: Families and Schizophrenia* by Lloyd H. Rogler and August B. Hollingshead. Copyright © 1965 by John Wiley & Sons, Inc. Reprinted by permission of John Wiley & Sons, Inc.]

Similarly, among the Zapotec Indians of Mexico, being crazy "had something to do with the soul and was symptomized by agitated motor behavior, ataraxia, violent purposeless movement and the inability to talk in ways that people could readily understand [Selby, 1974:41]." In each of these illustrations, mental illness is recognized when behaviors are so inappropriate that they defy explanation within any comprehensible category of behavior.

The examples presented thus far indicate that in a wide variety of times and places, behaviors that appear incomprehensible are labeled as mental illness. That all societies share a common view of mental illness need not stem from the existence of certain universal symptoms of psychosis (cf. Kiev, 1972). The particular behaviors that are perceived when labels of madness are applied are so diverse that they cannot be encompassed within common behavioral categories. Instead, the universal nature of categories of mental illness may result from the requisites of all social interaction. Whenever and wherever social interaction occurs, people must be able to find each other's behavior mutually comprehensible. Behaviors that observers label mentally ill strike at the basic properties of social interaction that are as necessary among the Eskimo as the Australian aborigines or among the medieval English as contemporary Americans. The universality of conceptions of mental illness may stem more from the basic requisites of social interaction than from universal features of psychiatric symptoms.

Because mental illness labeling is grounded in properties of everyday knowledge, it is not surprising that an easily recognizable stereotype of the mentally ill individual exists in a wide variety of times and places. Empirical research in contemporary Western societies shows that "incomprehensibility" is one of the major qualities of this stereotype (Townsend, 1978:45). When community members in contemporary societies are presented with a variety of hypothetical cases that psychiatrists believe represent mentally ill individuals, the community members typically identify only the most bizarre cases of schizophrenia as examples of mental illness (e.g. Star, 1955; Cumming and Cumming, 1957; Dohrenwend and Chin-Shong, 1967; D'Arcy and Brockman, 1976). These elements reproduce a more general stereotype of madness. For example, among the ancient Greeks,

> what was, as far as we can reconstruct it, the Greek stereotype of the madman? First, there are the physical signs: raving, roaming around or running wild, eyes rolling, sweating, drooling, foaming at the mouth. There is a greater emphasis on visual disturbances than on auditory ones: terrifying visual images cause or accompany madness. Also, madmen do things that are contrary to all good Greek custom, such as deeds that are harmful to their friends and helpful to their enemies [Simon, 1978:152].

The incomprehensible appearance of behaviors categorized by laypersons as mad leads them to see the mad person as unpredictable. For if behavior does not seem to be comprehensible, it cannot be predicted. This aspect of mental disorder is revealed in native Teutonic categories of madness in tenth-century England:

> Within the ideas of the "native Teutonic medicine" it was elfshot which was most related to psychiatric aetiology. But it was a "miscellaneous" category and provided for any sudden, unexpected and inexplicable disease of man or beast. Such disorders could be credited to elves as unpredictable agents [Clarke, 1975:46–47].

Psychiatrists and other researchers often conclude that the stereotypes of mental illness found among the lay public are mistaken and that the public is unable to recognize any but the most bizarre cases of mental illness (Joint Commission on Mental Illness and Health, 1961). This interpretation fails to realize the grounding of mental illness stereotypes in the nature of social interaction. The persistence of the stereotypical mad person in a variety of times and places stems from the necessity of rules for orderly social interaction. Because observers cannot attribute sensible motivations to the actions of the mentally ill, they cannot predict what a mad person might do. The predictability of social behavior that stems from a mutual comprehension of meaning appears absent. Therefore, people who are viewed as acting in incomprehensible ways are also expected to be bizarre, disorganized, unpredictable, and, often, violent. The illustrations presented above show that this stereotype cannot stem from the presentation of mental illness in the mass media, as is sometimes suggested (Nunnally, 1961; Scheff, 1966a). Instead, the stereotype of mental illness is grounded in the nature of the categories used to interpret social action in all societies.

While incomprehensibility is the central attribute of the stereotypical view of the mad person, most societies distinguish two major categories of mental illness: nonviolent eccentricities and violent forms of madness. For example, East African societies

> do not construe psychosis only in terms of flagrant, socially-disruptive actions. It should also be added that degrees of mental disorder less severe than psychosis are recognized in all 4 societies and these "neuroses" are characteristically defined in terms of socially benign or merely eccentric behavior [Edgerton, 1966:419].

Similarly, the ancient Greek writer Aretaeus noted two categories of madness, one "with whose madness joy is associated, laugh, play, dance night and day, and sometimes go openly to the market crowned, as if victors in some contest of skill; this form is inoffensive to those around [quoted in Rosen, 1968:98]"; while in the other, "madness is attended with anger and these sometimes rend their clothes and kill keepers, and lay violent hands upon themselves [quoted in Rosen, 1968:99]."

And among urban lower class Puerto Ricans,

> although most *locos* are violent, some are not. There is a type of "crazy" person referred to as a *loco tranquilo* (the crazy but quiet person), who is viewed not as a menace but as foolish, incapacitated, and childlike. Although his behavior is as bizarre as that of the violent *loco*, he is not considered to be a menace since he does not pose a threat of violence [Rogler and Hollingshead, 1965:216].

Because the violent and the eccentric types of mad persons seem to others to behave in incomprehensible ways, they are both encompassed in the more general category of mental illness.

Thus far, I have argued that the common element in the labeling of mental illness, whether among the Eskimo or ancient Greeks, African or Australian tribesmen, the contemporary public or Enlightenment philosophers, is the inability of observers to comprehend behavior within the categories of the particular culture. The motives behind the behavior of the mentally disordered appear senseless, purposeless, and without reason, and, hence, seem beyond the boundaries of comprehensibility. Across a wide variety of cultures, when ordinary knowledge fails to comprehend the motives behind individuals' actions, labels of mental illness are often applied to them. The core meaning of mental illness as a cultural label is the appearance of incomprehensibility, according to the particular cultural standards that are used to judge behavior.

The notion of mental illness as incomprehensibility is only descriptive of the standards of lay judgment. It does not establish a standard of correctness for applying mental illness labels. A psychiatrist, for example, might argue that many other forms of behavior that appear quite comprehensible are in actuality pathological. My concern here, however, is with the appearance of behaviors lay observers actually label as mentally disordered, not with establishing professional standards used to correct lay judgments. Nor does my position hold that all behaviors that are considered to indicate mental illness are also seen as incomprehensible. Many disturbances, such as psychosomatic symptoms, depression, or anxiety, may not necessarily appear incomprehensible. While in most cases these behaviors will also not be seen as signs of mental illness, if they sometimes are it does not mean that observers are mistaken in their labeling practices. Rather, it means that the core category of mental illness as incomprehensible behaviors is broadened in some settings to include other types of behaviors. This section, however, has not been concerned with these boundary cases. While there is much cultural variation as to whether one or another type of behavior is considered to be a sign of mental illness, there remains a central core of behavior that is universally viewed as mental illness.

## Mental Illness as Culturally Relative or Universal

I have argued that there is a universal quality to attributions of mental disorder. In the face of the widespread claims of social scientists that the nature of mental illness labeling is culturally relative (e.g., Sarbin, 1969; Scheff, 1975; Conrad and Schneider, 1980), how can this claim be maintained? When various senses of the term *culturally relative* are distinguished, the comprehensibility of behavior is always determined by the norms of particular cultures, but the standard of incomprehensibility itself is a universal one.

Ever since Ruth Benedict's classic paper, "Anthropology and the Abnormal" (1934), social scientists have usually taken a *relativist* view of mental illness. In the relativist position, what is called mental illness is not a culture-free phenomenon, but one that is culturally relative, varying from time to time and from place to place. Some behavior that is recognized as mentally disturbed in one society will be viewed as normal in another society and vice versa. Therefore, in the relativist view, it is impossible to establish any universal standards regarding the nature of mental illness.

Benedict argues that there is little cross-cultural consensus as to what is labeled mental illness. Among the Dobuans of Melanesia, for example, people with sunny and kindly dispositions may be labeled crazy while individuals who would be called paranoid in the United States are considered normal. Or, persons who would be judged by us as megalomaniacs are seen as normal and desirable among the Kwakutl of North America, who strive to outdo each other in competition for prestige. In other societies, people who fall into trances and claim to communicate with supernatural beings and who would be labeled schizophrenic in Western societies are placed in valued shamanistic and prophetic roles. Mental illness and mental health are therefore culturally relative definitions that are determined by culturally specific rather than by universal norms (Benedict, 1934).

In the relativist view, not only the content of symptoms, but even the major forms of the psychoses are culturally relative. In a more recent statement of the relativist position, Scheff (1975) discusses the nature of schizophrenia:

The language aberrations can obviously be seen as transgressions, not against the rules of nature, but of language, which are, of course, arbitrary. What about thought disorders and hallucinations and delusions? It has already been suggested that there are culturally derived rules about propriety. Similarly, it is suggested that there are culture-bound rules about thought and about reality [18].

Because the behaviors labeled mentally ill violate social norms, and are not departures from universal organic standards of functioning, and because these norms are relative to a particular time and place, the relativist position claims that it is impossible to maintain a universal conception of mental illness. The relativists believe that mental disorder is a social construction that depends on the particular norms of each society.

A problem in the relativist position is the failure to distinguish between the connotation and the denotation of mental illness labels. The *connotation* of these labels refers to the meaning of mental illness labels, whereas the *denotation* refers to the particular behaviors to which the labels are applied. It is obvious that the denotation of mental illness varies from time to time and from place to place. For example, the Yoruba tribesmen of Nigeria sometimes carry special boxes as protection against witchcraft and claim that these boxes contain their souls (Coulter, 1973:146). While this is considered normal behavior among the Yoruba, an American who made the same claim would be judged insane. However, that the specific behaviors that are called mentally ill in different cultures are diverse does not mean that the connotation of mental illness is culture-bound in the same way. Indeed, as the preceding section has illustrated, the connotation of mental illness labels is consistent in a wide variety of times and places, despite the variations in the particular behaviors to which this label is applied. Whatever the particular cultural standards of comprehensibility may be, mental illness labels are applied when observers cannot comprehend the meaning of behavior within the typical categories of the culture.

There are, however, several important senses in which the relativist position is correct in emphasizing the culturally relative nature of mental illness labels. The first is that no behavior can be judged as a sign of mental illness without considering the particular social context in which it occurs. The labeling of mental illness involves a search for the meaningful nature of the behavior within a socially recognizable framework of rules. This process is senseless apart from viewing the behavior within a particular social context. Virtually any behavior that is labeled as mental illness in one context might be viewed as normal in some other context while what seems normal in one setting may be labeled crazy in another.

Indigenous labelers are often aware of the context-bound nature of mental illness labeling. East African tribesmen, for example, note that

## 2. The Meaning of Mental Illness

eating feces, collecting trash, living in the bush, going naked, and all the other behaviors, are not necessarily psychotic. Each behavior can occur in exceptional circumstances, such as in ceremonies, or as the result of injury or illness, etc., without any suggestion of psychosis [Edgerton, 1966:419].

Talmudic scholars in ancient Israel debated the appropriate conditions for applying labels of mental illness. In one such debate, one scholar

proposed that a person who wandered about alone at night, who spent the night in a cemetery, or who tore his garments and destroyed what was given to him might be considered deranged—if such behavior appeared irrational. However, it was pointed out that otherwise normal persons could also behave in this way, e.g. one who spent the night in a cemetery might have done so to practice magic, or that another who tore his clothes might have done so in a fit of anger, or because he was a cynic philosopher exhibiting his contempt for material things [Rosen, 1968:67].

Whenever a plausible reason can be found for a behavior, it is no longer seen as a sign of mental disturbance. In this vein, Aristotle noted that when a strange behavior such as cannibalism occurs as part of a social pattern, as among savages, it is not a form of mental disorder; when it occurs in settings where there is no plausible social reason available, as when a man kills and eats his mother, the individual is mentally disturbed (cited in Rosen, 1970:174). A contemporary American sociologist makes the same point: "The delusions of a private can be the rights of a general; the obscene invitations of a man to a strange girl can be the spicy endearments of a husband to his wife; the wariness of a paranoid is the warranted practice of thousands of undercover agents [Goffman, 1971:356]." In other cases, behavior that is part of a recognizable social role, such as the hallucinations, delusions, and bizarreness of a shaman performing a healing ceremony, is not viewed as mental illness, while the same symptoms in the same culture performed outside of a recognized social role are labeled insane (Murphy, 1976).

The cultural and social context of an action is thus an intrinsic aspect of the labeling of mental disorder. What seems to indicate mentally disordered behavior is always inappropriate in a particular context, not inappropriate per se. Whenever a plausible motive such as the practice of magic, philosophical belief, custom, or a social role, is perceived to lie behind an action, it will not be labeled mental illness. In this sense, the particular behaviors labeled as mental illness are relative to a particular social context. This does not mean, however, that the meaning of mental illness differs from culture to culture nor that the rules used to label mental illness are arbitrary.

In addition to being context-bound, mental illness labels are culturally specific in several other important ways. The interpretations assigned to behaviors that are labeled as mentally ill widely diverge from culture to culture. Some cultures view mental illness as a sign from the gods, others as the product of witchcraft, some as sin, and others as disease. While all cultures label behaviors with the appearance of incomprehensibility as signs of mental illness, there is little commonality in how these behaviors, once labeled, are interpreted.

Mental illness labels are also culture-bound in the range of behaviors that they encompass. While behaviors that seem incomprehensible may always be labeled mentally ill, there is a wide periphery of behaviors that are called mentally disturbed in one culture but not in another. For example, highly educated contemporary Westerners view many more types of behaviors as signs of mental disturbance than is typical in other cultures. Contemporary psychiatrists, in particular, are likely to label a far greater number of behaviors than only incomprehensible ones as signs of mental illness. This means that while certain behaviors are universally judged as mental ill, other behaviors are labeled as mental illness in some cultures but not in others. While the core meaning of mental illness labels appears universal, the boundaries of these labels are culturally specific.

Finally, different observers may often not agree as to whether someone's actions are incomprehensible or not. Parents may commit their children to mental hospitals for smoking marijuana or joining religious cults (Torrey, 1974); official agents of social control may involuntarily hospitalize people for deviant political beliefs (Szasz, 1963); psychiatrists may not understand the behavior of individuals who are at a great cultural distance to them (Jewell, 1952). In these instances, the comprehensibility of behavior depends on the particular vantage point of the observer. While most labeling of mental illness may be consensual, there is sometimes conflict over whether someone's behavior is comprehensible or not, especially if the observer and the actor do not share common cultural values.

Because most of the social scientific literature has overemphasized the culturally relative nature of mental illness labeling, the focus here has been on the similarities of this labeling across cultures. However, because labels of mental illness are dependent on context, have variable interpretations and vague boundaries, and may depend on the vantage point of the observer, their universal aspect also should not be overemphasized. While all cultures have a special category to refer to persons who act in incomprehensible ways, the specific ways in which this category is used are highly variable.

24

## Mental Illness, Disease, and Deviance

One issue in the study of mental illness labeling is how the features of mental illness labels are related to labels of disease and of crime and deviance. Psychiatrists typically consider mental illness to share the major characteristics of disease, while sociologists are more likely to regard mental illness as behavior that violates social norms. While mental illness labeling is related in certain ways to labels of both disease and deviance, it is greatly different from both of those categories. It is most appropriate to regard characterizations of mental illness as a distinctive type of reaction to undesirable behavior.

The most obvious cases of mental illness are characterized by the appearance of incomprehensibility. How does this aspect of mental illness labeling relate to attributions of physical disease? The question does not involve whether or not psychiatric conditions are "really" illnesses or whether or not it is useful to treat mental symptoms as if they were signs of disease. Rather, my concern is with the everyday philosophies of ordinary people as they attempt to make sense of the world around them.

People are seen as having a physical disease when there is some disturbance in the normal functioning of the *body*. Because illness is located within the human body, it is viewed as part of the biological world of organic systems. This does not mean that the labeling of someone as physically ill is not a social construction, for all definitions of illness reflect the social value judgment that a condition is an undesirable one (Friedson, 1970; Mechanic, 1978). Yet the fundamental aspect of disease as a social construction is its nonsocial nature. People believe that diseases are part of the natural world. In this sense, disease is a social construction that is formulated in naturalistic terms (Aubert and Messinger, 1958). The physically ill are those whose organic systems do not function according to normal standards.

In contrast, the mentally ill are those whose problems seem to be located in their *minds*. The mentally disordered individual is someone who appears to be "out of his mind." For example, among the Eskimo, it is said that "something inside the person—the soul, the spirit, the mind—is out of order [Murphy, 1976:1022]."

The distinction between mental and physical illnesses is a fundamental one, because different commonsense frameworks are used to interpret each type of illness. The body is viewed as part of the physical world and is therefore subject to the laws of cause and effect. In the physical realm, things "happen" but are not intended. Unlike the body, however, the mind is viewed within a cultural framework of motives, actions, meanings, and responsibilities that are applied to social objects. Laypersons generally make a clear distinction between the body as operating according to laws of cause and effect and the mind as operating according to meanings, ends, and intentions. This dualism, however, is more characteristic of contemporary Western than of non-Western societies, which do not make this sharp distinction between mind and body, but often view both physical and mental illnesses as "spiritual" disorders interpreted within a common framework.

There is no absolute dichotomy between physical and mental illnesses. Many physical diseases, such as epilepsy, syphilis, or cancer have moral components; a number of mental disorders have physical aspects. Yet while there are many boundary cases of each type, the core cases of physical illness lie in the physical world while the core cases of mental illness are an aspect of the cultural world. This distinction has fundamental implications for the differences in the societal reaction to physical and mental illnesses.

Just as mental illnesses have critical differences from physical diseases, so are they distinct from other types of deviant behavior, especially criminal behavior. The concept of deviant behavior is a notoriously vague one (Gibbs, 1972b). Sometimes deviance refers to behavior that is statistically infrequent, sometimes to behavior that is undesirable, and sometimes to behavior that elicits a disapproving response. While any definition must be somewhat arbitrary, I define *deviance* as behavior that violates social norms. Deviant acts are ones that violate evaluative standards of proper and right behavior and are therefore judged to be undesirable. This conception of deviance is congruent both with most textbook definitions and with commonsense interpretations (McHugh, 1970).

The paradigmatic form of deviance is criminal behavior, especially the major crimes against persons and property. It is instructive to compare commonsense notions of crime with those of physical illness. In lay attributions, crimes are different from physical disease in virtually every important respect (see Aubert and Messinger, 1958; Flew, 1973). Criminals appear to be actors who choose to engage in crimes. They are viewed as having free will; that is, they intend to commit their actions and are capable of acting in a manner other than the way they do act. In contrast, incapacity is central to the notion of physical disease: Individuals do not choose to become ill; illness is something that involuntarily happens to them (Flew, 1973). When people are physically ill, their bodies seem incapable of performing according to normal standards. Even when illness is the consequence of an individual's own actions, as when a smoker develops lung cancer, disease is seen as something that an act of will cannot eliminate.

Because criminals appear to be goal-directed and strive to achieve some value such as money, respect, or pleasure, whereas people become sick in spite of wishing to be healthy, there is a distinct societal reaction toward the criminal and the sick. Criminals are viewed as agents of their actions, whereas the sick are considered victims of their illnesses. It follows that there is a fundamental distinction in the attribution of responsibility to the criminal and the sick. Because criminals appear to choose their actions, they are held responsible for them. Criminals are viewed as blameworthy and deserving of punishment. In contrast, the sick are viewed as victims of a disease process that is beyond their control. Hence they are not held responsible for their conditions, although they are considered to have the responsibility to try to get well (Parsons, 1951). While criminals appear to be deserving of punishment, the appropriate response to the sick seems to be humane treatment.

Does mental illness appear more like physical illness or criminal behavior? Many researchers, particularly those associated with the labeling perspective, view the mentally ill as more similar to social deviants than to the physically ill in the sense that the mentally ill appear to violate social, ethical, or legal norms, and not organic standards of bodily functioning (Szasz, 1961). Yet this position considerably oversimplifies the matter. Inherent in the notion of deviance is the sense that deviants have violated some norm that stipulates the rightness or wrongness of conduct (Gibbs, 1972b). Labels of deviance are invoked when individuals violate observers' evaluative standards. In order to be considered morally wrong, however, individuals must have chosen to break a norm.

In contrast to deviants, people who are seen as mentally disturbed are so labeled not when their behavior is seen as morally wrong but rather when it cannot be attributed to a comprehensible reason. Observers cannot make sense out of the behavior of the mentally ill. In contrast, most deviants violate social rules in such a way that observers can link the deviant act to the motive that is perceived to lead to the action. For example, society considers the thief as wishing to obtain valued goods in an illegal manner, the prostitute as wanting to make money, or the delinquent as desiring to gain status or thrills. Observers can comprehend the motives for these types of deviance but evaluate them as being wrong. Because deviants act to obtain some recognizable value, they are held responsible for their behavior.

In contrast to most deviants who willfully violate social norms, it is difficult for observers to hold the mentally ill responsible for their behavior. Consider the response to the *loco* in Puerto Rico:

> The fury of the *loco* is different from other kinds of violence, such as fist fights which are relatively common in slum and *caserio* life. Fist fights between men and hair pulling and scratching among women are focused acts of violence provoked by insinuations, breaches of proper conduct, or a show of disrespect. Indeed, to engage an opponent bravely in a proficient display of fisticuffs is a singular mark of a *macho*. The motives of the opponents are understandable and so is the form that the violence takes, but the violence of a *loco* is disorganized, unpredictable, and directed toward persons in general, not an identifiable culprit or opponent. Since a *loco* has not been provoked deliberately, it is difficult for others to understand the motives for his violence [Rogler and Hollingshead, 1965:216].

Because the motives behind the behaviors of the mentally ill appear incomprehensible, they do not seem to know what they are doing. While most deviants strive to obtain some value, the mentally ill do not appear to gain anything from their behavior; it seems pointless and purposeless. Thus the attribution of responsibility to the mentally ill is far more problematic than it is for most other deviants.

The considerations discussed indicate that mental illness is a special type of label (Feinberg, 1970). It seems to be something that affects the "soul" and therefore poses problems of intention, choice, and responsibility that are aspects of the social and not of the natural world. Individuals who are labeled mentally ill appear to violate the norms, conventions, and understandings of social interaction. Yet unlike most social actors, the mentally disturbed do not seem to strive toward goals or to gain anything from their behavior. Like the physically ill, they apparently are not agents of their behaviors but act in spite of their own best interests. The social disruption the mentally ill create indicates a punishment response, while at the same time, the appearance of inability to control the behavior indicates that a more humane response would be appropriate. This ambiguity in the status of the mentally ill makes the societal reaction to them highly problematic.

The label of mental illness is a unique kind of attribution with both similarities to and differences from disease and deviance, but it does not fit the essential qualities of either of those attributions. Because the core quality of mental illness attributions is incomprehensibility, it is no surprise that the reaction to the mentally ill is so varied or that mental illness creates some special problems of social control. The typical responses to mental illness diverge from those made both to disease and to crime and deviance. The chapters that follow consider these variations in the responses to persons who have been labeled mentally ill.

## Conclusion

This chapter has been concerned with the appearance of behaviors that are subject to labels of mental illness. The standard of incomprehensibility provides a rough comparative concept of mental illness as a social construction that captures the essential nature of mental illness labels in a wide variety of times and places. That all societies consider incomprehensible behaviors as signs of mental illness does not stem from any universal constitutional factors in humans, but from the basic requirements of social interaction. For social order to be possible, there must be a mutually perceived reliability and predictability in social action. The elementary nature of social interaction requires that individuals be able to make sense out of each other's behavior. This means locating any behavior within a socially recognizable framework of rules that the behavior follows. It is inevitable that all societies will have a special label for individuals whose behavior falls outside the boundaries of meaningful social interaction. The nature of social interaction, not of the human organism, is displayed in the apparent universality in the labeling of mental illness.

The topic of this chapter has been observers' categorizations of behavior, not the symptoms of individuals who are being categorized. Therefore, the universal nature of some mental illness labels has no implications for the etiology of mental illness. The reasons why individuals behave in incomprehensible ways, whether through biological, psychological, or sociological factors, is an entirely distinct question from the reasons why observers label them as mentally ill.

Incomprehensibility only indicates the common core of behaviors that all societies label as mentally ill. The major sociological task is to go beyond the conceptual level to predict and explain the application of these labels in everyday social interaction and in broader social and historical contexts. For these purposes, it is necessary to consider mental illness labeling as a variable rather than as a constant. Contemporary psychiatrists, for example, label as signs of mental illness many behaviors other than incomprehensible ones. Highly educated persons are likely to recognize more kinds of behavior as indicative of mental illness than will those who are less educated. The empirical goal is to predict and explain why some individuals and societies label a broader range and scope of behaviors as mentally ill than do others.

In addition, the labeling of mental illness is usually not a straightforward matter but a complex and ambiguous process that involves many shifts in interpretations. One theoretical task is to examine the factors that predict whether or not an observer will label someone mentally ill. The application of mental illness labels is affected by considerations such as the relational distance between the observer and the actor; whether a professional or a layperson is applying the label; and the power, social integration, and cultural conventionality of the labeler and labelee (Scheff, 1966a). The probability that an individual will recognize and label some behavior as mental illness is an empirical question that a theory of social control should predict.

An additional way that the category of mental illness varies across cultures lies in the framework used to interpret the behaviors that are so labeled. Depending on the time and place, the interpretations made of incomprehensible behaviors and the treatment accorded to people considered mentally ill are extremely diverse. In different cultures, magical, religious, moralistic, or scientific explanations have been used to interpret the behavior of the mentally ill. What type of interpretation is used in any particular setting is a variable to be predicted and explained. In addition, once the label of mentally ill is applied, the societal reaction to individuals so labeled is also varied. The mentally ill may be excluded from or maintained within the group, treated more or less coercively, or provided with more or less therapy. The kind of reaction that mental illness elicits is an empirical question that depends upon a number of social and individual characteristics.

For all of these reasons, incomprehensibility only provides a general integrating concept around which a great amount of variation occurs. This variation involves the scope and range of the behaviors recognized as mentally ill in various groups, the kinds of interpretations provided for mental illness, the probability of recognizing mental illness under different conditions, and the type of societal reaction elicited by the mentally ill. The remaining chapters consider the social variation in the recognition of and response to mental illness.

# 3

## The Recognition of Mental Illness

While all cultures have labels for people who act in incomprehensible ways, the actual application of these labels to particular individuals is highly variable. Only a few of the behaviors that eventually will be labeled as mental illness are initially seen to be clear signs of a psychological disturbance. Instead, symptoms of mental disorder are usually vague, ambiguous, and open to a number of varying interpretations. It is possible to interpret unusual behaviors in many ways; labels of "mental illness," "madness," or "psychological disturbance" are applied only after alternative interpretations have failed to make sense of the behavior. The recognition of mental illness is not a simple process but one that only becomes crystallized after a complex series of interpretations.

The following dialogue among a group of Sebei tribesmen in East Africa illustrates some of the complexities that are involved in the recognition of mental illness (Edgerton, 1969). The men are discussing the behavior of a young man who they observed talking nonsense, making excited, abrupt, and jerky movements, flapping his arms like a bird, and giggling like a child:

| | |
|---|---|
| SALIMU: | *He is a strange boy.* |
| SAYEKWA: | *He is a foolish boy. Why does he behave that way?* |
| SALIMU: | *He may be mad or he may be foolish* (mentally retarded). |
| SAYEKWA: | *It could also be bewitchment or a fever or something like a fit.* |

| SALIMU: | *What is his clan?* (Some clans are noted for epilepsy and mental illness.) |
|---|---|
| SAYEKWA: | *Is he circumcised? How old is he? He should not act that way.* |
| INTERPRETER: | *There is something wrong. People here smoke* bhang. *Perhaps he may be a* bhang *man.* |
| SAYEKWA: | *No. I don't think that. He is more like he is crazy.* |
| SALIMU: | *I think he may be a fool.* |
| INTERPRETER: | *It is impossible to know without knowing about his family. We could ask one of these people about him.* |
| ANTHROPOLOGIST: | *What is the difference between a fool and a madman?* |
| SALIMU: | *A fool was born without sense. A madman becomes senseless because of a disease or witchcraft. We would have to know his history to tell about this young man.* |
| ANTHROPOLOGIST: | *What will happen to him if he is crazy?* |
| SALIMU: | *I don't know.* |
| SAYEKWA: | *It would depend upon many things.* |
| ANTHROPOLOGIST: | *What do you mean?* |
| INTERPRETER: | *He means that so many things cannot be known. Who is his father? What clan does his mother come from? Does he have a disease or was he bewitched? Or spirits may be involved. Also it depends on what he does, whether he troubles people or is merely a silly fellow.* [Edgerton, 1969:59. This quotation and following quotations from Edgerton (1969) are from *Changing Perspectives in Mental Illness* edited by Stanley C. Plog and Robert B. Edgerton. Copyright © 1969 by Holt, Rinehart and Winston, Inc. Reprinted by permission of Holt, Rinehart and Winston.] |

Before these observers can decide whether the young man is mentally ill, mentally retarded, epileptic, bewitched, taking drugs, or in some other condition, they need more knowledge of factors such as his biography, family and clan history, and various situational contingencies. These complexities are present in even the simple society of the Sebei that has fairly well-defined and consensual norms regarding proper behavior. The complexities involved in labeling mental illness in modern societies that have competing and ambiguous norms are even greater than those in the Sebei illustration.

This chapter examines some of the circumstances under which individuals come to be recognized and labeled as mentally disturbed. This initial recognition of mental illness is the first stage in the social control of mental disorder. It involves a transition from a perception that individuals are acting in unusual or idiosyncratic ways to a more explicit view that they are mentally ill. The recognition that someone is mentally ill means that the individual in question is placed into a fairly distinct social category of persons who are regarded as mentally ill and is in some way treated as a member of this category. This recognition and labeling rarely occurs in a sudden realization; instead, it is usually the result of a gradual, shifting, and complex process.

The recognition of mental illness should be distinguished from other processes that are often confused with it. First, the recognition of mental illness is distinct from the tolerance of disordered behavior. Tolerance implies that individuals already have been recognized as mentally ill and that their behavior is ignored and not stigmatized. Before mentally ill individuals can be tolerated, however, they must already have been labeled mentally ill. Often, statements such as "families show a great tolerance for mental illness" may come up when the empirical material indicates that the family has not recognized that a member is mentally ill in the first place. Or, a statement such as "lower-class people tolerate more mental illness than middle-class people" may actually mean that members of the lower class recognize fewer behaviors as signs of mental illness than do those in the middle class, not that the former have a greater tolerance for behaviors that they do recognize as mentally ill (Dohrenwend and Chin-Shong, 1967). In this chapter, whenever possible, the recognition and labeling of mental illness is separated from the tolerance of this phenomenon.

The recognition and labeling of someone as mentally disturbed is also distinct from any particular type of reaction to the mentally ill. Once recognized as mentally ill, the reaction to an individual may be abuse or sympathy, coercion or tolerance, withdrawal or concern. While future chapters will be concerned with predicting the type of response made to those labeled mentally ill, this chapter only deals with the initial recognition that someone is mentally ill. This recognition is compatible with a wide variety of possible responses to labeled individuals.

The chapter develops several general propositions that predict the labeling of mental disorder over a range of social and cultural settings. I sacrifice the examination of the numerous complexities involved in the labeling process to achieve the goal of developing general propositions that represent the most simplified and abstract relationships between some sociological variables and the recognition of mental illness. These propositions order a number of empirical studies that address the question of the circumstances under which observers evoke labels of mental illness to explain behavior.

The initial recognition that someone is mentally ill usually occurs within the lay community. Psychiatric professionals do not seek out mentally ill individuals in the community, but respond to those whom others bring to their attention. Because professionals react to individuals who are already defined as probably being mentally ill, the initial labeling of mental illness is a process mainly shaped by lay conceptions about mental illness. The central dynamics of the labeling process therefore occur in the lay community rather than in professional psychiatric practice.

The vague and ambiguous nature of mental symptoms means that unusual behaviors can be interpreted in many ways. Unlike professionals, lay persons do not have well-established frameworks that provide interpretations of unusual behaviors. Instead, most lay persons use their common sense to understand bizarre behaviors and incorporate these behaviors into their established patterns of interpretation. A critical question in the study of the labeling of mental illness is the conditions under which lay persons employ labels of mental illness to explain unusual behavior.

The recognition of mental illness most simply can be conceptualized as involving two parties: first, the observers of the apparently disordered individual, and second, the person who is considered to be mentally ill. The discussion in Chapter 2 indicates that the major reason observers label people mentally ill is that they find their behavior incomprehensible. When laypersons cannot comprehend any socially recognizable motivation behind someone's actions, they are more likely to consider the individual to be mentally ill. The degree to which social action is regarded as comprehensible should be a function of the social distance between the observer and the actor. As used here, *social distance* refers to the degree of familiarity an observer has with an actor. When people share many common life experiences, world views, norms, and values, this distance is small; when they share few or none of these traits, the social distance is large.

The label of mental illness should be more likely to be applied as the social distance between the observer and the actor increases. Individuals at the closest distance to each other, such as family members, kinsmen, and tribesmen, share a common universe of meaning and usually employ the same conventions, rules, and understandings to interpret behavior. In contrast, persons at a great social distance from one another are more likely to use divergent frames of interpretation to comprehend behavior. Because the degree to which behavior appears comprehensible is a function of using shared frameworks of meaning, a growing social distance should lead to a greater appearance of incomprehensibility and hence to a greater likelihood of mental illness labeling.

Social distance can be divided into two components of relational distance and cultural distance. *Relational distance* refers to the extent of interpersonal involvement between people as indicated by factors such as the scope, frequency, length, and intimacy of their interaction (Black, 1976:40–41). An individual's family and kin are at the closest relational distance, followed by friends, neighbors, and acquaintances, and, at the farthest distance, strangers. In addition to relational distance, any relationship has a lesser or greater cultural distance. *Cultural distance* refers to the extent to which individuals share characteristics such as ethnicity, lifestyle, or religious and political beliefs. Cultural distance is small when individuals share many of these traits and large when they share few or none. While persons at a close relational distance are usually also at a close cultural distance, this is not always the case. For example, first generation immigrants and their assimilated offspring, or bourgeois parents and their bohemian children are relationally close but culturally distant. Conversely, strangers at a great relational distance may or may not be at a close cultural distance. Therefore, relational and cultural distance are treated as analytically distinct variables. First I will consider the correlation of relational distance and next of cultural distance to the recognition of mental illness. I expect that as both relational and cultural distance increase, the probability of mental illness labeling will grow.

## Relational Distance and the Recognition of Mental Illness

A central question in the labeling of mental illness is how the relational distance between the observer and the actor affects the probability that unusual behavior is called "mental disorder." Are certain types of observers more likely than others to label someone as mentally ill? Any answers to this question must be tentative because of the limited nature of the evidence. Most studies of the topic have been impressionistic rather than systematic, descriptive rather than explanatory, and have used small and nonrepresentative samples. In addition, nearly all studies begin with individuals who have already been formally labeled as mentally ill and then retrospectively trace back to the initial recognition process. This means that individuals who have comparable symptoms but are not recognized as mentally ill or those who have been informally labeled but who have never sought professional help are not part of the study sample. Therefore, much of our knowledge regarding the informal recognition process is inferential. The generalizations presented about the recognition of mental illness are tentative and speculative rather than well-founded conclusions drawn from an established body of data.

The probability that someone is recognized and labeled as mentally disturbed is summarized by the following proposition:

*The tendency to label an individual mentally ill
varies directly with the relational distance between the observer and the actor.*

This proposition indicates that people at a close relational distance
typically deny or normalize signs of mental illness while those at a greater
distance are more likely to label someone as mentally disturbed. As the
relational distance between people increases, so does the probability that
a label of mental illness is applied.

## RECOGNITION AMONG FAMILY MEMBERS

Most studies of the lay recognition of mental illness focus on the
recognition process at the closest relational distance, within nuclear
families. These studies almost uniformly indicate a widespread reluctance of family members to recognize and label mental illness and a common tendency to normalize bizarre behavior.

In their classic study, Clausen and Yarrow (1955) showed how wives
resist labeling their husbands' behavior as symptomatic of mental illness
for a number of years but instead use a number of techniques to normalize the behavior.

> The most obvious form of defense in the wife's response is the tendency to *nor-
> malize* the husband's neurotic and psychotic symptoms. His behavior is ex-
> plained, justified or made acceptable by seeing it also in herself or by assuring
> herself that the particular behavior occurs again and again among persons who
> are not ill. . . . When behavior cannot be normalized, it can be made to seem
> less severe or less important in a total picture than an outsider might see it. . . .
> By finding some grounds for the behavior or something explainable about it, the
> wife achieves at least momentary *attenuation* of the seriousness of it. By *balanc-
> ing* acceptable with unacceptable behavior or "strange" with "normal" behavior,
> some wives can conclude that the husband is not seriously disturbed. . . . Defense
> sometimes amounts to a thorough-going *denial*. This takes the form of denying
> that the behavior perceived can be interpreted in an emotional or psychiatric
> framework [Yarrow *et al.*, 1955:22–23].

According to Yarrow *et al.*, wives usually resisted applying a label of
mental illness to their husbands' behavior for long periods of time, usually over two years, until the husbands' behavior became so thoroughly
bizarre that any alternative definition was untenable. Even then, it was
often not the wife herself, but formal social control agents such as the
police, who actually applied the initial mental illness label after
husbands created disturbances in public places (Clausen and Yarrow,
1955).

## 3. The Recognition of Mental Illness

The wives in this study were able to normalize behavior by assuming it was typical in many people, that the unusual behavior was not serious and would quickly pass, balancing the strange behavior with normal behavior, or denying that anything was wrong with the behavior. The most common techniques used to normalize behavior included viewing the problem as a character defect such as laziness, drunkenness, shyness, or nervousness; as a somatic difficulty; or as a psychological disturbance of a transitory nature that did not indicate mental illness (Schwartz, 1957). Each of these interpretations places the behavior in question within a socially recognizable category and renders it more comprehensible.

Another intensive study of the reaction to mental illness among the husbands of schizophrenic wives in the United States also finds a great reluctance to label the behavior of a spouse as mentally ill. The authors conclude:

> We have seen that the study group wives were grossly disturbed for some time without being defined as mentally ill and without any kind of psychiatric or other professional care. Prior to hospitalization, the wife might have been severely depressed, immobilized, weeping, and withdrawn for weeks or even months; she might be unable to perform even routine duties as a housewife and mother most of the time over several years; she might express bizarre, delusional ideas or even noticeably carry on conversations with unseen people without provoking her husband or other relatives to seek professional care or hospitalization for her [Sampson *et al.*, 1964:121].

Despite the long-standing persistence of symptoms within the family, the husbands resisted becoming involved in their wives' problems and did not press for any kind of psychiatric treatment until there was a total breakdown of accommodation patterns in the family.

The denial of mental illness among family members is not limited to studies conducted in the United States but appears to be a more general process within families across cultures. In one study, for example, Greek spouses tended to normalize behavior and denied it was indicative of mental illness:

> A loving husband believed his wife's repeated complaints that the women in the neighborhood were gossiping about her, accusing her of being a prostitute. Every time she would complain about these gossips and accusations, he would go and reprimand the neighbors, disbelieving their denials of any kind of gossip. He finally stopped paying any attention to her crying and complaining when she started saying that the newspapers were also accusing and defaming her, a fact that he could easily and objectively check and find to be untrue. Only at this point did he define her behavior as deviant [Safilios-Rothschild, 1968:109].

In further support of the general proposition, this Greek study found that relational distance between spouses also affected the probability that they would apply a label of mental illness. While both satisfied and dissatisfied spouses normalized behavior for long periods of time, the greater the degree of the normal spouses' satisfaction with the marriage, the less their tendency to label the deviance of their husband or wife as a sign of mental illness (Safilios-Rothschild, 1968:116).

Other cross-cultural evidence shows a similar tendency of family members to deny the presence of mental illness. A study of unhospitalized schizophrenics among the Cape-Coloured population in South Africa concludes that "this group of unhospitalized schizophrenics was as deteriorated, untractable, and chronic as could be found anywhere, and *everybody but their relatives realized it* [Gillis and Keet, 1965:1062; italics in original]." Among urban lower-class families in Puerto Rico, only 1 person out of 20 whose spouses were schizophrenics asserted that the spouse was insane (Rogler and Hollingshead, 1965:221). Similarly, a study in Iraq reports that relatives do not recognize any but the most flagrant sorts of unprovoked violence, uncontrollable motor activity, or sexually shameful behavior as a sign of mental illness in a family member (Al-Issa and Al-Issa, 1969–1970).

Not only do spouses deny mental illness in one another, but parents typically deny the presence of mental illness in a child. In the United States, parents resist labeling their children mentally ill even after professionals have applied such a label (Silver, 1955; Bakwin, 1963). Instead they have an "unwillingness to recognize the serious disturbance in the child" and "a feeling that 'he will outgrow it' [Silver, 1955:210]." Similarly, a study in Japan concludes that "patients, especially the mother, may be the first to witness the expression of the son's emotional change, but the last to interpret it as a sickness (Sakamoto, 1969:372)." In one case among the Hehe tribe of East Africa, the father of a boy diagnosed as psychotic by a native doctor protested so vigorously that the doctor changed his diagnosis to bewitchment, stating: "They paid me little money. It was not that. But it is very important to them that the boy not be psychotic. Do you think I have no heart? [Edgerton, 1969:61]."

As parents are reluctant to label their children mentally ill, children also resist applying this label to their elderly parents. A study of the admissions of the elderly to California hospitals concludes:

> In short, though lay descriptions of these patients at the time of admission to the psychiatric ward were predominantly negative, they were not expressed in terms primarily indicative of mental illness. Yet these same collaterals reported abnormal symptoms in profusion in other sections of the interview. This may have been a further reflection of the wish to emphasize the normal (if difficult) rather

than the abnormal and presumably less comprehensible as reflected in the recurring remark, "he's not crazy, he's just old." We conclude that there is a deep-seated reluctance to allow the symptoms of mental illness to color the image of a parent or spouse. [Lowenthal, 1964:161–162. This quotation and following quotations from Lowenthal (1964) are from *Lives in Distress* by Marjorie Lowenthal. Copyright © 1964 by Basic Books. Used by permission of Basic Books, Inc., New York.]

The same phenomenon is found across three generations among the Sebei of East Africa. Of 21 adults and several children questioned about whether a certain member of the tribe was mentally ill, everyone except the man's grandson claimed that he was psychotic (Edgerton, 1969:56).

When relational distance is close, the recognition of mental illness is unlikely. Spouses are unlikely to label each other mentally ill, just as parents resist labeling their children and children their parents. The reluctance within the nuclear family to label behavior mentally ill explains the findings of numerous studies that clinical symptoms of mental illness are present for an average of about two years before hospitalization occurs (Yarrow *et al.*, 1955; Myers and Roberts, 1959; Wood *et al.*, 1960; Grad and Sainsbury, 1963; Sampson *et al.*, 1964; Lowenthal, 1964; Brody, Derbyshire, and Schliefer, 1967; Grove and Howell, 1974; Horwitz, 1977a). The consequence of this reluctance of intimates to recognize psychiatric symptoms is that most people do not enter psychiatric treatment until some dramatic incident occurs. By this time, they appear to be seriously disturbed. In addition, families must bear a large burden in dealing with the disruption created by psychiatric symptoms for extended periods of time.

The general unwillingness of close relations to label mental illness varies by a number of factors. For example, middle-class families recognize mental illness and seek psychiatric treatment more quickly than do lower-class families (Myers and Roberts, 1959; Gove and Howell, 1974); people in critical familial roles are labeled and treated sooner than those in noncritical roles (Hammer, 1963–1964); people with access to information about psychiatric facilities enter psychiatric treatment more rapidly than do those without access (Horwitz, 1977a). While there is considerable variation among families in the tendency to recognize and label mental symptoms, the general response of close relations is to resist the application of psychiatric labels and the seeking of psychiatric treatment.

The reluctance of family members to recognize problems as stemming from psychological disturbance is compatible with a wide variety of responses to the affected individual. Some studies indicate that families are extremely supportive to the individual and have tremendous sympathy for even the most bizarre and disruptive symptoms (Grad and Sainsbury, 1963; Gillis and Keet, 1965). Other studies find that spouses withdraw from each other, so that during the duration of symptoms their relationship is characterized by isolation, emotional distance, and a lack of demands on the part of either spouse (Sampson *et al.*, 1964). In other cases, the period before hospitalization is marked by hostility and frequent quarrelling within the family (Horwitz, 1978). Therefore, the reluctance of family members to recognize mental illness does not necessarily indicate tolerance for mental symptoms but may be accompanied by a variety of reactions to the disturbed individual. While family members may be more likely than others to think they understand the motives behind action, this comprehensibility is compatible with reactions of hostility, sympathy, or neglect.

The resistance of close relations to label mental illness does not mean that families do not eventually apply the initial label of mental illness. The evidence indicates that in a high percentage of cases the initial recognition of mental illness does occur within the family (Hollingshead and Redlich, 1958; E. Linn, 1961; Horwitz, 1977a; Fox, 1978). This is not surprising because of the great amount of contact and exposure the family has with the individual and the responsibility of family members to cope with disturbed behavior. Yet when families eventually apply the initial label of mental illness, it is usually only after both a long history of resistance to labeling mental illness and extreme precipitants.

The thesis that close relations tend to deny and normalize mental illness contradicts the belief that many persons enter mental hospitals because they have been rejected by families or other intimate relations. For example, Goffman (1961) speaks of the typical pathway into the mental hospital as a "betrayal funnel" in which a close relation persuades or traps the future patient into visiting a psychiatrist. The psychiatrist and next-of-kin then collude to define the patient as mentally ill, supposedly because it is in the patient's best interest. The patient then enters the hospital feeling betrayed and the victim of a conspiracy. While such processes may frequently precede the immediate entry into the mental hospital, what is neglected in this viewpoint is that the "betrayal" usually only occurs as the immediate precipitant to hospitalization, after a long period of normalization attempts. An emphasis on the appearance of betrayal in the immediate circumstances surrounding hospitalization does not contradict the typical long-standing denial of mental illness within the same families who might eventually betray one of their members. Yet most evidence indicates that even when they do commit a family member to a mental hospital, families initiate commitment reluctantly and with feelings of discomfort and dismay (Miller and Schwartz,

1966). Even when hospitalization eventually occurs, reluctance to exclude a member seems more prevalent than willing betrayal throughout the process preceding hospitalization. Close relations typically deny the presence of mental disorder and when they finally perceive a family member is mentally ill, they tend to do so unwillingly and with regret.

One important qualification to the general proposition is that the tendency of intimates to deny the presence of mental illness holds only for the *initial* recognition of mental illness. While family members may normalize unusual behaviors for many months or years, after a formal label of mental illness has been applied to a member they are less reluctant to view behavior within a mental illness framework (e.g., Freeman and Simmons, 1963; Angrist *et al.*, 1968). Once a psychiatric professional has labeled someone, instead of exhibiting the normalization tendencies that existed before the initial hospitalization, family members often interpret unusual behavior as indicative of mental illness. While before the formal label was applied, responders were likely to interpret strange behavior as stemming from a variety of sources, once a professional made a formal diagnosis of mental illness any future incidence of strange behavior would be explained within an illness framework. Symptoms that seemed to be ambiguous can then readily be located as signs of "mental illness" and the label provides a perceptual framework that offers a more crystallized explanation of the symptoms (Scheff, 1966a).

There are certain other exceptions to the tendency of individuals and relatives to deny the presence of mental illness in themselves or in close family members. These exceptions occur when a label of mental illness can serve the interests of the labeler. For example, individuals may label themselves as mentally ill if it allows them to evade military service, to obtain an abortion, or to reduce criminal liability (Halleck, 1971). Family members may also readily accept mental illness labels if there is some advantage in doing so. For example, among the Kamba tribe in East Africa, if an individual is found guilty of murder his clansmen must pay compensation to the clan of the murder victim. No compensation is required if the perpetrator is judged insane. When it was suggested to the clansmen of an accused murderer that he was insane:

> Mutiso's clansmen leaped at this interpretation (of insanity) with eager acceptance for if Mutiso were found to be insane, they would be required to pay little compensation (to the clan of the murdered girl), or perhaps none at all. The clansmen agreed among themselves to testify to Mutiso's madness, and they appear to have won Mutiso's agreement to such a plea. As one old man recalled it, "We told him that if the Europeans found him guilty of murder, he would hang. But if he were only insane, he would go away to the hospital in Nairobi." He agreed that he was insane [Edgerton, 1969:64].

In those rare circumstances when a label of mental illness is more attractive than alternatives or can gain some advantage for an individual or the family, it may be sought after rather than denied.

In other instances, a label of mental illness may serve the advantage of a close relative but not be in the best interest of the labeled individual. In ancient Rome, kinsmen might declare a relative insane in order to acquire his property (Rosen, 1968:126–129). Or, disinherited relatives may contest the sanity of their kinsman (Szasz, 1963:74–76). Sometimes social circumstances may change so that labeling rather than denial serves the interest of close kin. For example, a wife may resist labeling her husband as mentally ill until she finds a boyfriend; children may normalize the eccentricities of their parents until they move to another city and can no longer care for their parents (Goffman, 1961). While the general tendency of individuals and close relatives is to deny the presence of mental illness, when this label accomplishes some interest, this tendency may disappear.

## RECOGNITION AMONG MORE DISTANT RELATIONS

There is little evidence about the recognition process of mental illness for members of the social network more distant than the nuclear family. This is because families have to deal with the day-to-day problems of coping with the disturbed member. Nevertheless, the existing evidence shows that members outside the nuclear family, especially extended kin and friends, often play a significant role in the recognition process (Kadushin, 1969; Freidson, 1970; Horwitz, 1978). This evidence indicates that more distant members of the social network are less reluctant than family members to label someone as mentally ill.

In a study of elderly mental patients in the United States, as the social distance between the future patient and the audience increased, the willingness to cope with symptoms declined (Lowenthal, 1964). Spouses showed the most endurance for dealing with symptoms, followed by children for their parents, while more remote relatives (siblings, nephews, and nieces) and friends were least supportive. Remote relatives initiated mental hospitalization after milder precipitating episodes, used fewer alternatives to hospitalization, and endured symptoms for a shorter period of time than did close relatives (Lowenthal, 1964:52, 166–67). Other anecdotal evidence indicates that hospitalization may occur when members of intimate family networks are no longer able to care for an individual and responsibility is transferred to more distant relatives or friends (Lemert, 1946; Goffman, 1961). For example, Cumming and Cumming (1957) report the following Canadian case:

42

## 3. The Recognition of Mental Illness

This patient for some fifteen years had been convinced that she was being influenced by sex rays which came under her bedroom door at night. She suffered
also from more transitory delusional beliefs, one of which was that the clergyman
of her parish was making counterfeit money in the church basement. . . . She
lived with a sister to whom she habitually confided her ideas, and this sister had
always considered her somewhat eccentric. By the time she came under clinical
care she was thirty-seven years old, and the reason for her hospitalization was an
extended separation from her sister, who had been unexpectedly delayed in
returning from a holiday. The patient became anxious at her sister's failure to ar-
rive on schedule and discussed some of her delusions with a friend, who immediately placed her in medical hands [101–102].

Other studies in the United States also indicate that friends are somewhat
more likely than family members to interpret problems within a psychiatric framework and to make referrals to psychiatrists (Kadushin,
1969:296; Horwitz, 1978). Some case material indicates that close friends
use the same techniques of normalization and denial found within
families, while more distant acquaintances have a greater tendency to
label mental illness (Smith, 1978). A study of the recognition process in
Japan also finds "that people in the outside world such as friends,
relatives, or teachers have insight into the particular family member's illness before immediate family members [Sakamoto, 1969:370]."

The tendency to deny the presence of mental illness does not seem to
cross the boundaries of blood relationships outside of the nuclear family.
In-laws do not have the same reluctance as family members to apply
labels of mental illness. For example, in a study of schizophrenics in
Puerto Rico that showed close relatives denying mental illness, in-laws
were much more willing to apply mental illness labels (Rogler and Hollingshead, 1965). In one family, the parents-in-law of a schizophrenic
man took their daughter

out of earshot to inquire about his behavior; they repeatedly give her advice to
hide the knives, scissors, and razor blades, anything that her husband might use
to harm her, the children, or neighbors. [The daughter] rejects this advice
because to follow it would legitimize the idea that her husband is a dangerous
*loco*. This idea is intolerable to her, and from her point of view it is detrimental
to her husband [Rogler and Hollingshead, 372–373].

In another Puerto Rican family, the daughter called her mother "sick of
the nerves" in contrast to her husband who claimed his mother-in-law
was a *loca* (Rogler and Hollingshead, 1965:367). Among the Yoruba in
rural Ghana, "The wife of a schizophrenic husband is more often in-
clined to stay with and care for him, an impulse encouraged by his family
but not by hers [M. J. Field, 1960:454]." An American study also found
that relatives who were not closely related or involved with the patient,
such as stepparents, in-laws, and distant kin had a greater willingness

than close kin to label individuals mentally ill (Rose, 1959:201). Some unsystematic evidence also indicates that workmates have little resistance to label another employee mentally ill (Lemert, 1962; Rogler and Hollingshead, 1965:291; Horwitz, 1977b). In general, the sorts of behaviors that family members routinely normalize may appear incomprehensible to persons who are at a greater relational distance.

In a study that appears to contradict the general proposition, E. Linn (1961), from a sample of mental patients in Washington, D.C., concludes that close family members had less tolerance for mental symptoms than more distant family members. He bases his conclusion on the fact that people who lived with close family members were more likely to be hospitalized by these persons than were individuals who lived with more distant relatives. Linn's data, however, indicates that the proportion of persons hospitalized by all relatives is greater when patients live with more distant relatives than with close relatives. This may indicate, in support of the proposition, that more distant relatives are more likely than close relatives to apply labels of mental illness but will call upon closer relatives to initiate hospitalization. In any case, Linn's interpretation of his data contradicts the great bulk of evidence that shows that as the distance between the labelee and labeler of mental illness increases, the recognition of mental illness becomes more probable.

## RECOGNITION AMONG STRANGERS

All of the evidence reported above concerns the recognition of mental illness by persons who have some acquaintance with the individual who is presumed to be mentally ill. The general proposition indicates that strangers are more likely than either close or distant acquaintances to recognize mental illness. It is, however, difficult to examine the labeling behavior of strangers because of the lack of evidence. Most studies of the recognition of mental illness retrospectively examine the labeling processes that led to the entry into psychiatric treatment. Strangers will rarely be involved in the process because even if they recognize that someone is mentally ill, interactional norms usually prevent strangers from referring individuals into psychiatric treatment. While family members are involved in ongoing relationships with the disturbed person, strangers can ignore strange behavior, regardless of how they interpret it. Therefore, there is little evidence about the reaction of strangers to mental illness.

Some cases from the family studies reviewed above indicate that, in contrast to the normalization processes that occurred within the family, hospitalization commonly occurred when the individual was observed in a public place (Sampson *et al.*, 1964:82). For example, in several case studies in the Clausen and Yarrow (1955) data, the label of mental illness was only applied after the husband created a disturbance in a public place. Other inferential evidence indicating that strangers have a lower recognition quotient than closer network members stems from the types of behaviors family members and strangers refer for hospitalization. Several studies indicate that when strangers do initiate hospitalization, it is for behaviors less severe than those exhibited when closer network members are the initiators. For example, one study of the incidents that precipitated hospitalization in the United States finds that families initiated hospitalization for actually or potentially harmful behavior while strangers were more likely to initiate it for socially unacceptable behavior. The authors conclude that "if unacceptable behavior occurred at home, it was frequently tolerated. Members of the community were less tolerant possibly because of uncertainty as to whether the patient might become dangerous, or to guard the community standards of decency and order [Smith *et al.*, 1963:231]." A study of the labeling of mental illness in Jamaica also finds that strangers referred persons into psychiatric treatment for less severe precipitants than did family members (Horwitz, 1973). In this setting, while violence was involved in three-quarters of cases referred to mental hospitals from families, only one-half the cases referred from public places involved violence.

Lowenthal's (1964:123) study of the labeling of elderly mental patients in California shows that when strangers made the initial recognition of mental illness, direct action was usually taken to initiate psychiatric hospitalization. In contrast, when acquaintances made the initial recognition of mental illness, they tended to use professional alternatives to psychiatry. This may indicate that strangers, unlike relatives, are more likely to interpret behavior as a sign of mental illness. Similarly, in San Francisco between 1906 and 1929, individuals

> with relatives were more likely to have had longer attacks prior to commitment —doubtless because those living with or near relatives were tolerated longer than those who came into contact only with neighbors, landlords, employers, police, and doctors. Of those brought to court on an affidavit signed by police, for example, 40 percent had attacks lasting seven days or less, compared to 12 percent of those brought to court by relatives [R. W. Fox, 1978:129].

This tendency also exists among the members of four East African tribes (Edgerton, 1969). When asked whether certain individuals were mentally ill, unrelated persons were able to unanimously agree upon a diagnosis of mental illness; family members protested this interpretation.

While the evidence is both scanty and inferential, it indicates that, contrary to close acquaintances, strangers do not deny the presence of mental disorder. However, this does not indicate that strangers have a low tolerance for behavior that they do recognize as mentally disturbed. The relative infrequency of referrals into psychiatric treatment from public places indicates that strangers are not likely to take steps to initiate hospitalization but that they have a high tolerance for the strange behavior they observe.

There are several reasons why the recognition of mental illness grows as relational distance increases. In part, this association results from the application of mental illness labels when behavior appears incomprehensible. Strangers are less likely than intimates to share a common framework of meanings. Hence, they may view an individual's behavior within a stereotyped framework and fail to understand idiosyncratic behaviors. Persons in an intimate relationship are more likely to have a shared universe of meanings and a more complex picture of each other. Intimates can incorporate possible symptoms of mental disturbance into this framework without defining the essential nature of the person. In contrast, strangers have no framework of normality within which to assimilate the apparent symptoms and these symptoms may become the dominant trait used to define the person.

A second reason for the denial tendencies of intimates is that they have built over many years a common universe of shared social reality. The admission that one party does not share this universe would force a radical reinterpretation of the entire basis of the relationship. In contrast, the assumptive universe of strangers is not threatened when they make a diagnosis of mental illness.

Finally, intimates, unlike strangers, have a stake in maintaining normal definitions. A label of mental illness may discredit not only the identified patients but also those around them. While strangers have nothing to lose from applying a label of mental illness, family members may fear that feelings of stigma can spread from the labeled individual to themselves. In addition, parents or spouses may feel guilty if they perceive that they are to blame for the development of the mental illness. For all of these reasons, close relations usually avoid recognizing an intimate as mentally ill, in contrast to strangers who need not engage in normalizing techniques.

The tendency for the recognition of mental illness to increase as relational distance grows parallels the recognition of other kinds of deviance. For example, incidents that arise among intimates are less likely to be defined as crimes than those that occur among strangers (Black, 1979: 21). A striking by parents of their children is unlikely to be defined as an assault; the initiation of forcible sexual relations by a husband on a wife

46

is rarely considered rape; children who steal money from their siblings are not usually viewed as thieves. Similarly, civil disputes that arise among business people are not likely to be accorded a legal definition and litigated unless there is a great relational distance between the disputing parties (Macaulay, 1963). Just as intimates rarely define their disputes as appropriate for legal social control, they are not likely to define each other as mentally ill or in need of formal sources of psychiatric help. The recognition of all types of deviance seems lowest when relational distance is small.

## Cultural Distance and the Recognition of Mental Illness

Because the recognition of mental illness usually occurs within intimate social networks, the relational distance between the labeler and the labeled individual is usually low. Within these networks all individuals typically share the same cultural traits, so cultural distance is minimal. Sometimes, however, the labeling of mental illness becomes an issue when individuals of varying cultures confront one another. To what extent is the recognition of mental illness related to the cultural distance between individuals?

Labels of mental illness are applied when observers find behaviors incomprehensible. What appears as incomprehensible, however, is determined by the cultural understandings of the motivations that seem to lie behind actions. When these understandings are shared, the comprehensibility of behavior should be high; as cultural distance increases, the understanding of behavior should decline. This indicates the proposition that:

> *The tendency to label an individual mentally ill varies directly with the cultural distance between the observer and the actor.*

Individuals who share common ethnicity, lifestyles, or religious and political beliefs should be less likely than those without these shared traits to label each other mentally ill. This proposition holds for the labeling tendencies of both community members and psychiatric professionals.

When labelers are members of the conventional culture, individuals who are less conventional in all respects, whether ethnically, politically, religiously, or sexually, are at a greater risk of being labeled mentally ill than are more conventional individuals. Since the norms used by psychiatric professionals to define mental illness reflect those of the dominant culture, the application of these norms results in a greater probability that unconventional behavior will be labeled mentally ill.

Individuals at the greatest cultural distance from psychiatric professionals should have the greatest risk of being labeled mentally ill. For example, the values promoted by the mental hygiene movement in the first half of the twentieth century in the United States were those of upper middle-class, Protestant New Englanders. This meant that individuals most distant from this culture, who did not meet the standards of individual achievement and upward mobility, such as the poor and members of minority groups, were at the greatest risk of being labeled as pathological (Davis, 1938). The values of the nineteenth-century predecessors of this movement reflected those of Protestant, small-town America. Persons at the greatest distance from this culture were most likely to be labeled mentally ill:

> Psychiatric theories about mental health and disease, based on alleged psychological and physiological laws governing the human body, revealed a conception about the "good life" that was typical of the Protestant middle class from which psychiatrists came . . . Every man should conduct himself with moderation in all things; passions, desires for pleasure, intellectual activity, and physical exertions should be kept within bounds. The middle-class virtues of work, religious duty, self-control and self-abnegation were extolled, and imaginative thought, sensual delights, business speculation, excessive search for fame and glory, and self-indulgence were condemned as dangerous to mental health. Psychiatrists objected to a life whose primary aim was self-aggrandizement and pleasure. They criticized civilization, saying it caused insanity, but their criticism was based in part on prejudice against industrial development and the classes associated with it—capitalists and factory workers [Dain, 1964:207].

Similarly, when conceptions of conventionality derived from life in small towns dominate the culture, large cities will be seen as productive of mental illness, as well as many kinds of other pathologies (Mills, 1942).

Members of unconventional ethnic groups are more likely to be labeled mentally ill than more conventional persons. For example, in nineteenth-century America, immigrant groups were considered more prone to insanity than were native-born individuals (Schwab and Schwab, 1978:114). As the cultural distance between psychiatrists and the immigrant group increased, the more prone the group was considered to be to develop a mental illness. Irish immigrants, for example, were considered more prone to insanity than German ones because of their poverty, lack of education, and Catholicism (Dain, 1964:102). Observers at a great cultural distance from individuals are more likely to label their behavior as mentally ill. For example, in the early part of the twentieth century, some representative cases of persons picked up by the police included the following.

In 1908, for example, a 34-year-old Peruvian "merchant" who had been in the United States only six weeks was "arrested on the street for acting strangely; he was on his knees praying, making gestures, etc." In Peru, one might suppose, such spontaneous public worship may not have signified an unbalanced mind. In 1910 a German-born laborer went to the police station itself "complaining of being ejected from society." The police reported to the medical examiner that the man lectured them on socialism, leading the physician to conclude that he was suffering from "delusions of a socialistic nature." In 1925 another German, a 51-year-old baker, was arrested for vagrancy after losing his job. The examiners wrote that according to the police he "is a soap-box orator and is a Socialist." They added: "Wanders about streets and is noisy and disturbs peace and has unlimited nerve getting on without work." After one day in detention he was conducted to [a mental hospital]. In Germany, a laborer zealously pleading the socialist cause on a soap box or even in a police station, might have been considered rational, even if foolish or offensive [R. W. Fox, 1978:90–91].

Similarly, Jewell (1952) documents the case of a normal Navaho Indian who was labeled as mentally ill and incarcerated in a mental hospital for over a year until he was found by an anthropologist who understood his culture. Such cases appear to be more common when individuals are at a great cultural distance from psychiatrists (see also Kutner, 1962).

It is not only membership in culturally unconventional ethnic groups but also departures from conventional morality that can lead to labels of mental illness. For example, a common reason for declaring wills invalid because of mental incapacity is when the will violates

the *public sense of decency and right*. If the public sense of right is violated—as when a rich man disinherits his ailing widow and leaves his money to his mistress, or when a rich woman bestows all her property on a home for stray cats and disinherits her poor sisters, who are her only remaining heirs—then it is virtually certain that if the will is contested, the court will find that the testator lacked the capacity to execute a valid will [Szasz, 1963:76; italics in original].

Sometimes a great cultural distance between individuals can override a close relational distance between them. For example, Brazilian parents who aspire to upward social mobility and hold materialistic values may label their children mentally ill and initiate hospitalization when these youths reject parental values and adopt hedonistic and drug-oriented life styles (Velho, 1976). Similarly, some American parents in

49

the 1960s hospitalized their children when they discovered that they were members of drug-oriented countercultures.

The mother of the petitioner—he is a 26-year-old, self-professed "hippie"— following an altercation with her son which resulted in his arrest, filed a petition that he be adjudged incompetent. Testimony at the sanity hearing held pursuant to the petition disclosed that during the past 8 years the man had been in and out of several universities. In addition to his beliefs in love and nonviolence, he professed to be an atheist. His beliefs and personal conduct brought him into disagreeable conflict with his father as well as his mother and her husband. He fathered an illegitimate child, and resented the attitude of his mother and stepfather toward the child. Following the hearing and mental examination, the petitioner was declared incompetent and was committed. He appealed the court's determination [Torrey, 1974:88–89].

In nineteenth-century America, mental illness was also associated with unconventional culture; thus activities such as: "drinking, sex, smoking, snuff, novels, poetry, drama, imaginative thoughts, study, financial speculation, and luxurious living in general were either positively harmful (to mental stability) or became so if indulged beyond 'moderation' [Dain, 1964:91]." It was in this period that geniuses, particularly artists and poets, were thought to be exceptionally prone to insanity (Dain, 1964:8).

Labels of mental illness are also more likely to be applied when there is a great distance in political values between labelers and those who are labeled. In the Soviet Union, political dissidents are often diagnosed as insane and incarcerated in mental hospitals (Medvedev and Medvedev, 1971). Conservative interpreters of the American student revolts in the 1960s sometimes viewed these movements as the product of mental disturbance (see Torrey, 1974). On the other side of the political spectrum, the poet Ezra Pound was incarcerated in an American mental hospital after World War II because of his work on behalf of the Fascist cause (Szasz, 1963). Because the majority of psychiatrists in the United States have liberal political views (Rogow, 1970), they are more prone to label conservative than liberal politicians as mentally ill. A poll of psychiatrists taken by *Fact* magazine in 1964 found that by a vote of 1,189 to 657, respondents felt that the conservative Republican Barry Goldwater was unfit to be President of the United States because of his mental condition (Szasz, 1970:204). The majority felt that Goldwater suffered from paranoid schizophrenia or a similar condition. The use of mental illness to discredit political opponents is not new. For example, the ancient Roman poet Catullus "disposes of Ameana, mistress of Mamurra his political enemy, by questioning her sanity and urging that a doctor be called [Rosen, 1968:131]." By labeling a political opponent mentally ill, an individual can discredit the opponent's beliefs as incorrect and also as out of touch with reality.

Not only political but also religious distance between labelers and labelees can lead to a categorization of mental illness. In the early seventh century in England, for example, the Saxon king Eadbald rejected the Christian religion that his father had adopted. Christian missionaries stated that he was "troubled by frequent fits of insanity and 'by the attack of a foul spirit' after marrying his late father's second wife [Clarke, 1975:48]." In seventeenth-century Massachusetts, the Puritan minister Cotton Mather diagnosed the dissident Quakers who troubled the colony as "madmen—a sort of lunaticks, demoniacks and energuments [Rosen, 1970:186]." A member of the liberal establishment clergy in the nineteenth century claimed that while true religion would not cause mental illness, religious revivals assuredly produced insanity (Dain, 1964:190). In the contemporary United States, members of unconventional religious cults such as the Hari Krishnas or Children of God are also often viewed as suffering from mental illness by their parents and psychiatric professionals. Sometimes when labelers of mental illness themselves reject religious belief, religion itself can become symptomatic of pathology. Freud (1928), for example, considered belief in God to be a regression to an infantile mode of thought.

That behaviors of all sorts at a great cultural distance from observers are liable to labels of mental illness is understandable in light of the nature of stereotypes of mental illness. The comprehensibility of behavior is always contingent upon the cultural norms used to evaluate the behavior. Labelers of mental illness employ the familiar norms of their own culture and assume that they are universal. The result is that individuals who depart from conventional conceptions of politics, religion, sexuality, and so on are the ones at greatest risk of being labeled mentally ill. Just as increasing relational distance leads to a greater probability of mental illness labeling, so does a growing cultural distance increase the likelihood.

Because mental illness labels are applied to behaviors that appear incomprehensible, the labeling process can be manipulated to serve coercive social control purposes. When mental illness labels are applied to unconventional behaviors, these behaviors can be illegitimized. Individuals who engage in them are classified not only as deviant but so depart from conventional norms as to be considered thoroughly irrational. Departures from conventional norms become indicative of individual pathology, hence reaffirming the status quo of conventional behavior. In this way, labels of mental illness can, in certain cases, become powerful tools in discrediting unconventional actions.

## Psychiatric Professionals and the Recognition of Mental Illness

Most of the previous sections in this chapter have examined the typical lay recognition processes of mental illness. Because laypersons are nearly always the initial reactors to the mentally ill, lay recognition patterns are a critical part of the labeling process. However, once laypersons suspect that someone is mentally ill, the individual in question will typically go, or be brought, to a professional in order to confirm or deny lay judgments. If a label of mental illness is to "stick," a psychiatric professional must ratify lay suspicions of illness. I will now, therefore, examine the typical processes of recognition of mental illness among psychiatric professionals.

In contrast to community members, who use commonsense criteria to diagnose mental illness, professionals are trained to apply specialized knowledge in recognizing mental illness. There is no inherent reason why psychiatric professionals should recognize either a wider or a narrower range of individuals as mentally ill than laypersons. Some individuals that laypersons look on as insane may be considered sane by professionals and, conversely, some persons who remain unlabeled in the community may be viewed by professionals as mentally ill.

In fact, the response to mental illness among psychiatric professionals to possible cases of mental illness appears to reverse the tendency of laypersons:

*Labeling rather than denial of mental illness is the typical response of professionals to unusual behavior.*

While laypersons typically deny, rather than label, potential cases of mental illness, professionals routinely label individuals as mentally disturbed. Compared to laypersons, psychiatric professionals label a far greater amount of mental illness and consider a far greater range of behaviors as indicative of mental illness. Several bodies of evidence show that psychiatric professionals are more likely than laypersons to recognize and label mental illness.

One way to compare the labeling practices of the lay public with those of psychiatric professionals is to consider studies of the "true prevalence" of mental illness in the general population. While psychiatrists typically do not go into the community searching for mentally ill individuals, many epidemiological surveys have been conducted in which community members are asked whether they have experienced symptoms that psychiatrists consider to indicate the presence of mental illness. The results of these surveys indicate that psychiatrists would label a dramatically higher number of people as mentally ill than the lay public does. Typically, surveys in the United States find that about 20% of the general population are "severely" psychiatrically impaired (e.g., Srole *et al.*, 1962; Myers *et al.*, 1971). For example, in the Midtown Manhattan study, only 20% of respondents were considered to be symptom-free, almost 50% had "mild or moderate symptom formation," and nearly 25% were "impaired because of psychiatric illness" (Srole *et al.*, 1962). A very rough estimate of the relationship between the number of patients labeled mentally ill by community members to the number considered as such by psychiatrists is that there are 14 unlabeled cases in the community that would be labeled mentally ill by psychiatrists for every labeled patient (Scheff, 1966a:49). Comparative data show the same phenomenon. Studies in Nigeria and Nova Scotia found that psychiatrists judged 42% and 47% of these populations as impaired while about 20% were classified as having "psychiatric disorder with significant impairment" (Leighton, Lambo, Hughes, Leighton, Murphy and Macklin, 1963; Leighton, Harding, Macklin, Macmillan, and Leighton, 1963). One study in Ceylon asked village headmen to enumerate all mentally ill individuals, including doubtful cases; the results as given by the headmen found that "the obviously low and unlikely rate of 0.1 percent was returned for all mental disorders in the villages [Jayasundera, 1969:55]." A resurvey, using medical students trained to employ psychiatric criteria, found a prevalence rate between 4 and 10 times greater than that reported by the headmen. Epidemiological surveys consistently indicate that psychiatrists would find considerably more mental illness in the community than laypersons actually label.

Another common technique that allows for comparison between lay and professional judgments of mental illness is the presentation to community members of hypothetical case studies of individuals whom psychiatrists believe are mentally ill (e.g., Star, 1955; Cumming and Cumming, 1957; Dohrenwend and Chin-Shong, 1967; Crocetti *et al.*, 1974; D'Arcy and Brockman, 1976). Typically, subjects are asked whether individuals whose symptoms represent paranoid schizophrenia, simple schizophrenia, alcoholism, anxiety neurosis, juvenile character disorder, and compulsive phobia are mentally ill or not. In contrast to psychiatric professionals, who are virtually unanimous in their opinion that all are cases of mental illness, the lay public only displays wide agreement with the diagnosis of psychiatrists in the case of the paranoid schizophrenic. In contrast, about two-thirds of the lay public agrees that the simple schizophrenic is mentally ill, about one-half that the alcoholic is ill, and far less than one-half that the cases of anxiety neurosis, juvenile character disorder, and compulsive phobia represent mental illness (D'Arcy and Brockman, 1976). While researchers who use this technique usually conclude that the public is "unable" to identify mental illness and has a "distorted" conception of it, from the point of view of a theory of social control, these studies only indicate that psychiatric professionals recognize far more behaviors as mentally ill than do members of the lay community.

Both epidemiological surveys and hypothetical cases show that laypersons are far less likely than psychiatric professionals to label individuals as mentally ill. Another way to compare professional and lay labeling tendencies is to examine the reaction of professionals to individuals who have been brought to their attention as possibly being mentally ill. At this time, professionals are called upon to either confirm or deny lay suspicions of mental illness. Virtually without exception, studies indicate that professionals label as mentally ill virtually all individuals who are brought to their attention.

At every stage of the professional labeling funnel, professionals, including the police (Bittner, 1967), admitting psychiatrists (Rosenhan, 1973), psychiatric screening agencies (Wilde, 1968), and people involved in commitment proceedings (Scheff, 1964; Miller and Schwartz, 1966; Wenger and Fletcher, 1969), find signs of mental illness. Typical is Miller and Schwartz's (1966) study of commitment proceedings:

> The medical doctors recommended commitment in nearly all cases. In those cases where they did not, they found the defendant to be "emotionally disturbed" and in need of outpatient care. Thus, not one of the fifty-eight persons was given a clear bill of health by the examining professionals [28].

Other studies find that commitment proceedings occur in a routinized fashion, rarely lasting more than a few minutes (Scheff, 1964; Cohen, 1966; Maisel, 1970). Professionals habitually presume that individuals are mentally ill and search for indications that will confirm their presumptions.

Some detailed evidence that the presumption of mental illness among professionals is not limited to contemporary American society is provided by R. W. Fox's (1978) study of commitment practices in San Francisco over the period from 1906 to 1929. He finds that judges rotely followed the advice of medical examiners in recommending commitment and only four times in over 15,000 examinations did a judge discharge a patient against the advice of examiners. The examiners themselves recommended commitment in 8 out of 10 cases brought to their attention. When individuals were not recommended for commitment, however, it was not because they were thought to be mentally healthy.

Those individuals released by the examiners were by no means all considered mentally healthy. Only 20 percent of those discharged were clearly considered to be "sane" and in need of no further treatment. Twelve percent were sent to a general hospital for medical treatment, and another 12 percent to a public or private relief home for extended care. The remaining 56 percent of those released were felt to be in clear need of further psychiatric treatment or observation: 25 percent were put into the custody of relatives who, "warned of the patient's condition, promised to obtain medical treatment and to look out for him." Six percent were released to friends on a similar basis. Ten percent were put on "probation" for periods ranging from one week to three months. Fifteen percent were released because relatives or friends promised to have them committed to a private mental hospital—an alternative that both examiners and judges were bound to applaud, since it would allow the accused to be confined and treated at no cost to the state. A few individuals were released after relatives requested that they be allowed to apply for voluntary admission to a state hospital [R. W. Fox, 1978:101].

Far from being released because of a finding they are sane, the majority of individuals who were not committed owed this decision to the availability of alternative treatment arrangements.

The fact that psychiatric professionals routinely label mental illness does not mean that they also routinely hospitalize people who they believe are mentally disordered. Contrary to the position that the failure of professionals to hospitalize some individuals indicates a careful screening procedure to exclude individuals who are not ill (Gove, 1970, 1975), all studies indicate that even those individuals who are not hospitalized are usually considered to be mentally disturbed. Indeed, when less drastic control alternatives are available, hospitalization will be avoided. For example, Bittner (1967) found that the police resist hospitalizing individuals so that they can avoid the cumbersome procedure involved; they attempt to transfer responsibility to informal caretakers in the community. Similarly, Mendel and Rapport (1969) found that one hospital admitted only 41% of applicants but screened out individuals who were capable of being supported by family or friends. Like other social controls (Black, 1976:Ch. 6), formal psychiatric control is underutilized when informal social control is available. In addition, factors such as the lack of availability of psychiatric facilities (Haney and Michielutte, 1968), the presence of alternative types of psychiatric care (Wilde, 1968), the source of the referral agent (Mishler and Waxler, 1963), and the day and time of admission, type of admitting professional, and previous hospitalizations (Mendel and Rapport, 1969), all influence whether or not an individual will be admitted into psychiatric care. Nevertheless, even when they decide to forego recommending hospitalization, psychiatric professionals recognize signs of mental illness in the vast majority of individuals who are brought to their attention.

There is some variation in the labeling of mental illness among professionals. Some categories of psychiatric professionals are more likely than others to label individuals mentally ill. One experimental study found that psychiatrists were most likely to make diagnoses of psychosis and graduate students in clinical psychology least likely, with clinical psychologists falling between the extremes (Temerlin, 1968). The actual labeling practices of various psychiatric professionals confirm that psychiatrists are more likely than other professionals to diagnose mental illness. In a study of admissions to a California mental hospital, psychiatrists were significantly more likely than social workers to hospitalize individuals (Mendel and Rapport, 1969). Haney and Michielutte (1968) also find that screening committees that assess mental competency in Florida are more likely to find individuals mentally incompetent if they are composed entirely of psychiatrists than if they also have committee members who are not psychiatric personnel.

Some evidence also indicates that, parallel to lay labeling practices, as the social distance between the psychiatrist and the patient increases, the tendency to label mental illness grows. Judges in rural courts in the Midwestern United States who are acquainted with people who are allegedly mentally ill have a greater tendency to resist ordering hospitalization and, possibly, to resist recognizing the accused as mentally ill than judges in urban courts who are unfamiliar with the persons who come before them (Scheff, 1964). Similarly, campus psychiatrists who are acquainted with student culture are more likely than off-campus clinicians in private practice to normalize problems and less likely to interpret problems as indicative of psychiatric disorder (Kahne and Schwartz, 1978:471). Some inferential evidence also indicates that psychiatrists, who are typically of higher social status, white, and male, are somewhat more likely to label lower-class persons, blacks, and females mentally ill than do persons at a closer cultural distance (Wilkinson, 1975; Baldwin *et al.*, 1975; Cleary, 1980). As the similarity between psychiatrists and patients declines, the probability increases that a label of mental illness will be applied.

There are some exceptions to the tendency of psychiatrists to apply labels of mental illness. Whenever psychiatrists work within organizations that have an interest in the denial of mental illness, they will rarely make diagnoses of mental illness. One such setting is the military, where a label of mental illness can lead to discharge or to avoiding combat. The tendency of military psychiatrists in this setting

is particularly strong to find sanity rather than mental illness. Routine examinations for the administrative discharge are estimated as very brief (usually less than thirty minutes); and it is estimated that a psychiatric diagnosis of illness arises in about two in a thousand consultations [Daniels, 1972:161].

Similarly, physicians in the Soviet Union are agents of a state that strives to maintain a high level of production in the face of the desire of workers to use sickness as a means of escaping work (Field, 1957). In such circumstances, Soviet physicians and psychiatrists diagnose mental illness in only a very small number of cases. In the United States, when psychiatrists are employed by third parties such as private corporations, insurance companies, or criminal prosecutors, the result may be a minimalization of the amount of labeled mental illness (Szasz, 1970). In contrast to the typical labeling practices of psychiatric professionals, the denial, rather than the labeling, of mental illness may be common among professionals working in the service of third parties. In general, however, despite some variation and some exceptions, psychiatric professionals generally recognize signs of mental illness in persons who are brought to their attention.

## Conclusion

There is great variation in the probability that an observer will apply a label of mental illness. The general tendency of laypersons is to deny that someone is mentally ill. This is especially true among intimates, while the probability of recognition increases as relational distance grows. In addition, persons who engage in unconventional behaviors of all sorts are in greater danger of being labeled mentally ill. As the relational and cultural distance between the labeler and labelee increases, the probability of recognition of mental illness also grows.

In contrast to the typical labeling practices of laypersons, psychiatric professionals typically label as mentally ill persons who are suspected of being so, rather than denying it. The most important thing to consider about the fact that professionals routinely apply labels of mental illness is that the initial recognition of mental illness is made before individuals come to the attention of formal psychiatric personnel. The definition that someone is mentally ill is, in effect, made by laypersons such as disturbed individuals themselves, and their families, kin, and friends, or by nonpsychiatric professionals such as general physicians or clergy. Even when nonpsychiatric professionals apply the initial label of mental illness, it is usually after laypersons mobilize them to deal with disturbed behavior. In nearly every case, the initial labeling of mental disturbance occurs within the lay community, whose members bring the affected individual to professional services. Professionals mainly serve to ratify labels of mental illness among individuals that laypersons have already selected for psychiatric attention.

Why should laypersons tend to resist the recognition of mental illness while psychiatric professionals are far more likely to perceive and diagnose mental illness? In part, the tendency of professionals to label mental illness is a natural correlate to lay denial tendencies. Because laypersons generally deny the presence of mental illness for lengthy periods of time, by the time individuals are brought to psychiatric attention they usually appear to be in a severely disorganized state. When professionals come in contact with the affected individual, it is likely that signs of mental illness seem quite obvious. In addition, the circumstances under which professionals initially conduct their examination are often during a crisis when individuals seem highly agitated. This tends to exacerbate the appearance of mental pathology. The result of lay denial tendencies is to enhance the appearance of mental illness by the time professionals have contact with disordered persons.

A number of additional reasons make professionals more likely than laypersons to recognize and to label mental illness. Psychiatric professionals are trained to employ a framework that searches for what is strange, bizarre, and pathological, as these terms are defined by the norms of the psychiatric profession. When someone is brought to their attention for strange behavior, it is natural for them to regard the person as mentally ill. The natural tendency of laypersons, by contrast, is to try and find comprehensible explanations for unusual behavior and only to label behaviors mentally ill after alternative interpretations have failed. In addition, psychiatrists, like physicians, usually adopt the medical maxim of "better to be safe than sorry" and find it safer to err by calling behavior mentally ill that is normal, than to mislabel mentally ill behavior as normal (Scheff, 1966a). On the other hand, laypersons usually have more to lose than to gain by stigmatizing a close relation as mentally ill. Finally, members of the lay community have a greater familiarity with the character and background of the individuals in question and may be able to find reasons why their behavior is comprehensible. In contrast, psychiatrists view individuals as members of the general category of "patients" and apply presumably universal standards of mental health to their behavior (Schwartz, 1957). For all of these reasons, it is natural both that professionals are likely to find signs of mental illness and that laypersons are likely to find alternative interpretations for unusual behaviors.

This chapter has only examined the actual labeling practices of laypersons and professionals, it has not evaluated the consequences of these practices for the future behavior of the labeled individuals. Students of the labeling process generally have taken one of two evaluative positions regarding the labeling tendencies of professionals and the denial tendencies of laypersons. Defenders of the psychiatric profession find it alarming that the lay public sees such a narrow range of behaviors as mentally ill and advocate public education to make the knowledge of laypersons conform to the norms of the psychiatric profession (e.g., Joint Commission On Mental Illness and Health, 1961). From the medical point of view, early recognition and labeling of symptoms can lead to appropriate treatments that can control and eventually eliminate symptoms. The refusal of close relations to recognize mental illness can result in a progressive advancement of the disturbance so that by the time professional help is sought, the individual is likely to be severely disturbed. Early detection and intervention helps arrest the illness process, relieve the disruption created by symptoms, and obviate the need for severe control responses such as hospitalization.

An alternative position is that the recognition and labeling of mental illness serves to exacerbate symptoms; after labeling, both community members and professionals will respond to the individual as a member of the category of the mentally ill (Scheff, 1966a; Waxler, 1974). Even if the intentions of labelers are to help the individual, the crystallization of unusual behavior in the label of mental illness leads responders to expect the patient to act in an ill manner in the future. On the other hand, if mental illness is denied, the normal aspects of the individual's behavior are encouraged and the extent of symptoms minimized.

While it is possible to assess empirically whether denying or labeling an individual as mentally ill reduces or exacerbates the tendency for future symptoms to occur, little empirical research has adequately addressed this question. Such studies would require a longitudinal comparison of labeled and unlabeled individuals, controlled for the presence of initial psychiatric symptoms. Because few studies of this sort have been conducted, answers to what the consequences of lay and professional labeling tendencies are lie in the future.

Apart from the consequences of lay and professional recognition tendencies, each is an important topic of study in its own right. Laypersons and professionals approach the question of how to interpret behavior within radically different frameworks, one tending to incorporate the unusual within the bounds of normality, the other to interpret the unusual as pathological. The viewpoint of laypersons follows as naturally from their relationship to the individual as that of psychiatric professionals follows from their social role. Both the reasons for, as well as the consequences of, these viewpoints are important topics for future research.

# 4

## The Labelers of Mental Illness

The previous chapter considered how the relational and cultural distance between the observer and the actor and the nature of the observer, whether a layperson or a professional, influenced the recognition of mental illness. This chapter examines how various characteristics of observers, such as their social class, culture, and sex, are related to their recognition and labeling of mental illness. Depending on their social location, observers have a greater or lesser probability of labeling behaviors as indicative of mental illness. What factors predict the distribution of mental illness labeling among different types of individuals, groups, and societies?

Various individuals and groups demonstrate different *amounts* or degrees of likelihood of labeling mental illness. Faced with the same stimulus of comparable symptoms, some observers are more or less likely than others to apply labels of mental illness. Are upper- or lower-class people, men or women, or Jews or gentiles more likely to recognize and label mental illness? In addition to variation in the probability that the same symptoms will elicit a label of mental illness, there is variation in the *range* of mental illness labeling. The *range* refers to how many different types of behaviors are considered to indicate mental illness. The minimum range of mental illness labeling seems to be the core of incomprehensible behaviors discussed in Chapter 2. This core may expand to include a wide variety of conditions such as depression, anxiety, meaninglessness, or psychosomatic symptoms. The more types of behaviors that are recognized as indicating mental disturbance, the greater is the range of mental illness labeling. Different individuals and groups may vary in both the amount and range of their labeling practices.

In addition to a social location, every label of mental illness also has a *direction* in social space. When an individual is labeled by someone who shares the same social characteristics, mental illness labeling moves *within* social space. Examples are an upper-class person labeling another upper-class person, a woman another woman, or a white person another white person. Labels of mental illness may also move *between* different social groups, such as when an upper-class person labels a lower-class person, a woman labels a man, or a white person labels a black person. Whenever labeling moves between different social categories, there is a greater social distance involved in the labeling process than when it occurs among persons who share the same social characteristics. A central issue in the study of the direction of mental illness labeling is what sorts of individuals are likely to be labeled at a greater or lesser social distance.

The approach taken here contrasts with the bulk of research on the distribution of symptoms of mental illness within various social and cultural groups (e.g., Dohrenwend and Dohrenwend, 1969; Schwab and Schwab, 1978). That research assesses the incidence and prevalence of mental symptoms among different social classes, ethnic groups, sexes, and so on. For example, lower-class persons have more symptoms of mental illness than upper-class persons (Dohrenwend and Dohrenwend, 1969), women have more neurotic symptoms than men (Gove and Tudor, 1973), and single, divorced, or separated people display more mental symptoms than married people (Gove, 1972).

These epidemiological studies seek to find the "true" prevalence and incidence of mental illness in the population in order to make statements regarding the etiology of mental symptoms. Because significant numbers of persons with mental symptoms are never formally labeled as mentally ill and never seek psychiatric help, samples consisting only of persons who are recognized as mentally ill are inadequate for the study of the etiology of mental symptoms. Therefore, epidemiologists concerned with the causation of psychiatric symptoms must study the incidence and prevalence of mental symptoms in the population, whether or not these symptoms are recognized as signs of mental illness.

For the study of societal reaction, however, the amount of labeled mental illness does not mask the true amount of mental illness but is itself the topic of study. The research question is the conditions that affect whether someone will be labeled mentally ill, not those that affect whether mental symptoms develop in the first place. What is to be explained is the variation in observers' reaction to certain symptoms, not who is likely to display these symptoms.

A major problem in examining the variation in the recognition of mental illness is that most research in the area has focused on populations of treated psychiatric patients. Studies of treated psychiatric cases, however, confound the recognition of mental symptoms with the process of seeking help from professionals. The various steps involved in entering psychiatric treatment include the recognition of an emotional problem, the discussion of the problem with other members of the social network, the selection of a particular type of professional to deal with the problem, and the seeking of help from a provider of psychiatric treatment (Kadushin, 1958). Because people have been recognized as being mentally ill does not necessarily mean that they will then enter psychiatric treatment. They may remain in the community without consulting others or may seek help from nonpsychiatric personnel such as physicians, clergy, or spiritualists. In order to overcome the confounding of the recognition and help-seeking processes, the recognition of mental illness should be assessed independently of the propensity to seek help from psychiatric professionals. Unfortunately, studies that do so are rare. Therefore, I often will infer variation in the recognition of mental illness from variation in help-seeking patterns, although whenever possible I distinguish the two processes.

This chapter considers how the labeling of mental illness varies along several social dimensions. For each dimension, I construct tentative propositions that order the location and direction of the labeling of mental illness. Subsequent chapters then examine the response to individuals after they have been recognized and labeled as mentally ill.

## Social Class and the Labeling of Mental Illness

Most sociological studies of both the etiology and labeling of mental symptoms focus on social class. One of the most consistent findings regarding the etiology of mental symptoms has been the inverse relationship between social class and the presence of symptoms (e.g., Dohrenwend and Dohrenwend, 1969). For both psychoses and milder forms of psychological distress, the lowest social class consistently displays the greatest amount of mental illness while the highest social class usually shows the least amount. Therefore, if the patterns of labeling of mental illness mirrored the distribution of mental symptoms, there would also be an inverse relationship between social class and the labeling of mental illness.

In fact, however, studies of the labeling of mental illness indicate that:

*The recognition of mental illness varies directly with the social class of the labeler.*

The higher the social class status of labelers, the more likely they are to recognize and label mental illness. Conversely, as social class declines, so does the likelihood that observers will apply labels of mental illness. The relationship of social class with the recognition of mental illness is opposite to its relationship with the etiology of mental symptoms.

The most detailed study of social class and treated mental illness was undertaken by Hollingshead and Redlich (1958) in New Haven, Connecticut. They developed a scale of five social classes: Class I, the upper class, that contained 3.4% of the community's population; Class II, the upper middle class, with 9% of the population; Class III, the middle class, comprising 21.4% of the community; Class IV, the working class, representing 48.5% of the population; and Class V, the lower class, with 17.7% of individuals. The identity of persons who were labeled mentally ill seems to contradict the general proposition: The prevalence of labeled patients in all types of psychiatric treatment increased with declining social class from 1.0% in the highest social class to 7.0% to 13.7% to 40.1 and 38.2% in the lowest social classes (Hollingshead and Redlich, 1958:199). Like the presence of mental symptoms, the number of individuals who were labeled mentally ill was inversely, not directly, related to social class.

The opposite relationship, however, holds for the *labelers* of mental illness. When the source of referral into psychiatric treatment is considered as an indicator of the type of member who applies a label of mental illness, the source of psychiatric labels for all social classes is likely to be individuals of high class status. Members of the upper classes are likely to be self-labeled or labeled by family members or friends, while lower class persons have labels of mental illness imposed upon them by higher ranking professionals. For example, among psychotics, 79% of individuals from the two highest social classes were self-referred or referred by family or friends into psychiatric treatment, compared to 23% of the middle class, 11% of the working class, and 2% of the lower class (Hollingshead and Redlich, 1958:187). In contrast, members of the lower classes usually entered treatment through referrals and, presumably, labels by professionals. Because higher status individuals are self-labeled or labeled by other higher status persons, while lower status persons are usually labeled by higher status professionals, members of all social classes are likely to receive labels of mental illness from higher class individuals.

With ascending social class comes a greater correspondence in knowledge about mental illness among lay persons and professionals, a greater willingness to seek psychiatric treatment, and an enhanced tendency to label one's self as mentally ill. Hollingshead and Redlich (1958) conclude:

> class I and II persons are more aware of psychological problems than class IV and V persons. Class I and II persons are also more perceptive of personal frustration, failure, and critical intrapsychic conflicts than class IV and V persons. . . . As a consequence, we believe that far more abnormal behavior is tolerated by the lower classes, particularly class V, without any awareness that the motivations behind the behavior are pathological, even though the behavior may be disapproved by the class norms [172–173].

It should be pointed out, however, that the lower class does not "tolerate" more mental illness than higher classes do; members of the lower class are less likely to consider behavior indicative of mental illness in the first place (Dohrenwend and Chin-Shong, 1967). What these data indicate is that there is far more labeling of mental illness among higher than among lower class persons.

Because Hollingshead and Redlich only studied treated psychiatric patients, no definite conclusions about the recognition process can be drawn from their study. Yet their results receive consistent support from community studies of the recognition process. For example, in the Midtown Manhattan study, among a community sample of individuals who were rated as psychiatrically impaired, 52% of upper status persons had received psychiatric treatment at some time, compared to 23% of middle status individuals, and 21% of lower status persons (Srole *et al.*, 1962). This suggests a considerably greater willingness of high status persons to perceive the presence of a psychiatric disorder. The actual differences in labeling are much greater than these figures suggest because the lower status persons who had entered psychiatric treatment were likely to have been labeled by persons above them in class status. The greater willingness of higher class persons to view themselves and others as mentally ill and the reluctance of lower class individuals to use a psychiatric framework to interpret their problems is illustrated in the kinds of help these respondents said they would use for behavioral disturbances. Among upper status respondents, 52% said they would recommend the help of a psychiatrist, compared to 24% of middle status and 12% of lower status respondents. In contrast, 63% of lower status and 52% of middle status individuals but only 31% of upper status persons said they would seek no professional help (Michael, 1967).

The greater tendency of upper-class persons to label mental illness is also shown in the responses of community members to hypothetical cases that psychiatrists believe represent mental illness. One study that compared the responses of community leaders, including politicians, judges, businesspeople, and organizational leaders to those of a cross section of the community found that 64% of the leaders compared with 46% of the cross section found mental illness in more than two of six hypothetical cases (Dohrenwend and Chin-Shong, 1967). While 64% of the leaders recommended seeking help from mental health professionals for more than one-half of the six cases, only 28% of respondents in the cross section made this type of recommendation. Many other studies of North American communities also indicate that when education is used to indicate social class, those with a higher level of education identify more hypothetical cases as mentally ill (e.g., Cumming and Cumming, 1957; Lemkau and Crocetti, 1962; Phillips, 1967). These studies do not necessarily indicate that higher status people are more "correct" in their labeling practices than lower status ones, but only that there is more labeling of mental illness among higher-class persons. Given the same stimulus, upper-class persons are more likely than lower-class ones to invoke mental illness as an explanation for the behavior. The tendency of higher-class persons to be more likely than lower-class ones to seek psychiatric help not only reflects differences in their help-seeking practices but also differences in what they recognize as a psychiatric problem in the first place.

The upper classes not only label a greater amount of mental illness than the lower classes but also view a broader range of behaviors as signs of mental illness. In general, the lower classes only view the most bizarre and disturbed behaviors as signs of mental illness. For example, Myers and Roberts (1959) find that in New Haven, middle-class individuals seek professional help near the emergence of the first signs of serious disturbance while lower-class schizophrenics "did not come to the attention of a doctor until they displayed most extraordinary behavior, usually of a dangerous, violent, or irresponsible nature [213]." In contrast, milder types of symptoms such as depression and anxiety are more common precipitants to psychiatric treatment among upper status persons (Hollingshead and Redlich, 1958:240). Similarly, among a group of elderly mental patients, individuals of higher social class status were likely to enter psychiatric treatment with disturbances of thought and feeling in contrast to the violent and aggressive behavior displayed by the lower class (Lowenthal, 1964:35). Studies of the recognition process among individuals labeled neurotic also indicate that higher-class persons seek psychiatric help for a wide range of emotional and interpersonal disturbances while lower-class persons often interpret problems as symptomatic of physical disorders (e.g., Kadushin, 1969; Bart, 1968). In general, lower-class individuals limit their conception of mental illness to incomprehensible behaviors while persons of higher social class standing consider a greater range of behaviors as signs of mental illness.

The tendency of upper-class persons to label a greater amount and range of mental illness is not limited to the contemporary United States but holds both historically and cross-culturally. In the earlier history of both the United States and Europe, the application of mental illness labels to behaviors beyond the incomprehensible was limited to the upper social classes. In nineteenth-century America, for example, only upper-class individuals supported the movement of psychiatrists to view mental illness as a psychological disorder (Dain, 1964:Ch. 2). The primary supporters of psychological theories of mental illness that came to be applied to a wide range of behaviors in nineteenth-century Europe were also members of the upper class (Ellenberger, 1970). Throughout the twentieth century, the major psychologically oriented therapeutic movements such as the mental hygiene movement and psychoanalysis, have drawn their followers from a narrow segment of the upper social classes (Davis, 1938; Hale, 1971).

The same classes that have historically adopted a psychiatric framework in the Western world also recognize a greater amount and range of behavior as mentally ill in developing nations. Throughout the developing world, only members of the middle and upper classes are likely to label and bring to psychiatric attention cases other than the most severe psychoses. Studies in Egypt (El-Islam and El-Deeb, 1969), Malaysia (Teoh et al., 1972-1973), and India (Carstairs, 1969) all indicate that the recognition of states such as anxiety, depression, and general dissatisfaction as psychiatric in nature is associated with rising class status. For example, in Jamaica, the only patients who entered mental hospitals because of depression were from middle-class homes, while lower-class patients entered hospitals after a display of bizarre or violent behavior (Horwitz, 1973). Similarly, in Brazil, higher-class individuals are more likely than lower class ones to enter psychiatric treatment with a range of symptoms such as anxiety, depression, or failure to work (Brody, 1973:740). The findings from epidemiological surveys (see Dohrenwend et al., 1980) indicate that the higher treated rates of minor symptoms of disorder among the higher social classes do not stem from the actual presence of psychiatric symptoms, which are more likely to be found among the lower class, but from differential labeling tendencies.

**67**

Throughout the world, increasing social class status leads to a greater amount of labeled mental illness.

The labeling of mental illness has not only a location but also a direction in social space. When individuals of similar class status label one another mentally ill, labeling moves within social space; when labels are applied by a higher ranking person to a lower ranking one or vice versa, labels move between different segments of social space. When labels of mental illness are ordered on a continuum with self-labeling at the closest relational distance, followed by labels applied by family and friends and by professionals known to the actor, and, finally, by strangers and distant professionals, the following proposition orders the empirical evidence:

> *The relational distance between the person labeled as mentally ill and the person applying the label varies inversely with the social class of the person who is labeled mentally ill.*

Members of higher social classes are likely to be self-labeled or labeled by someone of similar class status while members of lower social classes are likely to be labeled by someone at a greater distance to them. This follows from the tendency of higher-class persons to recognize a greater amount of mental illness than lower-class ones.

The evidence from the New Haven study of Hollingshead and Redlich previously mentioned, strongly supports the proposition. Among psychotics, 79% of individuals in the two highest social classes were self-labeled or labeled by family and friends, compared to 23% of the middle class, 11% of the working class, and 2% of the lower class. Conversely, 85% of the lower class, 42% of the working class, 11% of the middle class, and no one in the upper two classes entered psychiatric treatment through referrals from distant professionals such as the police and courts, social agencies, or clinic physicians (Hollingshead and Redlich, 1958: 187). Among neurotics, distant professionals referred 50% of the lower class but only 9% of the working class, 7% of the middle class, and 1% of the upper two classes. On the other hand, 36% of the upper two classes, 32% of the middle class, 24% of the working class, and 5% of the lower class were self-labeled or labeled by family and friends (Hollingshead and Redlich, 1958:186).

Other studies support these findings. In one hospital in Washington State, Gove and Howell (1974) found that persons at a close relational distance initiated hospitalization for the higher income group (over $4000) while more distant persons were more likely to initiate hospitalization for low-income patients (under $4000). Among the higher income group, 65% of patients and 69% of spouses participated in the labeling process, compared to 48% of patients and 28% of spouses in the lower income group. In contrast, distant relatives and unrelated laypersons initiated hospitalization for 68% of the lower income group but for 30% of the higher income patients. Distant professionals initiated hospitalization for 32% of the lower income group and 13% of the higher income group (Gove and Howell, 1974). Lowenthal (1964) finds the same relationship between social class and the distance of the labeling process among elderly mental patients:

> Particularly striking was the social distance from the patient of persons taking the final action (to initiate hospitalization) among the three socioeconomic groups. The low and medium levels were almost identical in this respect, with nearly two-thirds of each having relatives involved. On the other hand, in the very low socio-economic group, more than half had final actions taken by institutional staff or other impersonals and only one-third had personal agents [125].

Similarly, members of minority groups such as blacks and Spanish-speaking Americans are also more likely than whites to be labeled by distant professionals, in particular, by the police (E. Linn, 1961; Brody *et al.*, 1967; Brody, 1973; Fox, 1978).

Several consequences stem from the fact that social class is inversely related to the relational distance at which mental illness labels are applied. When labeling occurs at a close relational distance, the labeled individual is more likely to share the values of the labeler, to be able to influence the labeling process, and to have a greater say in the future course of events. In contrast, labeling at a greater distance is likely to involve a clash of value perspectives that leads to a more coercive process whereby the individual involuntarily acquires an unwanted label. Like other social control processes, the labeling of mental illness is most coercive for lower-class individuals (Black, 1976:Ch. 2).

In addition to the coerciveness of the labeling process, a greater relational distance of labeling is associated with other deleterious consequences for lower-class individuals. Because they themselves or others close to them are unlikely to recognize the presence of mental symptoms, these symptoms are likely to persist for long periods of time. Treatment is often delayed until symptoms appear so bizarre or disruptive that recognition is unavoidable. Because of this, the psychiatric conditions of lower-class people are likely to be more severe than those of higher-class individuals when they finally enter professional treatment (Gove and Howell, 1974). In contrast, the greater control over the labeling process of higher-class persons allows them to seek psychiatric help quickly, and when they feel such help will be useful to them.

## Culture and the Labeling of Mental Illness

Social class is strongly related to both the location and the direction of the recognition process. Yet the notion of social class used in most studies of labeling is ambiguous and confounds two distinct aspects of social class. On the one hand, social class refers to the possession of valued goods such as wealth and other material resources, and of power. In this sense, social class refers to a vertical location in social space in which some individuals are more powerful than others (Black, 1976:Ch. 2). On the other hand, social class also refers to a location in cultural space in which persons of different social class status differ in their education, lifestyles, and value systems. Different social classes have varying material and cultural resources. The most common indicators of social class in empirical studies combine occupational status and education to form a single measure of social class (e.g., Hollingshead and Redlich, 1958; Srole *et al.*, 1962). In this way, both resources and culture are joined in one measure that makes the meaning of social class ambiguous. However, the evidence indicates that cultural differences between social classes, rather than material and power differences, are most responsible for the greater amount of mental illness labeling among the upper classes.

Studies that separate the relative impact of income and education on the location of mental illness labeling show that the latter has more impact on recognition than the former. For example, a nationwide survey of over 2000 people in the United States in 1956 found that there was no consistent relationship between rising income and the readiness to define problems as indicative of mental illness and to utilize psychiatric help (Gurin *et al.*, 1960:280–281; 289). In contrast, there was a direct relationship between rising education and the labeling of mental illness and willingness to seek psychiatric help: 15% of individuals with a grade school education, 25% with a high school education, and 31% of college graduates used a psychiatric framework to define problems (Gurin *et al.*, 1960:289). The actual use of psychiatrists in this sample followed a similar pattern. For individuals with incomes under $5000, as education increased from grade school to high school to college, the use of psychiatrists increased from 4% to 11% to 23%. Among those with income over $5000, the use of psychiatric help increased from 16% to 20% to 32% in the three educational groups (Gurin *et al.*, 1960:338). A resample of this group in 1976 also found that education was more

70

strongly associated than income with defining problems as psychiatric ones and with utilizing psychiatric help. By this time, the impact of income on mental illness labeling had disappeared, and all income groups were equally likely to label psychiatric problems and to use psychiatric services (Kulka *et al.*, 1979). Studies that present community members with hypothetical cases of individuals whom psychiatrists believe are mentally ill also find that education is more strongly related than income to a higher recognition rate (Rabkin, 1974). The greater recognition of mental illness and use of psychiatric help among the higher social classes appears more a product of their cultural orientation than of their greater material resources.

Even education is too broad a predictor of mental illness labeling. Not education in general, but a particular type of liberal and humanistic education, is associated with the recognition of mental illness. Kadushin (1969) found that the primary clients of outpatient psychiatric care in New York City go to plays, concerts, museums, and art galleries, and work in occupations that stress the artistic and psychological, such as the health professions, teaching, the arts, and communications. People in this social circle were more likely than others to define themselves and others as in need of psychiatric help, to solicit help from other people for emotional problems, and to seek voluntarily psychiatric care. Studies of college students also find that students who use psychiatric help are more likely than those who do not to major in the humanities or social sciences, particularly in psychology, to view foreign films, and to have "cosmopolitan" value systems (Scheff, 1966b; Linn, 1967; Greenley and Mechanic, 1976). Compared to other students, those who seek psychiatric help are aware of more lifestyles and ideologies, more self-questioning and introspective, and more concerned with questions regarding the meaning of life (L. S. Linn, 1967).

A nationwide sample of the patients of private psychiatrists in the United States supports the finding that a particular kind of humanistic and intellectual cultural orientation is most related to the recognition of psychiatric problems (Marmor, 1975). Individuals in the humanistic professions were far overrepresented as patients: professional, technical, and kindred workers accounted for 57% of psychoanalytic patients and 29% of all private patients, about 3.5 times their representation in the population (Marmor, 1975:38). Students comprised an additional 18% and housewives 25% of all private patients. Relative to their proportion in the population, lawyers were 13 times as likely to be in treatment, social workers 12 times, writers, artists, and entertainers 6.5 times, teachers 2.7 times, and nurses 2.2 times (Marmor, 1975:38). In contrast, professionals such as business executives, computer specialists, accountants, or engineers, who are less likely to be involved in humanistic pursuits, seem proportionately less likely to enter psychiatric treatment than other professionals (Marmor, 1975:33). This indicates that it is not education in itself, but a liberal and humanistic type of education, that is particularly related to the greater tendency to recognize mental illness.

Historically, intellectuals have had the greatest affinity to the ideas of the psychiatric profession. Young intellectuals in the urban centers of New York and Chicago were responsible for the spread and popularization of psychoanalysis in the first part of the twentieth century (Hale, 1971:398–399). The broadening range of psychiatric disorder is also associated with intellectuals. Commenting on the growth of the definition of psychiatric symptoms from the psychoses and well-defined neuroses, Hale (1971) observes:

> When these new problems first appeared is uncertain. The new symptoms can be observed among some of the intellectuals, writers, and artists who were psychoanalyzed before the Great War. In open rebellion against every canon of "civilized" morality, they complained to their psychoanalysts chiefly of unhappiness, unstable sexual relationships, longings for meaning and permanence [479].

In both Europe and the United States, the expansion of the notion of mental illness mainly occurred through intellectual circles (Ellenberger, 1970).

The greatest amount of mental illness labeling is found among psychiatric professionals. These professionals are not only likely to observe far more mental illness in other people (see Chapter 3) but also in themselves. Physicians, mostly psychiatrists, are 20 times as likely as their proportion in the population to enter private psychiatric care, more than members of any other profession (Marmor, 1975:38). Overall, physicians accounted for over one-half of all analytic patients, and nearly one-quarter of nonanalytic patients (Marmor, 1975:37). Another study of several thousand psychiatric professionals found that 81% of psychiatrists, 75% of clinical psychologists, and 63% of psychiatric social workers underwent psychiatric treatment (Marx and Spray, 1969). Among those professionals who sought psychiatric therapy primarily for personal problems were 31% of psychiatrists, 53% of clinical psychologists, and 75% of psychiatric social workers, far higher than any other group in the population (Marx and Spray, 1969).

These findings indicate that the location of mental illness labeling is not simply among persons of high occupational status or educational attainment, but among persons who share the values of psychiatric professionals:

## 4. The Labelers of Mental Illness

*The recognition of mental illness varies inversely
with the cultural distance between individuals
and psychiatric professionals.*

Where this distance disappears completely, in the case of psychiatric professionals themselves, the amount of recognized mental illness becomes highest of all.

Several other findings are related to the proposition that a cultural similarity to psychiatric professionals is associated with the tendency to label mental illness. One is the vast overutilization of psychiatric facilities by Jews, an ethnic group whose members are often likely to possess a cosmopolitan value orientation. In both Europe and the United States, Jews have been the ethnic group most prone to adopt psychiatric viewpoints, and the spread of psychiatry was to a great extent among Jewish practitioners and clients (Ellenberger, 1970). A nationwide study of psychiatrists in the United States in 1966 similarly found that 25% of all psychiatrists were Jewish (Rogow, 1970). A study of psychiatric professionals in New York City, Chicago, and Los Angeles found that 34% of therapists were Jewish (Marx and Spray, 1969).

The clients of psychotherapy are correspondingly more likely to be of Jewish ethnicity. In the Midtown Manhattan study, Jews were almost 4 times as likely as Catholics or Protestants to attend outpatient psychiatric facilities (Srole *et al.*, 1962:302). Among the members of the community sample judged to be severely psychiatrically impaired, Jews were 10 times as likely as Catholics and 2.5 times as likely as Protestants to enter psychiatric treatment (Srole *et al.*, 1962:302). In another study, 46% of the clients of psychiatrists and 48% of clients of clinical psychologists in New York, Chicago, and Los Angeles were Jewish (Marx and Spray, 1969). Jewish college students are also more likely than other students to utilize psychiatric facilities (Scheff, 1966b; Linn, 1967; Greenley and Mechanic, 1976). In addition, Jews are more likely than other ethnic groups to label mental illness when presented with hypothetical cases of psychiatric disorders: 51% of Jews compared to 38% of blacks, 22% of Puerto Ricans, and 17% of Irish found something wrong in all six cases of mental illness shown to them (Dohrenwend and Chin-Shong, 1967). All these findings are an implication of the proposition that a small cultural distance from psychiatrists predicts the recognition of mental illness.

In summary, the upper classes label far more mental illness than the lower classes. This tendency to recognize mental illness is most associated with education and, in particular, a humanistic and cosmopolitan value system. The most mental illness is labeled among those groups whose

73

values most closely correspond to those of the psychiatric profession: Jews, intellectuals, members of humanistic professions, and, especially, psychiatric professionals themselves. Whatever the scientific validity of the notions of mental illness found among the psychiatric profession, these notions have always appealed only to a fairly narrow segment of the population.

Several reasons account for the association of rising social class, education, and intellectuality with an increased recognition of mental illness. In modern Western societies, the notion of mental illness implies that some intrapsychic disturbance has caused one's problems. Those individuals who are most oriented toward scrutinizing their own thoughts and feelings and who have an introspective orientation are those who are most amenable to using a concept that locates some disturbance within the psyche. Numerous studies indicate that higher social class status is associated with an introspective orientation and that middle- and upper-class persons are more attuned to their own inner feelings and those of others (e.g., Bernstein, 1971). In contrast, members of the working and lower classes are less introspective and more oriented to external and formal rules in the outer environment (e.g., Kohn, 1959). They are less likely to scrutinize their own thoughts and feelings and so they do not naturally provide intrapsychic explanations of problems. Therefore, while higher status persons readily apply notions of mental illness to themselves and to others, when persons of lower status are labeled mentally ill it is usually not by themselves but by members of higher social classes.

In addition to the different social-psychological orientations of the various social classes, the upper classes have a greater knowledge and awareness of professional psychiatric viewpoints. Through formal education and participation in a social circle heavily influenced by psychiatric values, they have assimilated a psychiatric ideology that leads to a greater awareness of a mental illness framework as a cultural point of view (Kadushin, 1969). If the term *knowledge* is taken to mean the awareness and adoption of a particular frame of reference rather than a truthful body of information, then only members of the upper social classes acquire knowledge of professional psychiatric viewpoints.

Finally, in addition to socialization and awareness, the orientation of the different social classes to psychiatric professionals leads to varying patterns of recognition. Persons of higher social class status are most likely to have favorable attitudes toward professionals and to use professional services of all types (Mechanic, 1978). Hence, they are likely to have favorable viewpoints toward psychiatric professionals and to view their services as a valued good. Psychiatrists are seen as a source of help for psychic distress. In contrast, lower-class persons are more likely to view psychiatrists as coercive agents of social control more to be avoided than sought. This variation in the evaluation of psychiatric professionals makes the higher classes more amenable to the recognition framework of psychiatrists and the lower classes less prone to adopt psychiatric viewpoints. In this regard, the relationship between culture and the recognition of mental illness is similar to the recognition of medical problems of all sorts (Mechanic, 1978).

This interpretation of the relationship of social class and the recognition of mental illness contrasts with the one associated with the labeling theory of mental illness (Scheff, 1966a). The labeling view regards higher status persons as able to resist mental illness labeling because of their greater resources of wealth, power, and status. In contrast, lower-class persons are less able to resist being labeled mentally ill because of their powerless condition. This argument, however, is unable to account for why upper-class persons should so willingly apply mental illness frameworks to their own behavior and voluntarily seek psychiatric treatment. In contrast to the labeling explanation, it appears that the culture of the upper classes allows them to interpret mental illness and psychiatric treatment as not stigmatizing. The recognition of mental illness seems shaped more by the varying cultures of the social classes than by power differentials between the classes. As will be shown in the following chapter, however, the differential resources and power of the various social classes are more related to the different types of reactions to individuals who have been labeled mentally ill than to the initial recognition of mental illness.

## Gender and the Labeling of Mental Illness

Another factor that predicts the social location of mental illness labeling is the sex of the labeler:

> *Women are more likely than men to recognize*
> *and to label mental illness.*

To a certain extent, however, gender differences in labeling are related to the previous proposition about cultural differences.

In the United States, women are about twice as likely as men to enter self-initiated forms of psychiatric treatment (Chesler, 1972:312; Gove and Tudor, 1973; Tudor et al., 1977). For example, about two women are treated in public outpatient facilities for each man (Tudor *et al.*, 1977:106). About 60% of the patients of private practitioners in the United States are female (Marmor, 1975:29). Nationwide surveys of community populations also indicate that women are more likely than men to feel they could use or to have actually used psychiatric help (Gurin *et al.*, 1960:289). In contrast, men are less likely than women to recognize their problems as psychiatric ones and are more likely to enter psychiatric treatment through the advice of others rather than on their own initiative (Kadushin, 1969:197). One study of patients seeking help at a community mental health center found that women were about twice as likely as men to label problems as psychiatric on their own initiative (Horwitz, 1977b). In general, while female psychiatric patients are likely to be self-labeled, male patients are likely to be labeled by others.

The overrepresentation of women in self-initiated types of psychiatric treatment does not only result from differences in the prevalence of psychiatric symptoms but also from their greater tendency to recognize problems as indicative of psychiatric distress. A number of community surveys of distress show that women are more likely than men to translate psychological distress into the conscious recognition that they have an emotional problem (Kessler *et al.*, 1981). A substantial proportion of the overutilization of psychiatrists by women stems from their greater tendency to recognize that they have a mental health problem, over and above the presence of what psychiatrists recognize as mental symptoms.

Women also appear to be more likely to view the problems of men within a psychiatric framework than men are to view the problems of women in this way. A Puerto Rican study found that the wives of schizophrenic husbands "have considerable insight into both the inner turmoil from which the husbands suffer and the interpersonal conditions which aggravate their illness [Rogler and Hollingshead, 1965:302]." In contrast is the view these husbands take of their schizophrenic wives:

> If his wife fails to keep an orderly house it is because she is lazy and disorganized; if she is vociferous, argumentative, and explosive it is because she is *malcriada* (spoiled); if she meanders, it is because she is a gadabout. These explanations are often nothing more than pejorative descriptions of his wife's unacceptable behavior; in contrast to the well wives of sick husbands, these men have little or no insight into the mental illness [Rogler and Hollingshead, 1965:317].

There are also some indications from American family studies that wives are more likely than husbands to view the problems of their spouses as stemming from psychological problems (compare Clausen and Yarrow, 1955; Sampson *et al.*, 1964). Other studies indicate that women are more likely to label men as suffering from mental illness than are men to label women mentally ill (Kadushin, 1969; Horwitz, 1977b). Unfortunately, so few studies have compared the labeling practices of men and women that generalizations are tenuous.

In part, the apparent greater tendency of women to label mental illness may be related to the proposition about cultural differences already discussed, since women are more likely than men to adopt the introspective world view that is compatible with a psychiatric viewpoint (Gurin *et al.*, 1960:78; 210). Women have a greater tendency than men to internalize rather than externalize the location and source of problematic situations. In addition, women are more likely than men to be humanistically and artistically rather than technically and scientifically oriented. This indicates that there is some overlap between "feminine" culture and the cultural orientation compatible with a psychiatric point of view. To this extent, the greater recognition of mental illness among women may stem from their greater amenability to those aspects of psychiatric culture previously discussed. However, the extent to which women are more likely to recognize mental illness than men and the reasons for this tendency are mostly a matter of speculation.

There also appears to be some relationship between gender and the direction of mental illness labeling. Men appear to be more likely to be labeled mentally ill by women than women are by men. For example, in a study of help-seeking in Manhattan, Kadushin (1969:182) found that women were not only more likely than men to label themselves mentally ill but also to provide psychiatric advice to both men and women. A study in New Haven also found that women were more likely to label men than men were to label women (Horwitz, 1977b). Twenty-six percent of men compared to 13 percent of women were labeled mentally ill by spouses. A study of mental illness labeling in Greece also found that women were likely to be hospitalized on their own initiative while men were more likely to be forced by their wives or other relatives to enter the hospital (Safilios-Rothschild, 1968:112).

If these fragments of evidence indicate a more general tendency for men to be labeled by women than women by men, they apparently contradict the proposition stated that more powerful people are generally labeled at a closer relational distance than less powerful ones. Because men are, in general, more powerful than women, it would be expected from the proposition that they would be more likely to label women than women would be to label them. A more detailed examination of the evidence, however, indicates that sex differences in the direction of the labeling process are compatible with the social class differences reported above.

Men who are labeled mentally ill tend to be in relatively powerless social roles. For example, among diagnosed psychotics, while women have somewhat higher rates of hospitalization than men, men have higher rates than women during their younger years. Tudor *et al.* (1977:104) estimate that about four men for every three women are identified and treated as psychotic in their early twenties, while rates of treated psychoses among women overtake male rates with increasing age. This may indicate that men are likely to be labeled mentally ill when they are in a subordinate status to their parents, or, alternatively, are cut off from family ties and in a marginal social position (see also Rushing, 1979). Other studies also indicate that men who are labeled mentally ill are not in powerful positions but are young, unmarried, and in marginal positions (e.g., E. Linn, 1961; Brody *et al.*, 1967; Brody, 1973:521; R. W. Fox, 1978).

Even among the married, some evidence shows that men labeled mentally ill by their wives are in subordinate positions within the family. One study of sex differences in labeling found three typical situations when men were labeled mentally ill by their wives: (*a*) after losing their jobs and hence their basis of power in the family, (*b*) when they were elderly and their wives and children were able to form a coalition to enforce entry into psychiatric treatment, and (*c*) when they lived within strong in-law networks with no kin of their own (Horwitz, 1977b). In every case in which a wife successfully labeled her husband in need of psychiatric treatment, the man was in a relatively weak position of power.

While men in general may be more powerful than women, the particular men who women label mentally ill are in subordinate positions. When women label men mentally ill, the men are likely to be young or elderly, marginal or unemployed, and powerless. Therefore, sex differences in the direction of mental illness labeling do not refute the tendency of labels to move from higher to lower ranking individuals.

## Social Evolution and the Labeling of Mental Illness

Just as the amount of mental illness labeling is unevenly distributed among individuals in different locations in social space, the quantity of mental illness labeling also varies between societies. Different societies may label a greater or lesser range and amount of behaviors as indicative of mental illness. The discussion so far indicates that a number of factors predict the quantity of mental illness labeling. At the societal level:

*The recognition of mental illness varies directly*
*with the degree of cosmopolitan culture, societal*

*differentiation, and influence of psychiatric professionals.*

First, just as individuals who participate in cosmopolitan culture are most likely to recognize mental illness, an expansion of this culture should lead to more overall recognition of mental illness. Second, following from the fact that persons who are at a close relational distance to possibly mentally ill individuals are likely to normalize their behavior (see Chapter 3), societies such as tribal groups with a small aggregate amount of relational distance between members should recognize less mental illness than societies with a high degree of interaction between strangers. Third, the growing influence of the psychiatric profession should be related to an expanding use of mental illness labels. While it is not possible to specify the relative influence of each factor, all predict a growth of mental illness labeling over the course of social evolution.

Small tightly knit societies such as primitive tribes should have the least amount and range of mental illness labeling. All members of these groups share a common culture and laypersons and psychiatric healers are at a close distance to one another. While these societies recognize as mental illness what Western psychiatrists call psychoses, the notion of mental illness is mainly limited to the most severe manifestations of symptoms. Among the Yoruba of Nigeria, for example, the symptoms recognized as mental illness are

> composed of symptoms primarily associated with mental deficiency, schizophrenia, epilepsy, paresis, and other brain disorders. For the most part, symptoms characteristic of psychophysiologic, neurotic, personality, and sociopathic disorders were not included [Leighton, 1969:458–459].

The kinds of behaviors Western psychiatrists label as mental illness did exist, but the Yoruba did not consider them signs of mental illness. Leighton (1969) notes:

> For example, as soon as we described senile behavior, they said it was well known that older people become childish, do not answer questions properly, cannot remember things, "beat around the bush," and generally lose their capacities, but from the Yoruba viewpoint this kind of behavior is not "illness"; it is a normal part of life. Just as a child cannot do many things, so an older person cannot do many things; one does not take people to native healers for this kind of behavior because there is no treatment for it. It was apparent, then, that although the description of senile behavior was not volunteered under the category of mental illness it nevertheless was well known to our informants. Most psychoneurotic symptoms, certain manifestations of depression, and a good many kinds of personality disorders also were known but were not regarded as

illness; rather, they were considered to be uncomfortable, undesirable, impairing, and in some instances unusual [459].

Even those behaviors that are labeled mentally ill are not given a great deal of attention in these tribal societies (Waxler, 1974).

The breakdown of closely knit social structures and the emergence of less cohesive, industrialized, and urbanized societies is associated with the expansion of mental illness labeling. Through the end of the nineteenth century, in addition to the psychoses, only a small number of discrete, unwanted, and disturbing symptoms such as hysteria, phobias, and obsessive–compulsive preoccupations were labeled as mental illness (Leifer, 1969:107). In large part because of Freudian influence, the notion of mental illness expanded at the beginning of the twentieth century to include various forms of interpersonal disturbances, vague feelings of dissatisfaction, depression, anxiety, and other problems of living (Szasz, 1961). In the United States,

> while in the late nineteenth century "insanity" and "mental disease" tended to be interchangeable labels for a mysterious organic disease, the terms now began to acquire new, distinguishable meanings. "Mental disease," or more commonly "mental illness," became an umbrella concept that covered both "insanity" and a wide range of relatively minor mental and nervous disorders—disturbances increasingly viewed as both commonplace and transitory [R. W. Fox, 1978:15].

The psychiatrist William A. White emphasized that the concept of mental illness was enlarged at the beginning of the twentieth century so that "not only were the minor psychoses and the neuroses included, but all forms of social maladjustments and even unhappiness were seen to have mechanisms quite the same as the more serious conditions with which we were more familiar [quoted in R. W. Fox, 1978:184]."

By the 1960s, the typical psychiatric patient was far removed from any concrete form of mental illness. Instead,

> all experience is symptomatic now. People seek treatment because they sleep poorly, or have headaches, or feel apathetic toward loved ones, or because they are dissatisfied with their lives. Patients complain of the boredom and vacuity of their inner freedom, and desire to learn how to fill it by means of strategies that guarantee more direct satisfaction. [Rieff, 1961:334. This quotation and following quotations from Rieff (1961) are reprinted from *Freud: The Mind of the Moralist* © 1959, 1961, 1979 by Philip Rieff. Reprinted by permission of The University of Chicago Press.]

The range of behaviors now treated by professional psychiatrists have vastly increased to include

> hospitalized psychotics, criminal offenders, unhappy heterosexuals, happy and unhappy homosexuals, politicians, children who do not seem to want to learn,

unhappy couples seeking divorce, unhappy couples not seeking divorce, the poor, the aged, the retarded infants, narcotics addicts, problem drinkers, and patients suffering from such illnesses as ulcers. Psychiatrists at times consider it their proper task to deal with people who are excessively selfish and self-centered (narcissistic character disorders), people who are excessively private (schizoid character disorders), and people who just seem never to make it in life ("inadequate personality") [Simon, 1978:29].

It is not surprising that one prominent contemporary psychiatrist can state: "It is now accepted that most people have some degree of mental illness at some time, and may have a degree of mental illness most of the time [Menninger, 1963:33]." Corresponding to the growing range of disorders psychiatrists consider as mental illness is a growing range of mental illness labeling among the lay public. Between the 1950s and the 1970s, laypersons became increasingly more likely to identify instances of peculiar behavior as signs of mental illness (Rabkin, 1974).

The expansion of mental illness labeling is also occurring in the contemporary developing world. One psychiatrist, commenting upon the tremendous growth in the use of outpatient facilities in India notes:

During this relatively short period (between 1949 and 1964), the clientele has changed not only in numbers but also in diagnostic composition. Sixteen years ago many of the patients were suffering from severe brain damage or chronic schizophrenia; today, the majority are suffering from minor psychiatric disorders, including many cases of psychosomatic illness, anxiety states, and reactive depression. . . . I have been impressed particularly by the emergence of the awareness on the part of patients and their relatives that to suffer painful degrees of anxiety or depression is not simply an act of god, an affliction to be borne as best one may. . . . These complaints are beginning to be perceived as illness, susceptible of medical treatment. My Indian colleagues tell me that this tendency is still more marked among their private patients, who tend to be more sophisticated than the clinic clients. It seems, therefore, that in India and perhaps in other developing countries the relatively new specialty of psychiatry very soon will be confronted by a mounting tide of demand for attention and help [Carstairs, 1969:413].

While the pressures produced by social development may account for some of the growing rates of mental illness (Leighton, 1959; Fried, 1964), it is likely that increasing utilization rates of psychiatric facilities are more related to changing patterns of mental illness recognition than to a greater amount of mental illness. The same types of symptoms that once were defined in alternative ways are now coming to be labeled as indicative of mental illness.

A number of reasons account for the growth of mental illness labeling in recent times. One is the growth and expansion of cosmopolitan culture. Just as individuals involved in "high-brow" culture are most likely to recognize mental illness, a growth of this type of culture in a society predicts an increased amount and range of labeled mental illness. Psychoanalysis developed in a cosmopolitan center of its time, Vienna, and flourished to the greatest extent in the most culturally heterogeneous country, the United States. To the extent that the developing world assimilates this culture, the expansion of mental illness labeling will correspondingly grow.

The growth of societal differentiation, as well as of cosmopolitan culture, predicts an increase in labeled mental illness. As societies become more differentiated over time (Parsons, 1977), individuals are released from the bonds of extended kin and communal groups and more interaction occurs among strangers at a great relational distance from each other. While members of a tightly knit community share a common culture, strangers are less likely to share a common framework that interprets behavior, and so may apply more labels of mental illness to one another. The proposition that predicts that individuals at a great relational distance are more likely to label mental illness also implies that a growth of aggregate relational distance in a society leads to more mental illness labeling.

An additional correlate of the growing amount of mental illness labeling is the growing power of the psychiatric profession in contemporary societies. In the United States, for example, over the past 30 years the number of psychiatrists has increased from 1000 to over 25,000 (Torrey, 1974:25). In addition, a number of various types of psychiatric professionals have emerged, such as clinical psychologists, psychiatric social workers, psychiatric nurses, and others in related specialties. Psychiatrists have come to occupy important roles in the criminal justice system, the military, schools, guidance clinics, and all types of rehabilitation programs (Halleck, 1971; Kittrie, 1971). Because the range of behaviors viewed as mentally ill by psychiatric professionals is so much greater than that labeled by laypersons, as the power and influence of this profession increases, so does the amount of labeled mental illness.

Just as the labeling of mental illness increases among psychiatric professionals, individuals who participate in cosmopolitan culture, and those at a great relational distance from each other, societies with more of these people in their population will label more mental illness. As cultural and social heterogeneity, the growth of cosmopolitan culture, and the power of psychiatric professionals increase, the concept of mental illness expands. It is no surprise that the country where each of these factors is maximal, the United States, is also the one with the greatest amount and range of mental illness labeling. In addition, as these factors become more prevalent throughout the world, a greater amount of mental illness labeling results.

While psychiatric epidemiologists have long claimed that the growth of "civilization" brings with it an increase in the amount of mental illness, this claim has been a subject of controversy (Schwab and Schwab, 1978). What is beyond question, however, is that the amount and range of behaviors *labeled* as mentally ill have undergone a tremendous increase with the expansion of "civilization." If current trends of greater professional power, cultural heterogeneity, and structural differentiation continue, the amount of mental illness labeling should also continue to expand. A theory of social control, not of mental illness, predicts the evolution and growth of the concept of mental illness over time.

## Conclusion

An individual's location in social space predicts the probability that he or she will recognize and label mental illness. Higher social class, more education, cosmopolitan culture, and female gender all are associated with more labeling of mental illness. The most labeling of mental illness occurs among a small group of urban, cosmopolitan intellectuals, Jews, and humanistic professionals. As the values of individuals approach those of psychiatric professionals, they are more likely to recognize a greater amount and range of behaviors as mentally ill. This does not mean that their conception of mental illness is necessarily a more correct one, but only that they share the labeling practices and values of psychiatric professionals. In addition, the expansion and spread of cosmopolitan culture, societal differentiation, and psychiatric influence over the course of the twentieth century has led to a growing amount and range of mental illness labeling on the societal level.

The amount of labeled mental illness is distinct from the presence of mental symptoms, as these symptoms are measured by the psychiatric profession. The best predictors of mental illness labeling, such as social class, education, or Jewish ethnicity, are directly related to the labeling of mental illness but inversely related to the presence of mental symptoms. Upper-class individuals, for example, are most likely to recognize the presence of mental illness in themselves and in others but least likely to have psychiatric symptoms. Even when there is an empirical overlap between the presence of symptoms and the recognition process, as in the case of gender, the factors that predict the recognition of mental symptoms are distinct from those that lead to the development of these symptoms. Therefore, the greater amount of mental illness labeling in certain groups cannot be explained by the presence of more "real" mental illness in these groups. Instead, the recognition of mental illness is a process worthy of study in its own right. The factors that predict the recognition and labeling of mental illness are distinct from those associated with the development of mental symptoms.

# 5

## The Reaction to Mental Illness

The preceding chapter examined some of the conditions under which individuals are labeled mentally ill. Once these labels have been applied, there are many possible responses to the individuals. They may be pitied or scorned, excluded from the group or maintained within it, ignored or treated. A theory of social control should predict the circumstances under which various kinds of reactions to the mentally ill will occur. This chapter examines the social variation in the response to individuals who have been labeled mentally ill.

One way to order the reaction to the mentally ill is along a continuum of exclusion or inclusion. On one end of this continuum is a coercive, stigmatizing, and rejecting view of the mentally ill whereby they are excluded from the group. Formal, institutionalized methods are used to isolate the mentally ill and they are not seen as ordinary members of the community. On the other end of the continuum is a sympathetic, caring reaction in which the mentally ill are maintained within the community and little is made of their conditions. They continue to be viewed as members of the group. Between these end points are varying combinations of exclusion or inclusion.

The continuum between exclusion and inclusion is not a one-dimensional one but has two major aspects. The first is the degree to which the societal reaction involves informal or formal means of handling the mentally ill. At one extreme, affected individuals may remain in the community without using any special services for the mentally ill; at the other extreme they may enter an institution that separates them from the community. A second aspect of exclusion or inclusion is the degree of coerciveness of the societal reaction. The reaction to the mentally ill may range from a harshly rejecting and stigmatizing response to a sympathetic and accepting attitude. The informal and accepting responses are considered "inclusive" and the formal and rejecting reactions "exclusive." Yet the degree of coerciveness and the use of formal institutions do not always overlap. In some cases in which an individual is hospitalized in a formal institution, the reaction may be one of concern, as when a family places one of its members in the institution in the belief that it suits the ill person's best interests. Or, hospitalization may be the most humane alternative for persons without family or friends. In other cases, mentally ill members may be maintained within the informal network yet coercively treated, as when they are chained and locked in closets or cellars. Usually, however, an exclusion reaction will be more coercive than an inclusive one. My use of the term *exclusion* encompasses both the degree of coerciveness and the use of formal means of social control. Whenever appropriate, I distinguish between these two aspects of exclusion.

There have been three major explanations of the treatment accorded to the mentally ill. The first is the behaviorist position that views the type of behavior displayed by the mentally ill as the best predictor of the societal reaction to them (Murphy, 1976). According to this view, the social control of the mentally ill shows neither constant progress nor growing exclusion over time but has remained relatively constant in most cultures. Murphy (1976) summarizes this position.

> There is apparently a common range of possible responses to the mentally ill person, and the portion of the range brought to bear regarding a particular person is determined more by the nature of his behavior than by a preexisting cultural set to respond in a uniform way to whatever is labeled mental illness. If the behavior indicates helplessness, help tends to be given, especially food and clothes. If the behavior appears foolish or incongruous . . . , laughter is the response. If the behavior is noisy and agitated, the response may be to try to quiet, sometimes by herbs and sometimes by other means. If the behavior is violent or threatening, the response is to restrain or subdue [1025].

In the behaviorist view, the social characteristics of the deviant and controller, the nature of the community, or the control technology are relatively unimportant determinants of the reaction to the mentally ill. Instead, the behavior of the mentally ill, which has similar manifestations in all cultures, is seen as evoking a universal range of responses.

## 5. The Reaction to Mental Illness

A second approach, usually found in traditional medical histories, finds a progressive evolutionary dynamic in the reaction to the mentally ill (e.g., Zilboorg, 1941; Ackerknecht, 1959; Alexander and Selesnick, 1966; Wing, 1978). Until the advent of a modern medical viewpoint about mental illness, the mentally ill were consistently feared, mistreated, and loathed (Dain, 1964:xii). Supernatural and demonological beliefs prevailed, which led to the persecution and mistreatment of the mentally ill. Not until the enlightened changes in treatment brought about by Tuke and Pinel in the late eighteenth and nineteenth centuries did the mentally ill come to be treated in a humanitarian fashion. The initial development of mental hospitals reflected a progressive concern for the mentally ill and a desire to remove them from intolerable conditions in jails, workhouses, or the community (Wing, 1978). Another major change was brought about by the development and implementation of Freudian theory. Freud is often credited as the first major figure who "introduced a sound and scientific kind of psychological reasoning that did not appear to threaten medicine with relapse into its magical and animistic origins [Alexander and Selesnick, 1966:23]." Particularly important was the growing belief that mental illness was a disease similar to physical illness:

> The most significant and perhaps the only real advance registered by mankind in evolving a rational and humane method of handling behavioral aberrations has been in substituting a concept of disease for the demonological and retributional doctrines regarding their nature and etiology that flourished until comparatively recent times [Ausebel, 1961:71].

The contemporary treatment of the mentally ill by medically trained psychiatrists who use scientific methods is viewed as the culmination of two centuries of evolutionary progress from the fear and loathing of the mentally ill to their current humanitarian and scientific treatment.

A third view of the societal reaction to the mentally disordered contrasts with the progressive view. This perspective finds growing coerciveness in the treatment of the mentally ill over time rather than growing enlightenment (e.g., Foucault, 1965; Rothman, 1971; Scull, 1979). In this view, the treatment of the mentally ill was relatively benign before formal institutions developed to exclude them, and the last several hundred years of Western history have been marked by a growing rejection of the mentally ill. The medical ideology that justifies the contemporary treatment of the mentally ill, according to this perspective, is a gloss on the coercive methods of social control actually in use (Szasz, 1963). Advocates of this view believe that the social control of mental illness is imposed by formal authorities in an attempt to restrain powerless groups and impose social order, and that the changing ideologies of elite groups regarding the most adequate ways to insure community cohesion produced the separation of the mentally ill from the rest of society (Rothman, 1971). Like other forms of social control, this perspective sees the reaction to mental illness as reflecting the interests of the elite at the expense of other groups. Where the evolutionary view finds a growing humanitarianism in the reaction to the mentally ill, the critical view finds an elaboration of institutionalized methods of exclusion.

Despite the clear differences between the progressive and critical views, they share certain assumptions. The first is that both find the major determinant of societal reaction in the changing consciousness of elite groups, whether in humanitarian ideals and the concept of disease according to the progressive view, or in notions of order and reason according to the critical view. This emphasis on ideas, however, overlooks underlying social structural changes that may lead to greater or lesser capacities for inclusion or exclusion. A second shared assumption of both views is that elite groups, especially medical and other agents of social control, are the major shapers of societal reaction. This emphasis on the elite ignores the basically reactive nature of formal institutions of the control of mental disorder. Members of informal groups usually make the decision to exclude the mentally ill and then bring the affected individual to official attention. While lay consciousness is to some extent influenced by the values of psychiatric authorities, to a greater extent it reflects indigenous values. The key to understanding the societal reaction to the mentally ill should lie more in the nature of informal networks and their interaction with formal institutions than in the consciousness of the psychiatric elite.

The central thesis of this chapter diverges from each of the three common views about societal reaction to mental illness. I do not find the major determinants of societal reaction in the behavior of the mentally ill, the ideas of the psychiatric profession, or the needs of formal agents of social control. Instead, I use the strength of social resources and social control within informal groups such as families, neighborhoods, and communities to predict the degree of exclusion of the mentally ill. When informal networks possess the resources to take care of the mentally ill, they will rarely reject them or rely on formal means of social control. In contrast, the breakdown of control resources within informal networks predicts the rejection of the mentally ill and the development and use of formal means to exclude them. For the most part, formal systems of social control of mental illness respond to the changing demands for social control by families and communities. This thesis is a deduction from the general nature of formal social control: formal systems of social control are stronger when informal control is weaker and are rarely used when alternative means of social control are available (Black, 1976:Ch. 6). To understand the reaction to the mentally ill, the focus here will be on the nature of social groups, not on psychiatric professionals or other formal agents of social control, or on the behavior of the mentally ill themselves.

## Social Variation in the Reaction to Mental Illness

One way to categorize social groups is by their degree of social cohesiveness (also see Chapter 7). A communal group is one with a high degree of cohesiveness that features many ties between its members and a value system that emphasizes the welfare of the group. Structurally, a communal group has a tightly intertwined network of interaction among its members (Bott, 1957). Culturally, communal groups maintain value systems oriented to the solidarity of the collectivity rather than to the welfare of individual members (Dumont, 1976). The degree of cultural distance between members is low. The opposite of the communal group is the individualistic group. When the group is individualistic, there are few ties between group members, the value system stresses the autonomy of each individual, and the cultural distance between members is often high.

The distinction between communal and individualistic groups underlies many of the most fundamental typologies of societies in social science including mechanical and organic solidarity (Durkheim, 1893/ 1964), gemeinschaft and gesellschaft (Tonnies, 1887/1963), folk and urban character (Redfield, 1947), and status and contract relationships (Maine, 1861/1963). In contrast to these distinctions, however, communal and individualistic group structures are not viewed here from an evolutionary perspective. While individualistic societies are almost exclusively limited to the modern West, all modern societies have pockets of cohesiveness such as some urban ethnic communities and some small towns. In addition, the distinction between communal and individualistic groups is used here not only for total societies but also for communities within societies, interpersonal networks, and families. Communal groups are found whenever there is a high degree of cohesiveness among group members. Just as a tribal society is more cohesive than a modern one, a homogeneous ethnic community is more cohesive than a heterogeneous suburb, and an extended kin group more cohesive than a number of isolated nuclear families.

The degree of group cohesiveness, whether within societies, communities, interpersonal networks, or families, predicts the reaction to the mentally ill:

> *The degree of exclusion of people who have been labeled mentally ill varies inversely with the cohesiveness of the social group.*

When groups have strong social and symbolic bonds between their members they will tend to react to the mentally ill with attempts to maintain them within the group and with a minimum of coercion. In contrast, individualistic groups will be more likely to exclude the individual from the group and to adopt a more coercive reaction. In certain ways, this thesis reverses Durkheim's (1893/1964) association of repressive social control with mechanical solidarity and restitutive social control with organic solidarity. Instead, it hypothesizes that tightly knit communal groups respond to deviance through attempts to integrate the deviant into the group while individualistic groups are more likely to reject the deviant.

There are several sources of the greater ability of communal groups to contain the mentally disordered. First, cohesive groups have a greater availability of informal resources that allow them to care for the mentally ill without recourse to formal mechanisms of exclusion. Because of the high degree of exchange of goods and services within tightly knit networks, a low role performance of one member can have less impact on group functioning as a whole. In addition, communal groups have a greater ability than individualistic ones to provide role replacements so that the tasks of the mentally ill member may be assumed by other members of the group. Finally, the members of communal groups are in contact with each other and thus can unite in efforts of informal social control of the disruptive behavior. In these ways, communal groups are better able than individualistic ones to absorb and contain the disruptive behavior that stems from mental disorder.

The cohesiveness of the group is not the only factor that predicts the type of reaction to the mentally ill. In addition to the degree of informal resources of social groups, the capacity of the group to *normalize* the symptoms of mental illness has a strong impact on the type of societal reaction. Whenever cultural interpretations, social roles, or treatment technologies that reduce the degree of bizarreness and disruption of mental symptoms are available and used, exclusion becomes a less likely reaction. Groups may normalize symptoms of mental illness in a number of ways. First, certain cultural interpretations of mental disorder may lead to a greater tolerance than other interpretations. For example, viewing mental symptoms as a sign of divine inspiration makes symptoms more acceptable than viewing them as signs of wickedness or laziness. Second, some groups have culturally defined roles for the mentally disordered, such as shaman, prophet, or spiritualist, that are not present in other groups. Such roles provide an alternative to an exclusion reaction. Finally, certain technologies such as drug treatment or psychotherapy may control the most disruptive symptoms of mental illness. Groups that possess such technologies can maintain disordered members more easily than those that do not.

To some extent, communal groups should have a greater capacity than individualistic groups to normalize symptoms of mental illness because the cultural distance between members is smaller. This follows from the proposition that the recognition of mental illness is directly related to the cultural distance between members (see Chapter 3). Yet in other respects, communal groups do not necessarily have greater normalization capacities than individualistic ones. Normalization technologies such as drug therapy, for example, develop independently of the structure of the social group. Therefore, the reaction to the mentally disordered is not solely related to the cohesiveness of the group but is also reflective of factors such as the effectiveness of treatment technologies, the availability of defined social roles for the mentally ill, and the cultural interpretation of symptoms. The lowest degree of exclusion of the mentally ill occurs when both informal resources and normalization capacities are high; the greatest degree of exclusion occurs when both of these factors are weak or absent. When informal resources or normalization capacities, but not both, are available, the reaction to the mentally ill should be intermediate between inclusion and exclusion.

## THE REACTION TO THE MENTALLY ILL IN TRIBAL SOCIETIES

The prototypical communal community is a small, tribal society. While there are tremendous variations between different tribal social structures compared to modern societies, they provide an "ideal type" of communal social group. Individuals are typically bound to a small number of kinsmen and tribesmen throughout their lives, are encompassed within an interlocking network of social relationships, and are devalued relative to the kin or tribal group. In these societies, the typical reaction to mental illness is to respond to ill persons sympathetically, attempt to maintain them within the group, deemphasize the difference between the mentally ill and other members of the community, and avoid stigmatizing persons who are labeled mentally ill.

A typical reaction to the mentally ill in tribal groups is illustrated by the response to an attack of *malgri*, a psychosis found among the aborigines of the Wellesley Islands, near Australia.

> When the cry goes out that somebody has fallen victim to *malgri*, everybody runs to help. A fire is made near the prostrate victim. From the throng emerges a native practitioner or other elder with knowledge. Kneeling, he massages his axillary sweat into the victim's body. A grass or hair belt is unraveled to provide a long cord, which is tied by one end to the victim's foot while the other is run down to the water in order to point the way home for the intruding spirit. The healer commences the song of exorcism; its innumerable verses are sung through the night, while the assembled people scan the sky for a shooting star. The shooting star is the incarnation of *malgri's* eye, at last diving from the sky to indicate *malgri's* dispossession and banishment. The string is then snapped. The victim recovers. So runs the procedure for treatment [Cawte, 1974:110].

This incident illustrates several typical aspects of the treatment of mental illness in tribal groups. The response focuses on healing ceremonies whose goal is designed to integrate the patient into the social group (Berndt, 1964; Levi-Strauss, 1964; Obeyesekere, 1970). To this end, the entire group is often mobilized to deal with the problem. Therapy occurs in settings that involve collective activities, during which the affected individual is placed at the center of group attention (Kaplan and Johnson, 1964; Turner, 1968). The extreme of group involvement is illustrated by the Navaho Indians of North America: "When hot pokers were applied to the patient's body, the others would receive the same treatment [Kiev, 1964:25–26]." The healing ceremony serves to reaffirm the similarity of the afflicted members to others in the group, not to exclude the individual from the group.

There is little stigma placed on the mentally ill within tribal groups; instead, the group is mobilized to care for the individual. An example is the reaction of relatives to schizophrenics among the Yoruba of rural Ghana:

> The majority of chronic schizophrenics in rural districts are treated with such patient and sustained kindness by their relatives and tolerance by their neighbors that the prognosis for their recovery is probably better than it would be were they herded with other patients in understaffed mental hospitals. If they have phases of destructive violence or of wandering off into the bush they are usually either locked up or fettered to a log during these phases but are released at the earliest moment. . . . The younger schizophrenics are always cared for by their parents, the mothers especially displaying impressively uncomplaining devotion. After the parents' death the brothers and sisters take over [M. J. Field, 1960:453–454].

The tightly knit bonds between members of these societies serve to maintain the ill person with a minimum of exclusion.

As the previously mentioned case indicates, even when a mentally ill member becomes uncontrollably violent, the degree of exclusion is minimal. In another case among the Yoruba,

> an insane man was permitted to roam about a village at will. When he became too disturbed, the villagers would counsel his family and he would be taken either to a bush hamlet for a few days or locked in his own special room. This room had an outside door so that he could come and go without disturbing his family [Osborne, 1969:192].

A similar mode of response to the mentally ill is found among the Ifaluk, a small tribe of natives in the Caroline Islands in the South Seas. Spiro (1950) provides a detailed case study of a native who engaged in behaviors characteristic of a paranoid schizophrenic, such as bizarre actions, unintelligible speech, attempts to burn down houses, fighting, and thievery. After outbursts of violence, this man would be mildly restrained but would be released almost immediately and allowed to rejoin the activities in the village. At one point, he had attacked several villagers:

> By this time people were angrier than I had ever thought they could possibly become. Until now they had all been patient with him, exhibiting the greatest restraints in their treatment of him. But this, apparently, was the stimulus that evoked all their pent-up hostility. Tom was so angry that he slapped Tarev [the mentally ill man] in the face—an unheard of act of aggression in this culture. Their anger was soon dissipated, however, and in the evening a number of people went to visit Tarev and asked if they could do anything for him. Tom told me that he was terribly sorry for what he had done and had invited Tarev to sleep in his house [Spiro, 1950:200].

While the ethnographer attributes the particular type of reaction to mental illness in this group to the nonaggressive nature of South Sea Islanders, their response appears to be more characteristic of tribal groups in general.

A number of factors account for the generally nonstigmatizing, accepting, and inclusive reaction to the mentally ill among tribal groups. The first lies in the high degree of resources available for the care of the mentally ill individual. The relatives of ill individuals feel strongly responsible for their welfare and assist them in many ways, such as performing tasks and chores, taking responsibility for disruptive behavior in the community, and providing goods and services. In all of this, the strong informal resources of a communal group can be put into the service of maintaining the mentally ill person within the informal network.

Despite the fact that the mentally ill are highly visible in small tribal groups, their behavior is given little notice and reaction to it is minimal.

In addition to providing resources to the affected member, tribal groups may respond to mental illness by reducing role responsibilities. For example, among the Gururumba tribe of Highland, New Guinea, a young man may sometimes suddenly engage in "wild man" behavior in which "he rushes about from place to place, gesticulates a great deal, attacks, shouts, scatters objects and breaks into groups of people [Newman, 1964:6]." After such attacks:

> There are no recriminations against a wild man after he has gone wild, and no one in his clan or village will mention the episode to him . . . there is an observable reduction in the expectations others have of the degree he will participate in exchange transactions and a corresponding reduction in the intensity of demands made on him. He may still have debts, but repayment is not pressed aggressively . . . The outcome of wild man behavior is thus a reduction of demands made without loss of social support. The wild man does not become an outcast or deviant in the eyes of others; he becomes a man now known to be incapable of, or unwilling to participate in, certain affairs with the same degree of intensity as others, but still a man who can participate to some degree [Newman, 1964: 16–17].

It is likely that in tribal societies, where members are interdependent on one another for goods and services and where there is a strong sense of collective responsibility, the reduction of role responsibilities can be absorbed by the social network more easily than in individualistic groups.

An additional reason for the inclusive reaction to the mentally ill among tribal peoples lies in their ability to normalize the symptoms of mental disorder. In these groups, after an individual has been treated for mental disorder, recovery is assumed to be complete and the patient is expected to return to normality. Waxler (1974:380), speaking of the peasant culture of Ceylon, reports:

> What accounts for these observations that in a peasant society like Ceylon the patient who has suffered a psychosis can so easily and quickly return to normal? . . . Traditional Ceylonese beliefs about mental illness center upon supernatural causes—demon possession, witchcraft, bad influence of the planets; if a person is supernaturally affected he can be easily treated by prescribed standard rituals carried out by exorcists and priests. The sick person, himself, is not believed to be responsible for the illness; his body or soul may be possessed but his "self" remains unchanged. If he follows the appropriate prescriptions, then it is believed that his symptoms will disappear and he will quickly and easily return to normal. There is no stigma attached to mental illness; no one believes that the patient is "different" and should be treated in a new way after his symptoms have gone. Thus, the way people formulate the illness calls forth certain societal expectations and responses which, in the Ceylonese case, seem to allow the patient to drop the sick role quickly and easily. [Reprinted by permission from "Culture and mental ill-

ness: A social labeling perspective" by Nancy E. Waxler in the *Journal of Nervous and Mental Disease* (1974) 159:379-395. Copyright © 1974 The Williams & Wilkins Co., Baltimore.]

Because of the expectation of a quick return to normality, symptoms of mental illness are generally of briefer duration and of less chronicity in tribal societies, allowing mentally ill individuals to avoid the stigmatizing social role they sometimes take on in modern Western societies (Scheff, 1966a).

The normalization reaction typical of tribal groups is also illustrated in the response of arctic Eskimoes to *pibloktoq*, a state in which the victim becomes wildly excited, tears off his or her clothing, breaks furniture, shouts obscenely, throws objects, and eats feces. Wallace (1972) notes that

> an attack of *pibloktoq* is not automatically taken as a sign of the individual's general incompetency. The victim is, if necessary, prevented from injuring himself or others; otherwise he is left alone while the attack spends itself. The attack may be the subject of good-humored joking later but is not used to justify restriction of the victim's social participation. There is, in other words, little or no stigma; the attack is treated as an isolated event rather than as a symptom of deeper illness [379].

The view of mental illness as an episodic occurrence that does not change the fundamental nature of the person appears to be an effective normalization technique that allows the mentally ill person in a tribal society avoid assuming the role of a chronic patient.

Because of the effectiveness of normalization techniques, labels of mental illness typically do not have the negative and long-standing consequences that modern Western societies often associate with them. For example, an ethnographer of the Zapotec Indians of Mexico noted that after months of fieldwork regarding Zapotec conceptions of deviance, he had collected no material about mental illness (Selby, 1974). On further questioning, he found that

> crazy people ate, drank, and socialized with everyone else, and most of the time their behavior was unremarkable. One man regularly went into psychotic states and equally regularly emerged from them, but the villagers were not that interested in his condition. Another man sometimes had to be restrained within the house, if barring the door of a bamboo hut can be called restraint. Crazy people were not stigmatized in any way, even though it was judged unlikely that they would be elected to a powerful political office; but in any case, they would not seek office. If they had delusional symptoms, no one was particularly interested in them or felt that they had special powers of any kind [Selby, 1974:41-42].

In a study of the reaction to mental illness among four East African tribes, Edgerton (1969) also found a high degree of consensus that nothing should be done about the behavior of the mentally ill. Instead, they were allowed to wander through villages and engage in bizarre behavior without any coercive reaction being taken against them.

Tribal groups may also react to the mentally ill not by ignoring their differences from others but by emphasizing these differences and placing them in valued healing roles. For example, Benedict (1934) finds that among the Shasta Indians of California,

> it is clear that, so far from regarding cataleptic seizures as blots upon the family escutcheon and as evidences of dreaded disease, cultural approval had seized upon them and made of them the pathway to authority over one's fellows. They were the outstanding characteristic of the most respected social type, the type which functioned with most honor and reward in the community. It was precisely the cataleptic individuals who in this culture were singled out for the authority and leadership [61–62].

Similarly, Benedict (1934) reports that in Siberia,

> the shamans of Siberia dominate their communities. According to the ideas of these peoples, they are individuals who by submission to the will of the spirits have been cured of a grievous illness—the onset of the seizures—and have acquired by this means great supernatural power and incomparable vigor and health [62].

In other tribal groups someone who has undergone an episode of mental illness may become a member of a healing cult that collectively treats cases of mental illness (Messing, 1959; Dawson, 1964; Constantinodes, 1977). The mobilization of the mentally ill in the service of a valued social end enables them to avoid a negatively defined social role and to be maintained within the group.

The bulk of evidence indicates that the treatment of mental disorder in tribal groups minimizes the significance of the disorder and the stigma connected with it. The response to affected individuals focuses on returning them to normal or, occasionally, valued roles as quickly as possible. The energies of the community are mobilized to integrate them into the mainstream of community life. In extreme cases, coercion may be applied but even then it is usually of brief duration and of minimal scope. While formal mechanisms of institutionalization are not available to these societies, many alternatives such as isolation, banishment, or death would be possible. The rarity of these responses testifies to the inclusive reaction of tribal societies to their mentally disordered members.

## 5. The Reaction to Mental Illness

All of the elements that predict an inclusive reaction to mental disorder—the presence of strong informal resources to care for the individual, a high capacity to normalize behavior, and the ability to reduce role obligations or provide alternative nondeviant roles—are found in tribal groups. Hence, small, tribal societies lie on the most inclusive end of the reaction spectrum. In other settings, where varying combinations of these factors are present, the reaction to the mentally ill becomes more complex.

### THE REACTION TO THE MENTALLY ILL IN OTHER COMMUNAL SETTINGS

The general proposition indicates that the reaction to mental disorder found in tribal groups stems from the cohesive nature of tribal societies. If so, the general style of reacting to the mentally ill found in tribal groups should also be found in communal social groups in a wide variety of historical and cultural settings. Of course, there are also dramatic differences in culture and personality between tribal and other communal groups that lead to many differences, as well as similarities, in the societal reaction to the mentally ill. Nevertheless, because members of communal groups of all sorts have continuing relationships with one another, the use of coercive sanctions can lead to lasting alienation between members that destroys the solidarity on which tightly knit groups depend. Therefore, the reaction to the mentally ill, as to other types of deviants in communal groups, should be an inclusive one.

Evidence from various types of communal societies and communities indicate that the inclusive response to mental disorder found among tribal peoples is a more general response in communal groups. For example, the People's Republic of China under the leadership of Mao Zedong was one large, contemporary society marked by a strong orientation to the group, a collective ideology, and tightly knit social structures organized around groups called *"hsiao-tsu"* (Whyte, 1974). The reaction to the mentally ill in China reflects this collective emphasis through the use of shared ideology to attach the patient to the group and the mobilization of the social network to help deal with the patient's problems (Sidel, 1975; Lu, 1978). Chinese mental patients are not excluded from the group; instead, group ties are mobilized to integrate the patient with the community. According to one sociological observer, the Chinese treatment of mental patients provides

all those concerned with a sense of group participation and group belonging which may broaden individuals' self-identity and enhance their strength and feeling of self-esteem. This sense of national community is a strong driving force

97

in promoting the mental health program in China. . . . Instead of depending completely on mental health professionals, the system uses a social network approach which relies heavily on the communities, on others significant to the patients in all areas of their lives, as well as on the patients themselves for support in modifying and changing attitudes and behavior [Lu, 1978:10].

When even modern societies are oriented to a common ideology and emphasize group over individual purposes, they are able to integrate, rather than expel, the mentally ill.

A number of studies also indicate that communities marked by tight bonds between members make inclusive responses to the mentally ill. The Hutterite communities in the Northern United States and Southern Canada are examples of small communities isolated from the larger society, held together by a common religious ideology and a tightly knit social structure. In an intensive study of mental illness among the Hutterites, Eaton and Weil (1955) found that despite a rate of mental illness roughly equivalent to other societies, no Hutterite had ever been hospitalized. Instead, the group adopted a supportive and sympathetic attitude toward its mentally ill members and maintained them within the community.

The Hutterite patient, unlike the average American patient, is not socially isolated. . . . The community reaction among the Hutterites is generally more accepting. The patient becomes a center of attention. The immediate family makes arrangements to guard and nurse him at all times; the colony gives whatever support is needed [Eaton and Weil, 1955:168].

Similarly, the mentally ill in colonial America were cared for within the family and community. Grob (1973) notes: "Until the middle of the eighteenth century there were no hospitals in any of the colonies that could provide either therapy or custodial care for the insane persons. The best that such individuals received therefore, was kind and humane care by those who loved and cared for them [10]." There is, however, little evidence regarding the degree of coercion involved in the care of the mentally ill in colonial America.

Studies of urban ethnic groups in the United States that are marked by extended kinship and friendship ties also show that these groups are reluctant to exclude the mentally ill through hospitalization and attempt to maintain them within the community. A study of an Italian subculture in Boston found that persons who were considered mentally ill were maintained within the group through an emphasis on conformity to group norms and on group solidarity (Gans, 1962:266). In Italy itself, the emphasis on family cohesion and maintaining the mentally ill in the community in Southern Italy leads this part of the country to have a rate of mental hospitalization less than one-half that of the more industrialized North (Lemkau and de Santis, 1950). Mexican-Americans in the United States also have a utilization rate of psychiatric facilities far below their proportion in the general population, in part because of close and interdependent family structures that provide them with support and protect them from exclusion (Torrey, 1972:Ch. 8). A study of the Japanese-American community in Los Angeles also notes that the strong family systems and cohesiveness of this community leads to an extremely low rate of psychiatric utilization. Families go to elaborate lengths to protect the mentally ill, including. "high tolerance for 'crazy behavior,' a redefinition of family roles, and, finally, the use of external resources only if the effects of the deviant behavior caused major disruption in the family (Kitano, 1969:273)." In this tightly knit community, even individuals without families may be sheltered within the community and protected from outside intervention:

> For example, there is the case of an elderly Issei woman who died recently. During her lifetime she was rather widely known for her eccentric behavior—talking to animals, communicating with spirits, and displaying extremely erratic behavior in conducting her business. She was a widow left with running a small store; her absent-mindedness, her eccentric buying and spending habits and her extreme emotionality would have meant immediate failure for most stores. Instead, her loyal employees protected her, gradually taking over and handling her as they would a child. There was no thought of sending her for any psychiatric treatment (who could talk to her in Japanese?), no thought of hospitalization, and a rather amused tolerance for her odd and eccentric ways [Kitano, 1969: 278–279].

Even within highly individuated societies, when communities are cohesive, the reaction to the mentally ill tends to be inclusive.

As in tribal societies, the typical response to mental illness in modern close-knit communities is inclusive. There is a strong normative emphasis on the collective responsibility to care for a disordered member and a corresponding reluctance to release the person to formal agents of control. To the end of informal maintenance, aid and services are provided that allow the individual to function at a low level. Yet, the strong capacity to normalize symptoms of disorder found in tribal groups seems to be largely absent in modern ethnic communities. Hence, if members of these subcultures eventually do come to enter psychiatric treatment, they may show severe symptoms of disorder. The inclusive response of modern close-knit communities to the mentally ill seems to result more from the availability of informal resources and a sense of collective responsibility than from the ability to normalize symptoms of mental disorder.

## THE REACTION TO THE MENTALLY ILL WITH THE
## BREAKDOWN OF COHESIVE COMMUNITIES

While an inclusive reaction to the mentally ill occurs within communal groups, the breakdown of tightly knit groups predicts their exclusion. This is illustrated in ancient Greece, Israel and Rome. The development of growing social complexity in these societies led to a lessening toleration for the mentally ill. In fifth-century Greece,

> it is clear from various sources that the madman, even when regarded as in some way touched by the divine was a person to be shunned. Contact with holiness, like contact with its opposite uncleanness, was perilous and to be avoided. In fifth century Greece, madness was widely considered the consequence of a divine curse, and an insane person was therefore polluted and a thing of evil omen [Rosen, 1968:86].

This attitude toward the mentally ill, however, was the product of the development of Greek civilization. Socrates in Plato's *Phaedrus* noted that "madness was accounted no shame nor disgrace by the men of old," implying that the earlier, more tightly knit, Greek communities did not reject the mad (Rosen, 1968:87). In ancient Israel, "Madmen who were not violent wandered about, roaming the streets in towns and the roads of the countryside. Not infrequently they were followed by children or street loafers who mocked, ridiculed and abused them, and often threw stones at them [Rosen, 1968:64]." Nevertheless, there were no formal institutions within which the mentally ill were contained in ancient societies.

In medieval Europe, the typical reaction to the mentally ill illustrates varying degrees of inclusion and exclusion. On the one hand, the mentally disordered did not participate in community life, were often stigmatized, and treated harshly. On the other hand, they were left to roam the countryside at liberty, as long as they caused no disturbance: "Harmless lunatics were permitted to roam the streets and roads; others were whipped out of town [Rosen, 1968:152]." According to Foucault (1965), until the Renaissance, the mentally ill were viewed as part of the order of things and "man's dispute with madness was a dramatic debate in which he confronted the secret powers of the world [xii]." Mad people exerted a fascination for normal consciousness and were highly visible in the societies of the time. Thus, the mentally disordered were an aspect of the everyday landscape, were not excluded from public consciousness, and no institutions existed for their confinement.

The partial tolerance shown the mentally ill in the medieval period may stem from several factors. The cultural conception of madness

**100**

allowed the public to feel that the mad had a kind of special participation in the world of the spirit and, in the myths and literature of the time, they often symbolically engaged in a dialogue with accepted wisdom (Foucault, 1965). While this participation was not mobilized in any valued social role, as in some tribal societies, it allowed the mentally ill to have a definite place in public consciousness, thereby partially normalizing their behavior. In addition, during this time the requirements for subsistence were minimal. There was little emphasis on productivity and people who were not able to work could minimally subsist through begging without grossly offending public morality. Both the cultural conception of madness and the standards of role performance, however, were to change rapidly, resulting in a drastic shift in the response to the mentally ill.

The breakdown of social cohesiveness in Western societies resulted in a more dramatic exclusion of the mentally disturbed. Confinement in mental institutions arose between the sixteenth and nineteenth centuries in Western Europe concomitant with the emergence of the capitalist market economy (Foucault, 1965; Rosen, 1968; Scull, 1979). To some extent there is a direct relationship between capitalism and the rise of the asylum because the new emphasis on rationality and productivity lessened the normalization capacities and increased the requirements for performance found in the earlier period. The ideological emphasis on rationality left little room for viewing mental symptoms as manifestations of spiritual power. In addition, the emphasis on productive role performance for all individuals made low functioners such as the mentally ill, as well as all those who could not or would not work, vulnerable to formal social control. In these respects, the conditions of early capitalist societies maximized the probability of the exclusion of the mentally ill.

Yet, the importance of capitalism per se in leading to the rise of the asylum should not be overemphasized. The new social system led to the breakdown of informal control systems that earlier had been able to contain the mentally ill. Old feudal forms of social solidarity were destroyed, migration increased, large cities expanded, and a new class of persons emerged who were marginal to the social order. A detailed and careful study of admissions to asylums in Lancashire, England between 1848 and 1850 concludes:

> If we view mental illness as effectively socially defined, we find that the important variables are migration patterns, family structure and economy, and the scale of urban living. Large cities whose growth was fuelled by long-distance migration, and whose inhabitants lacked the solidarity which soon arose from shared work experiences and, perhaps, a disciplined industrial environment,

were generous providers of lunatics for the new custodial institutions. In the smaller towns and industrial villages, where kin and migrants from the same village were accessible and the workplace built up a supportive friendship network of its own, the working-class family was better able to deal with the problem of what was coming to be seen as insanity than it had been in a countryside dominated by scattered small holdings. This analysis of the distribution of asylum admissions, then, provides support for the contention that the really disruptive effects of early industrialization arose less from the coming of the factory system than from the sprawling, uncontrolled great cities whose economies were still organized largely on traditional lines [Walton, 1979:18].

During this later period of capitalist development, the breakdown of communal groups, more than the development of a capitalist economic system, was responsible for the growing use of asylums as a means of controlling the mentally ill. Regardless of the nature of the economic system, it would have been difficult for the society to contain these marginal individuals in informal networks, without resort to formal exclusion. A changing social system marked by migration and urbanization resulted in a shift of social control functions from the family to external institutions such as mental hospitals.

In the United States, as well as in Europe, the breakdown of cohesive communities led to the exclusion of the mentally ill. Mental hospitals emerged in the first half of the nineteenth century as a response to the growing urbanization, geographic mobility, and immigration of various ethnic groups that split apart the cohesiveness of earlier American communities (Grob, 1973). Before 1810, in the entire country only 500 patients were kept in one public and a few private hospitals. By 1860, 28 of the 33 states had public institutions that contained the insane. The informal control provided by families and communities in a newly industrializing and urbanizing society no longer provided an adequate response to the mentally ill. The source of care shifted to formal institutions that isolated them from the community but, at the same time, provided them with the means of survival in a harsh social environment.

The same factors that led to the development of exclusion in Europe and the United States are currently occurring in both capitalist and non-capitalist societies in the developing world. These societies have traditionally maintained the mentally ill within kin and communal groups. As informal ties break down with growing urbanization throughout the developing world, mental hospitals are increasingly used as a means of handling the mentally disturbed (Mehryar and Khyjavi, 1975). Increased rates of mental hospitalization are one result of the changing social control needs of modernizing societies.

## 5. The Reaction to Mental Illness

More systematic evidence that community cohesiveness predicts the type of reaction to the mentally ill is found in a study that compared the extent of exclusion of the mentally ill in heterogeneous and in homogeneous communities in the state of Washington (Linsky, 1970a). Exclusion was measured by the ratio of involuntary to voluntary commitments to mental hospitals. Hence, in this study, the term *exclusion* refers to the relative degree of coerciveness of the societal reaction rather than to the use of formal institutions. Community heterogeneity was indicated by low political consensus, few common economic interests and values, and a high diversity of racial and ethnic composition. Despite having a lower overall rate of mental illness, heterogeneous communities had a higher ratio of involuntary to voluntary commitments to mental hospitals. This indicates that the less social cohesion in a community, the greater the extent of coercion applied to the mentally ill in that community (see also Gibbs, 1962; Levy and Rowitz, 1972).

### THE REACTION TO THE MENTALLY ILL IN INTERPERSONAL NETWORKS

The proposition that predicts communal societies and communities are more likely than atomized ones to make an inclusive reaction to the mentally ill also predicts the societal reaction within informal social networks and families. Kinship and friendship networks as well as nuclear families that have strong ties among their members are more likely than less cohesive networks to maintain the mentally ill within them.

A number of studies show that communal social networks respond to all types of illnesses through inclusion rather than exclusion (Freidson, 1970:Ch. 13). Studies of help-seeking for mental illness illustrate the same phenomenon. For example, elderly patients with strong relational networks who were hospitalized in California entered mental hospitals after longer periods of time and with more severe disorders than those with weaker networks (Lowenthal, 1964:34–35). Persons with high contact with kin and interlocking friendship groups who sought help at a community mental health center in New Haven received more emotional support and advice for psychiatric problems than those with weaker kinship networks and looser friendship networks (Horwitz, 1978). The structure of the social network provided the kind of support that led individuals with strong networks to delay seeking psychiatric help until they had developed severe psychiatric symptoms (Horwitz, 1977a). The same pattern of support is found in the reaction to the mentally ill among lower-class urban families in Puerto Rico:

Financial aid constitutes a small portion of the material help and benefits that sick families receive from their relatives. The Lebrons were given a house by his mother. Every week the Cardones are given vegetables and fruit by her father. Services, such as transportation, child care, and therapeutic messages, are performed for the sick family members who also receive advice and orientation [Rogler and Hollingshead, 1965:371].

The extensive network of services exchanged within these strong extended family networks helped to maintain the mentally ill within the community without resort to hospitalization. However, this informal maintenance can also have negative consequences. Individuals from tightly knit networks tend to avoid entering psychiatric treatment until their disorders appear quite severe, and so do not receive whatever benefits are available from professional treatment.

Within families, individuals who seem mentally ill who have strong family structures are less likely to be excluded than those whose family ties are weak or nonexistent. One study in New York City found that households with interconnected ties among members, compared to those without such ties, provided more personal care and reacted with less hostility, coercion, and severance of ties after the emergence of mental symptoms (Hammer, 1963–1964). Similarly, in ancient Greece, strong family structures encapsulated their mentally ill members while individuals without families were subject to stoning, scorn, and abuse (Rosen, 1968:89).

A study in South Africa finds that the degree of family organization is the best predictor of the maintenance of the mentally ill in the community (Gillis and Keet, 1965). A group of 16 chronic schizophrenics who had never been hospitalized were compared to a hospitalized control group. Each group had the same degree of bizarre, impulsive, and violent behavior. Those individuals maintained within the family were a tremendous burden, needed constant attention, and often were destructive, overactive, and impulsive (Gillis and Keet, 1965:1061). The major difference between the hospitalized and nonhospitalized groups was the tight and communal family structures in the community group that contained the mentally ill members within them. Especially important was the presence of a close bond with a key relative. The authors conclude that "non-hospitalization was found to be associated with good domestic organization, residential stability, and an almost complete absence of manifest family disorganization and disruptive behavior [Gillis and Keet, 1965:1061]." In contrast to the families that maintained the mentally ill within the community were those that hospitalized their members. In the South African study, the families of the hospitalized patients were marked by a high degree of residential instability and marked disorganization such as fighting, drinking, and divorce (Gillis and Keet, 1965: 1061).

The breakdown of strong family systems leads to a greater tendency to exclude the mentally ill through hospitalization. For example, in 1900, the superintendent of the Binghampton State Hospital in New York, Charles Wagner, commented:

> We are receiving every year a large number of old people, some of them very old, who are simply suffering from the mental decay incident to extreme old age. A little mental confusion, forgetfulness, and garrulity are sometimes the only symptoms exhibited, but the patient is duly certified to us as insane and has no one at home capable or possessed of the means to care for him [quoted in Grob, 1977:37].

The unavailability or unwillingness of relatives to care for the elderly led to an increase of about 3 million to about 9 million in the number of persons 65 and over who were hospitalized between 1900 and 1940, a far higher rate than the increase of population (Grob, 1977:37). A more recent study in California found that about 10% of all admissions of elderly patients to mental hospitals were precipitated by a breakdown in the ability or willingness of family members to care for the patient. A typical case was

> Mr. F., a sixty-four-year old man, who had had a stroke two years prior to admission, was completely paralyzed and needed constant nursing care (his diagnosis was chronic brain syndrome/arteriosclerosis). His wife had to work four days a week to support the family, and a married daughter who lived in the city took over his care at those times. The precipitating factor leading to the decision for hospitalization was the transfer of the daughter's husband to another part of the state [Lowenthal, 1964:44–45].

Other anecdotal evidence also indicates that a weakening of family cohesion can lead to mental hospitalization. For example, Goffman (1961) notes that a wife hospitalized her husband after she found a boyfriend, and children hospitalized their elderly parents after they moved to a new city. As long as the group remains intact, it may maintain its mentally ill members in the community; a fragmentation of the group can lead to the exclusion of the mentally ill.

Other factors determining whether families hospitalize their members are the need for role performance and the availability of role replacements. Single persons who are mentally ill and who live with their parents, for example, are maintained within the family for longer periods of time than spouses, because the former have no critical roles to play (Dinitz *et al.*, 1961). Similarly, persons who play critical roles within families are hospitalized sooner than those who have noncritical roles (Hammer, 1963–1964). The availability of role replacements is one factor that determines the criticalness of a role. For example, mentally disturbed women who have mothers or mothers-in-law available to carry on with household chores and child care remain in the community for longer periods of time than those with no available role replacements (Dinitz *et al.*, 1961). In general, communal groups should be associated with the availability of more role replacements and a corresponding lower demand for role performance from the mentally ill member.

Just as the degree of family cohesion predicts which families will utilize hospitalization or maintain the affected member within the group, it also predicts the development of the institutionalized exclusion of the mentally ill in mental hospitals. In England, mental hospitals developed in the sixteenth century only for persons whose families were no longer able or willing to care for them or for individuals without families at all (Clarke, 1975:216). On the European continent as well, the breakdown of informal family control led to the emergence and spread of mental hospitals as a means of containment for the mentally ill (Rosen, 1968:Ch. 5). In the United States, the strong family structures of colonial America allowed for the maintenance of the mentally disturbed within the family during this period, while the breakdown of these structures in Jacksonian America, caused by urbanization, immigration, and mobility led to the development of mental hospitals (Grob, 1973). The breakdown of family control systems not only predicts the types of families that exclude their members but also the conditions under which mental hospitals develop.

Just as informal networks tend to utilize formal means of control only when network ties are weak or broken, formal controllers tend to initiate hospitalization only when informal means of control are weak or unavailable. This tendency is found at every stage of the psychiatric processing system. The police resist hospitalizing disturbed persons when caretakers in the community can be found and only initiate hospitalization when there are no informal resources (Bittner, 1967). Similarly, individuals without relatives or friends are more likely to be admitted and confined in mental hospitals than those who do not have community resources (Mendel and Rapport, 1969). Once they have entered the hospital, individuals who have families willing to take care of them are released sooner than those who do not (Greenley, 1972). Indeed, the family willingness to care for the individual is a stronger predictor of release from the hospital than both patient desires and the degree of psychiatric impairment. At every stage, psychiatric control agents reflect the tendency of all formal social control to be utilized only when informal alternatives are weak or unavailable (Black, 1976:Ch. 6).

## 5. The Reaction to Mental Illness

Whether the point of reference is societies, communities, networks, or families, communal groups maintain the mentally disturbed within the group and usually react to them with less hostility and rejection than individualistic groups. In contrast, the weakening and breakdown of communal structures leads to the exclusion of the mentally ill and their confinement within formal institutions. The proposition that the exclusion of the mentally ill varies inversely with the cohesion of social groups has a wide range of application. It predicts that tribal societies are less rejecting of the mentally ill than modern ones; that cohesive communities within modern societies are less exclusive than heterogeneous communities in reacting to the mentally ill; and that mental hospitals develop with the breakdown of informal social groups. In addition, it predicts the conditions under which formal networks will utilize mental hospitals and the use of formal means of exclusion when informal social control weakens.

### A NOTE ON "COMMUNITY CARE"

One development that appears to contradict the general proposition is the trend toward "community care" of the mentally ill over the past two decades in Western societies. This trend represents a decline of exclusion without any corresponding increase of social cohesiveness. For example, in the United States, the number of persons confined in mental hospitals per 100,000 population declined from 405.5 in 1950 to 351.3 in 1960 to 213.5 in 1970 (Kramer, 1977:21). In addition to the decline in the number of patients residing in mental hospitals at any given time, there was a drop in the admission rate to mental hospitals in every year between 1971 and 1978 (Milazzo-Sayre, 1978). Similarly, in England and Wales the hospital population declined from 344 per 100,000 population in 1954 to 202 per 100,000 population in 1978 (Wing, 1978:200). Because the declining population of mental hospitals has occurred without a corresponding increase in social cohesion, it apparently cannot be predicted with the proposition.

However, studies of this trend indicate that it is, in large part, more representative of a change in the form of exclusion than in the amount of exclusion. To a great extent, the declining hospital population represents a dramatic decline in the hospitalization of the elderly. For example, in 1962 in the United States persons 65 years and older had a first admission rate of 163.7 per 100,000, the highest of all seven age groups. By 1975, the admission rate of this group declined to 36.7 per 100,000 population, the lowest rate of any group except for children under 15 (Milazzo-Sayre, 1978:6). This trend does not represent a lessening of exclusion but instead the development of an extensive system of nursing homes and other types of formal institutions that care for the elderly. While the elderly, for the most part, have been released from mental hospitals, they have not returned to the community but to alternative types of institutional care.

Other studies of the movement to community care also find that it is more representative of a change in the type of, rather than in the presence of, exclusion. In California, for example, the state where the deinstitutionalization movement has been most extensive, communities have commonly resisted including the mentally ill within them, with the result that the mentally ill often have moved from "the back wards of hospitals . . . to the back alleys of communities [Aviram and Segal, 1973:131]." Another study finds that release from mental hospitals has been accompanied by movement to boarding homes in deteriorated areas of cities that are "like small long-term state hospital wards isolated from the community [Lamb and Goertzel, 1971:31]." Deinstitutionalization has not resulted in community care but rather in the isolation of patients from the community in welfare hotels, boarding houses, or flophouses in the slum areas of cities. Many observers have concluded that, given the lack of support they receive outside the hospital, many patients would be better off within an institution than outside of one (Wing, 1978).

It is predictable from the general proposition that attempts at community care in individualistic societies will fail. Because cohesive communities are becoming less and less common in modern societies, there are no communal groups into which the mentally ill can be integrated. As societies become more fragmented, the exclusion of the mentally ill should increase.

Yet, the widespread removal of the mentally ill from mental institutions does represent a dramatic shift in the societal reaction to them. This shift does not reflect a change in social cohesiveness but, in part, the increased capacity to normalize mental symptoms brought about by new drug technologies. Psychotropic drugs suppress the most disruptive and bizarre symptoms of mental disorder. In the United States, this allows patients to be released from mental institutions after short stays that now average about 41 days (Gove, 1975:58). But because the increased ability to normalize symptoms has not been accompanied by an increased capacity of informal networks to maintain disordered members, the decline in formal exclusion has not resulted in the integration of the mentally ill into the community. While psychiatric technologies can, to some degree, normalize symptoms, they cannot create the interpersonal ties necessary for community integration.

The same factors that predict the initial development of mental hospitals also predict the failure of community care. Only social groups that have cohesive and extensive bonds among their members can provide the level of support necessary to maintain the mentally ill within them. The high degree of continuing interaction and the strong ties between members of communal groups prevent an exclusion reaction that could tear the group apart. The nature of group solidarity limits the degree of rejection of the mentally ill. Just as "normal" members of cohesive communities resolve their disputes through conciliation or compensation rather than coercion (Black, 1976), the mentally ill in these communities are not rejected but are maintained within the group. In contrast, the growing individuation of social structure leads to a decline in the informal resources available to encapsulate the mentally ill. The use of repressive law of all types increases (Spitzer, 1975; Black, 1976), including the use of formal means to exclude the mentally ill. While normalization technologies have, in part, reduced the degree of exclusion, the underlying social structure prevents a return to the inclusive care of the mentally disordered.

## Individual Variation in the Reaction to Mental Illness

When societies such as tribal groups are homogeneous with few social differences between members, there is little differentiation in the reaction to the mentally ill. With the evolution of societies, however, various social classes, cultures, and occupational and ethnic groups emerge. The reaction to the mentally ill becomes differentiated according to a variety of individual characteristics. This section considers how characteristics of disordered individuals, such as their social integration, culture, social class, and gender shapes the societal reaction to them.

### SOCIAL INTEGRATION

Just as certain kinds of groups more or less readily expel their mentally disturbed members, certain types of individuals within these groups have a greater or lesser probability of being excluded. While groups with looser ties between members are more likely to exclude the mentally ill than groups with stronger ties, those individuals who are most marginal to social groups are the ones who are most likely to be expelled:

*The degree of exclusion of individuals who are labeled mentally ill varies directly with their social marginality.*

109

Social marginality refers to the degree to which an individual is tied into social groups (Black, 1976:Ch. 3). Marginal people have few ties to social groups; integrated people have many ties. People who are married are more integrated than the single or divorced, employed people more than the unemployed, people with community and family ties more integrated than those without them. Whatever particular referent of social integration is used, people who are more marginal to the community are more likely than the integrated to be excluded if they are labeled mentally ill.

Socially marginal individuals who are considered mentally ill have always been subject to the most exclusionary treatment. In ancient Israel, Greece, and Rome, before the development of mental hospitals, persons without families were left to roam the streets, while individuals with family ties were cared for within the home (Rosen, 1968:64, 89, 129). Other findings show that compared to residents of communities, nonresidents have a higher probability of receiving coercive treatment. In medieval Europe, mentaly ill members of communities were left at liberty, as long as they caused no severe disturbance, while the insane from other communities were expelled from towns and, not infrequently, were whipped before being transported (Rosen, 198:139–140). With the emergence of mental hospitals, the unemployed, vagrants, and other persons without family and community ties were most likely to suffer confinement (Foucault, 1965; Rosen, 1968; Scull, 1977).

The same process occurred in the United States. In colonial America, the reaction to the mentally ill was sharply differentiated by whether the ill person was a resident on nonresident of the community (Rothman, 1971:5). Residents were provided for by their own families or, sometimes, by funds provided by the community. The insane who had not established legal residency in a community, however, were commonly expelled from the community. Deutsch (1949) notes: "the most repressive measures were adopted to keep out poor strangers, including the dependent insane, through the medium of harsh settlement laws [44]." While members of cohesive communities received an inclusive reaction, nonmembers were harshly excluded. Similarly, in the first three decades of the twentieth century, individuals who entered mental hospitals through commitments by the police were disproportionately likely to lack relatives in the city, be unmarried, and be recent arrivals in the city (R. W. Fox, 1978:87).

In the contemporary United States, the most marginal individuals are also the ones most likely to suffer an exclusionary and coercive reaction if they are labeled mentally ill. For example, among young vagrants in Berkeley, California, who have no family, friendship, or job ties, 75%

of hospitalizations are involuntary and initiated by the police (Segal *et al.*, 1977). These youths experience hospitalization as a coercive reaction.

> Disturbed street people, however, have not asked for therapy. They may define themselves as poor, as outcast, as politically disagreeable, but they rarely perceive themselves as 'crazy.' Yet, against their wishes, they become mental patients. Thus, they may come to identify the hospital with jail, and hospital personnel with jailers [Segal *et al.*, 1977:395–396].

The strength of ties to the community is also a good predictor of whether an individual will enter mental hospitals voluntarily or involuntarily. While the distinction between "voluntary" and "involuntary" commitment may often be only a matter of legal terminology, it does provide a crude indication of the degree of coerciveness of societal reaction. When the degree of exclusion is indicated by the ratio of involuntary to voluntary hospitalizations, individuals who are not in the labor force have nearly twice the exclusion ratio as those with jobs (Linsky, 1970b). Within occupational groups, migrant farm workers, the most marginal group of all, have the highest ratio of involuntary to voluntary commitments (Rushing, 1971). The exclusion ratio for migrant farm workers is 4.1 compared to 2.0 for other nonfarm laborers, 1.5 for farmers, 1.1 for managers, and .95 for professionals. Even within the category of migrant workers, the degree of marginality predicts the exclusion rate. Married farm workers have a ratio of 2.1 involuntary to voluntary admissions, divorced and separated workers a 3.25 ratio, and single farm workers a 7.7 ratio (Rushing, 1971). The fewer the ties to conventional society, the greater the likelihood that the societal reaction is coercive and exclusionary.

Just as individuals with fewer community ties are more likely to be excluded, so are the single and divorced, compared to the married. Unmarried people are more than twice as likely as the married to be involuntarily, rather than voluntarily, committed to mental hospitals (Linsky, 1970b). The exclusion ratio is highest for the never married, intermediate for separated, divorced, and widowed individuals, and lowest for married people (Rushing, 1971). The relationship between marital resources and exclusion is particularly strong when the perceived degree of impairment is not severe (Rushing and Esco, 1977). The degree of marital integration also predicts the degree of police involvement in hospitalization, indicating a coercive response to the mentally ill. One study in the state of Washington shows that the police initiated hospitalization for 32 % of single people, 19 % of the divorced and separated group, and 9 % of the married group (Gove and Howell, 1974). Other studies of urban populations indicate that single males are especially vulnerable to police intervention (Linn, 1961; Brody *et al.*, 1967; R. W. Fox, 1978:87). The greater degree of exclusion of single people holds within different social classes (Rushing, 1971) and different age groups (Rushing and Esco, 1977).

In all of the studies just mentioned, exclusion refers not to the use of formal institutions but to the degree of coerciveness of the societal reaction. Whatever measure of social integration is used, the fewer an individual's ties to conventional society, the more coercive is the societal reaction. Nonresidents of communities, vagrants, the unemployed, the unmarried, or the divorced all tend to be treated more coercively than more integrated individuals. This tendency partly reflects the lack of informal control and support available to marginal members of society. They are less likely than the integrated to have anyone willing to assume responsibility for their care, so they are more vulnerable to the coercive intervention of formal control agents. In this regard, the social control of mental disorder mirrors that of other social controls: Individuals on the margins of society are more subject to coercive styles of social control for all types of deviant behavior (Black, 1976:59).

CULTURAL DISTANCE

Not only their social integration but also their cultural distance from conventional groups predicts the reaction to the mentally ill:

*The degree of exclusion of individuals who are labeled mentally ill varies directly with their cultural distance from conventional groups.*

Cultural distance refers to the location of individuals relative to the mainstream culture (see Black, 1976:68). Immigrants have a greater distance from the mainstream than the native born, blacks than whites, bohemians than bourgeoisie. The greater their distance from mainstream culture, the greater the probability that the mentally ill will suffer an exclusion reaction.

In a study of hospitalization in Washington State, Linsky (1970b) found an almost perfect correlation between a measure of the social distance that whites feel toward members of various ethnic groups and the degree of exclusion of the mentally ill. The social distance scores, with a negative score indicating a greater degree of rejection, where .85 for Caucasians, $-.56$ and $-.57$ for Japanese and Chinese, $-.96$ for Filipinos, $-1.09$ for American Indians, and $-1.79$ for blacks. The ratio of involuntary to voluntary commitments to mental hospitals was 2.4 for whites, 4.9 and 5.1 for Japanese and Chinese, 5.1 for American Indians, 6.3 for Filipinos and 10.1 for blacks. Similarly, in the mid-nineteenth century, Edward Jarvis, a prominent psychiatric authority at the time, estimated that 43% of the insane poor who were native-born white Americans were placed in state mental institutions compared to virtually every foreign-born individual who was judged insane (Rothman, 1971: 283). In the early decades of the twentieth century in San Francisco, the police were twice as likely to initiate commitment for foreign-born than for native-born persons (R. W. Fox, 1978:87). Even controlled for the presence of relatives and occupational position, the foreign born were more likely to be coercively committed. In addition, while about 1 out of 20 persons entered state hospitals voluntarily in this period, not a single Italian, East European, Asian, or Mexican entered a mental hospital voluntarily (R. W. Fox, 1978:95–96).

The expanding use of mental hospitals as a means of social control in the United States is directly linked to an increase in the number of immigrants distant from the dominant Protestant and British culture. Over the course of the nineteenth century, mental hospitals became disproportionately filled with the foreign born. Grob (1973:231) notes that

> as a result of population growth from immigration and births, the number of institutionalized patients began to increase (a fact that also reflected the establishment of new hospitals and the expansion of older ones). The rise in patient populations at public hospitals was often accompanied by a disproportionately high number of lower-class patients from minority ethnic groups. At the New York City Lunatic Asylum on Blackwell's Island—to cite the most extreme illustration—8,620 out of the 11,141 persons admitted between 1847 and 1870 were immigrants; of this number 5,219 were from Ireland and 2,056 from Germany. In the single year of 1850, 534 patients were foreign-born and only 121 were native Americans—this despite the fact that the foreign-born constituted slightly less than half of the city's population. Similarly, at the Longview Asylum, which served Cincinnati, 68 percent of the resident patients in 1875 were foreign-born, although this group constituted only 32 percent of the population. Urban institutions in particular, including those in New York, Boston, Philadelphia, Cincinnati, and St. Louis, had high percentages of foreign-born inmates, as did state institutions in Massachusetts. [This quotation and following quotations from Grob (1973) are reprinted with permission from *Mental Institutions in America: Social Policy to 1875* by Gerald N. Grob. Copyright © 1973 by The Free Press, a Division of Macmillan Publishing Co., Inc.]

Even among the mentally ill within institutions, it was felt that the foreign born should be separated from native Americans because of the distaste that the native patients felt for foreigners (Dain, 1964:102).

The most coercive treatment among persons labeled mentally ill is received by members of the most distant ethnic groups. In the United

States, this means that blacks are treated more coercively than other ethnic groups. When mental hospitals emerged in the nineteenth century, most states either had separate wards or separate mental institutions for blacks (Grob, 1973:243-255). Within these segregated facilities was found the harshest treatment of the mentally ill. Whereas today blacks are no longer segregated from whites, they are still subject to more coercive treatment if they are labeled mentally ill. In Washington State, for example, there are 2.4 involuntary commitments for each voluntary commitment for whites but 10.1 involuntary for every voluntary commitment for blacks (Linsky, 1970b). In Baltimore, 75% of black females compared to 35% of white females (no figures are provided for males) enter mental hospitals through police intervention (Brody et al., 1967). In Washington, D.C., among the unmarried, the police initiated hospitalization for 19% of white males and 28% of white females but for 53% of black males and 52% of black females (Linn, 1961).

While epidemiological studies do not find that blacks have higher rates of mental illness than whites (Dohrenwend and Dohrenwend, 1969; Fisher, 1969; Warheit et al., 1975), they are considerably more likely than whites to be placed in mental institutions. In 1970, nonwhite males were 1.8 times as likely as white males to be confined in a mental institution and nonwhite females 1.4 times as likely as white females (Kramer, 1977:19). On the other hand, blacks rarely initiate noncoercive forms of psychiatric treatment. Ninety-seven percent of the patients of private psychiatrists are white and only 2% are black (Marmor, 1975). Even those blacks who do use outpatient treatment are more likely than whites to enter through unsolicited advice from other people (Kadushin, 1969:197). While the mentally ill who are distant from the norms of conventional society receive the most coercive treatment, those who are most distant are the most likely of all to be excluded.

The greater exclusion of culturally distant individuals reflects several factors. First, there is a lack of shared norms between themselves and official controllers. Because of this, their symptoms may appear to controllers as more threatening and disruptive than the symptoms of more conventional persons. In addition, members of culturally distant groups are less likely than others to seek psychiatric services voluntarily, so their symptoms may deteriorate until they appear highly bizarre. Therefore, they may elicit a more coercive response from controllers. Finally, culturally distant individuals usually are also powerless and their treatment reflects that accorded people who lack material resources and influence. The greater exclusion of culturally distant individuals reflects the greater vulnerability of unconventional persons to formal social control of all sorts (Black, 1976:Ch. 4).

## 5. The Reaction to Mental Illness

To some extent, both marginality and cultural distance indicate a powerless status. Nevertheless, individuals' positions in a vertical hierarchy of power are analytically distinct from their social integration and cultural distance. Power also predicts the probability that individuals are excluded from the group if they are labeled mentally ill:

> *The degree of exclusion of individuals who are labeled mentally ill varies inversely with their power.*

The term *power* refers to the amount of social resources individuals possess and in empirical research is usually indicated by social class or income.

Powerless people have always been subject to harsher treatment than the powerful if they are labeled as mentally ill. In ancient societies, the mentally ill who were wealthy were cared for by personal physicians while the poor were left to roam the streets (Rosen, 1968). In ancient Israel, for example,

the practice of allowing the insane who were not violent to roam the streets was followed only by the lower classes and those who had no family. Members of well-to-do, noble families were placed in the care of a personal attendant or were confined at home [Rosen, 1968:64].

Mental hospitals developed, in part, as a response to a new underclass of the poor who had been displaced by the emergence of the capitalist economic system (Foucault, 1965; Scull, 1977). In the United States, public mental hospitals developed for the poor underclass, while the wealthy were served by private institutions with intensive treatment programs (Dain, 1964; Grob, 1973).

Compared to the upper classes, lower-class people are more likely to enter psychiatric treatment through the intervention of coercive agents of social control. In a study of all treated psychiatric patients in New Haven, Hollingshead and Redlich (1958:189) found that referrals into psychiatric treatment for schizophrenics from the police and courts accounted for over 50% of all referrals in the lowest social class, 25% of referrals in the working class, 7% in the middle class, and none in the highest two classes. Similar, although less dramatic, results were found for neurotics (Hollingshead and Redlich, 1958:186). A study in the state of Washington also found that the police were about twice as likely to initiate hospitalization for members of the group with income under $4000

**115**

compared to those making over $4000 (Gove and Howell, 1974). The exclusion ratio of involuntary to voluntary commitments to mental hospitals is also related to social class status. A study in Washington State shows that as class status declines from Class I to Class V, the ratio of involuntary to voluntary commitments rises from 1.02 and .94 to 1.32, 1.45 and 2.23 (Rushing, 1971). There is also a strong relationship between education and the probability that an individual will be hospitalized through a court commitment, rather than voluntarily. A study of all first admissions into Tennessee mental hospitals for patients between the ages of 21 and 64 during the period 1956 to 1965 found a direct relationship between years of education and probability of court commitment for both males and females. At the extremes, 46% of males and 51% of females with more than a high school education were involuntarily committed, compared to 88% of males and 87% of females with 4 years or less of education (Rushing, 1978:527). The relationship between education and type of admission did not disappear when controlled for severity of diagnosis, although it was especially large for nonorganic and mild disorders (Rushing, 1978).

There is some evidence that there is an interaction between social class and marginality in the reaction to the mentally ill. Among the married, only members of the lowest social class have a significantly greater exclusion rate compared to the other four social classes (Rushing, 1971). In contrast, there is a more direct relationship between class status and exclusion among those who are single or those whose marital relationships have been disrupted (Rushing, 1971). This may indicate that more social integration can offset the negative effect of low social power, except for the lowest social class, while marginal individuals are particularly vulnerable to coercive control as their power declines. While there is little doubt that the most exclusive and coercive reactions occur towards the most marginal, culturally distant, and powerless individuals, and the gentlest and most inclusive among the integrated, conventional, and powerful, there is little evidence to specify how the three statuses—social integration, conventionality and power—interact.

One reason for the more inclusive reaction to the disorders of more powerful persons lies in their greater ability to normalize their symptoms. Unlike the less powerful, they have the resources to pay for psychiatric services and techniques that control their symptoms at an early stage as well as a value system that leads them to seek help voluntarily for disorders that are relatively benign. Because of this, their symptoms rarely seem as disruptive as those of lower ranking persons, and they can more readily be maintained within the group. In addition, as with the response to all types of deviant behavior, control agents are less reluctant to deal coercively with powerless people, while they avoid harsh treatment of the powerful. The use of coercive control for mental disorder is mainly reserved for the powerless, who are not able to control their symptoms in alternative ways or to resist the power of official agents of social control.

## GENDER

An additional factor that predicts the degree of exclusion of the mentally ill is the gender of the labeled individual.

*Males are more likely than females to suffer exclusion if they are labeled mentally ill.*

While this phenomenon can partly be predicted from the propositions already presented, it is treated separately here.

Men who appear to be mentally disturbed are more likely than women to be excluded. For example, in Washington State, the ratio of involuntary to voluntary commitments to mental hospitals is twice as high for men as for women (Linsky, 1970b). In a study of over 10,000 mental hospital admissions in Tennessee during the period 1956–1965, Rushing (1979) found three voluntary female admissions for every two voluntary male admissions, but three involuntary admissions for males for every two involuntary admissions for females. Numerous studies of the nationwide pattern of psychiatric treatment in the United States indicate that women predominate in all types of voluntary psychiatric treatment, while men are considerably more likely than women to be confined in mental hospitals (Chesler, 1972; Gove and Tudor, 1973; Marmor, 1975; Milazzo-Sayre, 1978). Women generally constitute from 60 to 67% of voluntary outpatients (Chesler, 1972:312). In contrast, in 1975, the rate per 100,000 men confined in state and county mental hospitals was 78.6 compared to 37.0 for women (Milazzo-Sayre, 1978).

Studies of the patterns of admissions to psychiatric treatment also indicate that men enter through more coercive pathways than women. In Manhattan, a study of admissions to a number of outpatient facilities showed that men were more likely than women to enter treatment through the unsolicited advice of others (Kadushin, 1969:197). Another study of patients entering psychiatric treatment at a community mental health center in New Haven found that women were twice as likely as men to say that they wanted to enter treatment. Men, in contrast, were more likely to enter treatment after being coerced by employers or spouses (Horwitz, 1977b). A study of labeling processes in Greece simi-

117

larly found that 75% of women patients were hospitalized on their own initiative or consented to their husbands' suggestions. In contrast, 56% of men were hospitalized against their will, often "being forced by their wives and other relatives who often employed deception in order to get them to enter a hospital [Safilios-Rothschild, 1968:112]." Men are also more likely than women to be hospitalized at an earlier age and spend more time in the hospital once they have entered it (Tudor *et al.*, 1977). In addition, studies that present community members with hypothetical cases of mental illness find a greater degree of exclusion when the case presents a male rather than a female (Phillips, 1964).

The findings of a harsher reaction to males than to females can, in part, be predicted by the proposition regarding marginality. Men who are hospitalized may be more likely than women to lack community ties. For example, Rushing (1979) found that the ratio of involuntary to voluntary admissions among men is especially high for the 20-to-24-year-old age group. This group might be especially likely to be cut off from family ties and to be residentially transient. Women, by contrast, traditionally have been more integrated into informal social groups. In addition, because women are more likely than men to seek voluntary psychiatric help at an early stage of symptom development, their symptoms can be normalized sooner and may not appear as bizarre as those of men. Therefore, the deviance of men may appear to be more threatening than that of women, leading parents, employers, or the police to react to them more forcefully. Finally, women are subject to a greater amount of informal social control than men, while men are more vulnerable to formal means of social control (Black, 1980). While it is not possible to specify what factors account for this fact, men are more likely than women to be excluded if they are labeled mentally ill. In this regard, the social control of mental illness mirrors all other forms of formal social control. Males are more vulnerable to coercive social control of all sorts and the social control of mental illness is no exception.

## Conclusion

The characteristics of social groups and individuals predict the societal reaction to the mentally ill. The least coercive reaction to the mentally ill is found within groups that are most cohesive, least stratified, and culturally homogeneous. The exclusion of the mentally ill develops as the social structure becomes atomized, stratification increases, and cultural heterogeneity grows. Exclusion becomes an increasingly likely reaction with growing marginality and cultural distance and declining power. It remains a task for future research to determine the interactions among these various factors.

The propositions presented here that predict the reaction to the mentally ill themselves are related to more general propositions regarding the behavior of social control. Cohesive societies and communities respond to all types of disputes and deviance through conciliatory and compensatory mechanisms that minimize the degree of alienation produced by a conflict (Gluckman, 1967; Chambliss and Seidman, 1971:Ch. 4; Black, 1976:Ch. 3). Similarly, the breakdown of social cohesion brought about by an individuation of social ties and increasing stratification leads to a more repressive response to deviance (Spitzer, 1975; Black, 1976). The exclusion of the mentally ill within formal institutions and a coercive reaction toward them is predicted by the same social forces that lead to the growth of all types of legal social control.

The reaction to individuals who are labeled mentally ill also mirrors the reaction to other types of deviants. Socially marginal, culturally distant, and powerless people, as well as males, are subject to more exclusion in the social control used over them for all types of deviant activity (Black, 1976). The lack of social resources among these individuals renders them more expendable to expulsion and more vulnerable to the operation of formal control systems. The integrated, conventional, and powerful, in contrast, are less subject to the intervention of formal agents of control and, if intervention does occur, less likely to be reacted to in an exclusionary fashion.

There are, however, advantages as well as disadvantages to both exclusion reactions and inclusion reactions. For many individuals, institutionalization, even if purely custodial, provides a minimal standard of living and protection from exploitation in the community. Indeed, recent trends to deinstitutionalize the mentally ill in the United States may have resulted in greater harm to the most marginal and powerless segments of the patient population compared to institutional care. Conversely, maintaining a disordered individual within the informal network in some cases leads to a deterioration of symptoms and a delay in seeking professional help. While inclusion may often be a more beneficial response to the mentally ill, there are positive and negative consequences to both styles of responding to mental illness.

The evidence summarized in this chapter indicates certain weaknesses in the dominant explanations of the societal reaction to mental illness. The behaviorist view that finds few differences in the way various societies respond to mental disorder ignores vast historical and cultural differences in the social response to the mentally disordered. While the response to mental illness obviously is shaped in part by the nature and

**119**

degree of disordered behavior, of greater sociological interest is how structural and cultural factors produce differences in the societal reaction to the mentally ill. The view that finds a progressive evolution in the reaction to mental illness is also inadequate. While more effective control of symptoms through improved drug technologies has developed in recent decades, there is no evidence that these changes are related to prior developments in psychiatry such as psychoanalysis or institutional care. Nor is there evidence that the contemporary treatment of mental illness is more effective than that in many more "primitive" settings. In addition, the progressive view overemphasizes the importance of psychiatric techniques and gives insufficient attention to the resources for care available within informal networks. Finally, the critical approach is also seriously flawed. It overstates the degree to which social control is imposed from the top down and understates the reactive nature of formal control to informal networks. This tendency leads the critical view to overemphasize how elite ideologies affect the response to the mentally ill and to devalue the importance of informal resources and changing capacities for normalization of symptoms.

A better explanation for the variation in the societal reaction to mental illness lies in the nature of the social group, and in particular, in the form of social solidarity. The degree to which informal networks possess the resources for social support and social control predicts whether the mentally ill will be excluded from the community or included within it. An understanding of the social response to mental illness requires an understanding of the changing capacities for social support and control within families, neighborhoods, communities, and societies.

# 6

## The Nature of Therapeutic Social Control

Once individuals have been recognized and labeled mentally ill, they may remain in the community or enter formal institutions. In addition to exclusion or inclusion, another aspect of the societal reaction to the mentally ill is the kind of psychiatric treatment they receive. In particular, my concern here is with the nature of *psychotherapy* as one type of response to the mentally ill. I will address questions such as: What distinguishes psychotherapy from other styles of responses to mental illness? Under what conditions is a psychotherapeutic or some other response accorded the mentally ill? What styles of psychotherapy emerge in what kinds of social structures? This chapter delineates the basic elements of psychotherapy and compares it to other forms of social control. Propositions are developed that predict the use of psychotherapy as a response to mental illness. The following two chapters then discuss how the major styles of psychotherapy arise within particular types of social settings and are grounded in the nature of social solidarity.

### The Elements of Therapeutic Social Control

The nature of mental illness leads to certain unique problems of social control. A central problem in the social control of mental illness is to make intelligible the incomprehensible behaviors of the mentally ill.

The aim of therapeutic control, therefore, is to provide order and intelligibility to the chaotic expressions of mental illness. Therapeutic control must provide accounts to both the patient and the community for behavior that appears to be mad, strange, and without meaning. The actions of the mentally ill threaten the schemes of interpretability within a culture and they must be made explicable within known cultural frames of meaning. Psychotherapy gives sufferers and those around them an interpretative frame that provides meaning to their distress. The goal of therapy as a system of social control is to make intelligible the manifestations of mental illness to the patient and the social group.

A central task of a theory of therapeutic social control is to predict when this style of social control is used and how it varies across social space and time. The first requirement of such a theory is that it be grounded in an adequate concept of therapeutic social control. Like all concepts, a concept of therapeutic control is not true or false but only more or less useful for the purpose at hand (Brodbeck, 1968). For the purpose of developing a general theory of therapeutic control, the concept of psychotherapy must not be limited to the particular techniques that are called "psychotherapy" in contemporary Western culture but must encompass all generically similar techniques in a broad cross-cultural perspective.

Because the term *psychotherapy* has been used in many different ways (see Szasz, 1979:Ch. 12), it is necessary to specify how it is used in this work. First, I limit the term *psychotherapy* to techniques that attempt to change *personalities*, not bodies, and will not consider any types of physical therapies. In addition, in order to keep the subject matter manageable, the concept will be limited to *intentional* efforts at social control. I will not, therefore, be concerned with broader social and cultural arrangements that may be "therapeutic" in their effects (e.g., Parsons, 1951; Rieff, 1966). Finally, to keep therapeutic control from encompassing the field of socialization, I will only be concerned with intentional efforts to control *deviant* or undesirable states of mind.

Therapeutic social control has several properties that differentiate it from other types of social control. Before delineating these properties, it is useful to review briefly the other major styles of social control and to locate therapeutic control as one style of response to deviant behavior.

One of the earliest attempts to distinguish styles of social control is found in Emile Durkheim's *Division of Labor in Society* (1893/1964). Durkheim developed the thesis that types of social control systems reproduce the principal forms of social solidarity. He predicted that societies based on mechanical solidarity, in which each member is similar to the others, develop repressive forms of social control. In repressive control, suffering is imposed upon wrongdoers to deprive them of something of value such as money, liberty, honor, or life. On the other hand, societies held together by organic solidarity, marked by a differentiation of individuals, develop restitutive forms of social control. In restitutive control, wrongdoers are forced to compensate their victims for the harm that they have done.

While Durkheim sharply differentiated repressive and restitutive styles of social control, in a broader sense both are coercive forms of social control that are imposed upon offenders. In both styles, parties to a dispute vie against each other, there is a winner and a loser, and a decision is imposed upon the parties regardless of their wishes (Black, 1976:4). In addition, both styles are associated with the law of the state, the criminal law illustrating the repressive style and parts of the civil law such as contracts and torts representing the restitutive style. Most sociological studies in the area of social control focus on these coercive styles of social control.

By contrast, most anthropologists who have studied social control have emphasized conciliatory styles of social control (Gluckman, 1967; Nader, 1969; Black and Mileski, 1973). Conciliatory social control uses mechanisms of dispute processing such as mediation and negotiation that do not impose decisions upon disputants but rely on solutions cooperatively agreed upon by all parties (Black, 1976:5). Unlike coercive forms of control, there are no winners or losers; each party to the dispute "gives a little and gets a little" in the interest of compromise and consensus (Nader, 1969). The goal in conciliatory control is not the punishment of offenders but the attainment of social harmony. While coercive styles of social control are usually embedded in legal systems and are found when disputes arise among strangers, conciliatory styles of social control are commonly found in informal settings when disputes arise among intimates (Black, 1976:47).

Despite their differences, one factor shared by coercive and conciliatory styles of social control is that they are directed at the control of *conduct*. Both are used only after some behavioral deviation has occurred and both are satisfied when conformity in the outwardly visible conduct of the offenders has been achieved. Indeed, the notion of social control itself is usually defined as control over nonconforming behavior rather than control over nonobservable states of individual personality (e.g., Clark and Gibbs, 1965; Toby, 1973; Gibbs, 1977). For example, in his influential work, LaPiere (1954) states that "the proper concern of social control is with how persons act overtly rather than with their private selves [56]." In this view, whatever is open to public scrutiny is subject to social control while whatever is within the "inner self" is solely of private concern and not subject to social control.

The unfortunate consequence of identifying the study of social control with the control of overt conduct has been the neglect of the study of the social control of personality systems. With few exceptions (e.g., Parsons, 1951:Ch. 6), sociologists have been unconcerned with the social control of personality systems and, by default, have left the field to psychiatrists and psychologists who are unconcerned with sociological questions regarding this topic. Yet there is no reason why the control of personalities is any less important a topic for sociological exploration than the control of conduct.

The purpose of the typology in Figure 6.1 is not to construct an exhaustive grouping of social control systems but to illustrate the distinctive aspects of psychotherapeutic social control. I define *therapeutic social control* as the *persuasive social control of the personality.* As Figure 6.1 indicates, this definition stems from dividing styles of social control along two dimensions: whether the control is coercive or persuasive and whether it is directed at changing conduct or the personality.

The first dimension involves the voluntariness of the control: It is imposed upon parties regardless of their wishes, or is a solution reached through persuasive means? Whenever coercive efforts to change conduct are imposed by third parties and are ultimately backed by coercive force, the style of social control is *adjudicatory* (Weber, 1925/1954; Felstiner, 1975). Adjudicatory control encompasses both the repressive and restitutive styles of social control. When persuasive means are used to secure conformity in conduct, as in mediation or negotiation, a *conciliatory* style of social control is present (Black, 1976).

There are analogies to both adjudicatory and conciliatory styles of social control in the response to mental illness. Sometimes coercive tech-

| | Relationship between parties | |
|---|---|---|
| | Coercive | Persuasive |
| Conduct: | Adjudicatory | Conciliatory |
| Focus of control effort | | |
| Personality: | Indoctrinatory | Therapeutic |

**Figure 6.1.** Styles of social control systems.

niques, such as electric shock, the forced administration of drugs, operations such as lobotomies, or physical restraints are used as a means of control. None require the cooperation of patients and all can be imposed on them against their wills. On the other hand, some techniques that operate directly on the body are administered to willing patients, such as the voluntary taking of medication. In both styles, the control effort acts directly upon the physical organism and does not use symbolic means to affect the personality. Hence, they are not considered to be instances of psychotherapy, as this term is used here.

In addition to whether the control effort is coercive or persuasive, a second dimension that distinguishes styles of social control is their focus: Is the control effort directed at changing the outward conduct of individuals or at their personalities? Both adjudicatory and conciliatory social control accomplish their purposes through efforts to change overt conduct. In the case of mental illness, these techniques would operate on either the brain (e.g., shock treatment, lobotomies, drugs) or on the body (e.g., straitjackets, chains). Social control can also attempt to change motives, ideas, values, emotions, meaning systems, and the like. I use the term *personality* in its broadest sense to refer to all of these states that are defined as existing "inside" of the individual. For my purposes, the terms *mind, self, identity* or *soul*, are interchangeable with the term *personality*, and I will sometimes use them as such.

There is no sharp distinction between the social control of conduct and of personality. When the control effort is directed at the personality, the ultimate goal may be to change the conduct of the deviant. However, this goal is always achieved through changing the personality. Similarly, adjudicatory and conciliatory control may alter the personality, but they do this through the mechanism of changing conduct. In the response to mental illness, there is a central difference between the manipulation of the body and of the mind. When techniques are directed at changing the body, the patient need not participate actively in the change effort or even be conscious of the effort at all. In contrast, when the focus is on the personality, the patient must participate actively in the change effort if the personality can be altered. While the distinction between the social control of conduct and of personality should not be overemphasized, it is nevertheless a useful one.

When the distinction between coercive and persuasive styles of social control is applied to the control of personalities, two additional styles of control emerge, the *indoctrinatory* and the *therapeutic*. Indoctrinatory social control refers to the coercive control of the personality. It occurs whenever controllers attempt to change the attitudes, beliefs, motivations, and so on of unwilling deviants. Religious inquisitions (Ladurie, 1978), brainwashing (Frank, 1973:Ch. 4), and political indoctrination (Parsons, 1942) are instances of indoctrinatory social control. In addition, all contemporary "rehabilitation" programs that attempt to change the personalities of unwilling deviants such as delinquents, criminals, drug addicts, and alcoholics are forms of indoctrinatory, rather than of therapeutic, control. While these programs are sometimes associated with the rise of the "therapeutic" state (Kittrie, 1971), my definition views any involuntary therapy as a contradiction in terms.

There are a number of inherent differences between coercive and persuasive styles of personality change that should keep these two styles from being assimilated into the same category of social control. The dynamics of indoctrinatory control are different than those of therapeutic control. While changes in conduct can be imposed upon individuals regardless of their wishes, coercive changes in personality are more difficult to accomplish. The personality is, by definition, not observable to control agents, so it is always possible for deviants inwardly to resist control efforts while outwardly to conform to them. In addition, if deviants resist the attempts of controllers to change their personalities, there is little controllers can do except to resort to coercive control over conduct. With some exceptions, such as some forms of drug treatment, changes in personality cannot be coerced but require cooperation between controllers and deviants. Because controllers find it extremely difficult to produce changes in the personalities of unwilling deviants, there is a tendency for coercive attempts to change personalities to become coercive attempts to change behavior, so pure cases of indoctrinatory social control are rare. Therefore, I reserve the label *therapeutic* for *persuasive* attempts to change the personality. This maintains both the spirit of the word and the scientific necessity to create homogeneous categories.

Several elements distinguish psychotherapy from other forms of social control. First, because it is directed at changing personality systems, therapeutic control can only occur through the manipulation of *symbols*. Therapeutic control attempts to change attitudes and beliefs so that patients are persuaded to think and feel differently than in the past. Changes in the self can only come about when the therapeutic techniques are meaningful to the individual undergoing the change attempt. This means that therapeutic social control must rely mainly on the power of *language* to achieve conformity. Words, rather than force, are the major mechanism of social control (Entralgo, 1970). While the social control of behavior need not be understood by deviants, changes in their personalities can only be accomplished through the use of cultural symbols.

## 6. The Nature of Therapeutic Social Control

A second aspect of therapeutic control is that the seeker of therapy must *believe in* the efficacy of the therapeutic technique (Frank, 1973). Because the symbolic reorganization of the personality is impossible without belief, all schools of therapy find it impossible to cure someone who is skeptical about the efficacy of the particular therapeutic orientation. Hence, the practitioners of therapy must be people who are able to mobilize the belief necessary for effective therapy. The association of formal therapeutic agents with medical and religious roles in a wide variety of social settings is understandable in light of this fact, for in all groups medical and religious healers occupy roles that mobilize symbolic commitments (Parsons, 1942).

A third element of therapeutic control is that a relationship of *trust* must be established between patients and therapists (Parsons, 1942; Frank, 1973). Because therapeutic control is not backed by coercive sanctions, patients will only accept therapists' authority if they trust their therapists. Without the condition of trust, patients would not provide therapists access to the inner thoughts, feelings, and emotions that are the object of the control effort. If patients do not trust their therapists and fear sanctions for revealing their personalities, they can simply refuse to engage in the therapeutic effort, rendering therapeutic control inoperative.

Because therapeutic control involves the use of symbols and requires belief in the therapy and trust in the therapist, it necessarily must be a *voluntary* form of social control. Changes in meaning systems, belief, and trust cannot be achieved without the willing consent and participation of deviants. While punishment can occur regardless of the wishes of deviants, therapy can achieve its aims only with the active participation of patients. If a change in personality is to occur, patients and therapists must cooperate to bring about the change. For all these reasons, I define *therapeutic control* as the persuasive social control of the personality.

Psychotherapy is one style of response to mental illness that involves a cooperative relationship between patients and healers in which therapists use persuasive means to change the personalities of patients. In addition, controllers may respond to mental illness through coercive means to change the personality or through coercive or persuasive attempts to change the physical organism. In the following chapters, the central concern will be with psychotherapy rather than alternative techniques as a response to mental illness. A theory of therapeutic control should predict when a therapeutic or some other response will be made to mental illness. This involves examining the conditions under which a therapeutic relationship can develop between patients and therapists.

## The Application of Therapeutic Social Control

For psychotherapy to go on, patients and therapists must be able to communicate with each other through a common symbolic system. Therapists must be able to understand patients, maintain rapport, and empathize with them (Frank, 1973). These conditions set psychotherapy apart from both coercive forms of social control, which can be imposed against the will of the deviant, and from medicine, which can proceed through the purely physical manipulation of the body. The nature of the therapeutic relationship indicates the following proposition:

*The application of psychotherapy varies inversely with the cultural distance between therapists and patients.*

If a cooperative relationship oriented at changing the personality is to develop, therapists and patients must share a common culture. Conversely, as the cultural distance between therapists and patients increases, the conditions for the cooperative change of the personality deteriorate. Because of its use of symbols and need for belief and trust, psychotherapy is far more likely to occur within narrow cultural distances rather than across wide ones.

The proposition indicates that a therapeutic relationship has the greatest chance of developing when therapists and patients share similar cultural characteristics. In contemporary American society, psychiatric professionals, including psychiatrists, clinical psychologists, and psychiatric social workers, are distributed within a fairly narrow cultural space. Most are of upper middle-class social origins. One nationwide study in the United States found that the fathers of over 12% of psychiatrists were physicians, an additional 6% were sons of teachers or professors, and 42% had fathers in business or in white-collar occupations (Rogow, 1970:57). In contrast, only 12% of psychiatrists came from working or lower-class backgrounds. Psychiatric professionals are also much more likely to be Jewish, agnostic, or atheists than the general population. A study of therapists in Chicago, Los Angeles, and New York, found that about one-half were of Jewish ethnicity and that one-third stated their current religion was Jewish (Marx and Spray, 1969). In addition, 36% of therapists claimed to be atheists or agnostics, a far higher proportion than the general public. Psychiatric professionals are also likely to participate in "highbrow" culture, to read intellectual journals, and to hold politically liberal beliefs (Rogow, 1970:60).

As the proposition predicts, the clients of psychiatric professionals are likely to share a common cultural space with therapists: They are typically well-educated professionals, intellectuals, and of Jewish ethnicity (also see Chapter 4). For example, one study of 250 psychiatrists in private practice in the United States during the 1960s reports on the characteristics of their clients:

> Most of these patients are white and from the business, professional, or white-collar occupations; more than half of them are women. About a third of the analysts do not have any Catholic patients. A fifth of the analysts, on the other hand, have Jewish patients to the extent of between 75 and 100 percent of their practice, and for another quarter of the analysts Jews constitute between 50 and 75 percent of their total practice. Among the analysts there are no Puerto Rican, Mexican, or Indian patients, and only three analysts have any Negro patients; in these instances, the Negro patient percentage is less than 5 percent of the total number of patients. [Rogow, 1970:78. This quotation and following quotations from Rogow (1970) are reprinted by permission from *The Psychiatrists* by Arnold A. Rogow. Copyright © 1970 by G. P. Putnam's Sons.]

In another study of psychiatric patients in private therapy in New York, Chicago, and Los Angeles, Jews were far overrepresented and Catholics and Protestants far underrepresented as patients. Forty-six percent of the patients of psychiatrists were Jewish, while Catholics made up only 19% and Protestants only 35% of the clientele (Marx and Spray, 1972). The clients of clinical psychologists were also of similar ethnicity. These therapists tended to select into therapy patients with the same religious affiliation as themselves. Jewish therapists and therapists with no religious affiliation overselected Jewish patients while Christian therapists overselected Catholics and Protestants (Marx and Spray, 1972). In this study, religious affiliation was the most important factor that predicted the formation of patient-therapist relationships.

Chapter 4 demonstrated that, in the United States, therapeutic relationships are likely to form only among a narrow group of persons who hold humanistic and intellectual cultural orientations. A nationwide study of the patients of private psychiatrists found that individuals in the humanistic professions were far overrepresented as patients with professional, technical, and kindred workers accounting for 57% of psychoanalytic patients and 29% of all private patients, about 3.5 times their representation in the population (Marmor, 1975:38). Relative to their proportion in the population, lawyers were 13 times as likely to be in treatment, social workers 12 times, writers, artists, and entertainers 6.5 times, teachers 2.7 times, and nurses 2.2 times (Marmor, 1975:38). The greatest overrepresentation of patients was found at the absolute closest cultural distance, among psychiatric professionals themselves. Physicians, mostly psychiatrists, are 20 times as likely as their proportion in the population to enter private psychiatric care, accounting for over one-half of all analytic patients and nearly one-quarter of nonanalytic patients (Marmor, 1975:37–38). Another study of several thousand psychiatric professionals found that 81% of psychiatrists, 75% of clinical psychologists, and 63% of psychiatric social workers had themselves undergone psychiatric treatment (Marx and Spray, 1969).

While therapy flourishes among individuals who share a similar culture, it is unlikely to arise when there is a wide cultural distance between professional and patient. Therapists commonly assume that individuals at a great cultural distance from themselves cannot be reached through psychotherapeutic methods. One psychiatrist, for example, notes:

> "When I first came here I had high hopes of doing something about the neglected people who are sick—the Negroes, Mexicans, Puerto Ricans, the poor in general. But I've become sort of disillusioned. Most of them really can't be reached, because they live in cultures where 'acting out' is habitual, where you don't talk much and practically never in intimate terms about yourself. So when I tried to discuss things with them, they just wouldn't discuss. 'Look Doc,' they'd say, 'forget the horseshit. I know all that. Just give me something to get through the day so I don't lose my temper so much.' Well, what can you do [quoted in Rogow, 1970:73]?"

When there is a wide cultural distance between therapists and patients it is unlikely that a therapeutic relationship will be established. One study compared the treatment experiences of black and white schizophrenics admitted to Philadelphia hospitals between 1956 and 1962 who were matched on social class, age, and type of illness. It found that 62% of blacks but only 39% of whites received drug therapy alone while 19% of blacks but 41% of whites received psychotherapy (Singer, 1967). In addition, whites were likely to receive varying forms of treatment depending upon the nature of their symptoms, while blacks were treated more homogeneously regardless of the types of symptoms they presented (Singer, 1967). Not surprisingly, only 2% of the patients of private psychiatrists are black, 1% Latin American, and 1% other ethnic minorities (Marmor, 1975:40).

The history of American psychiatry also illustrates the principle that psychotherapeutic relationships are inversely related to the distance between therapist and patient. The emergence and decline of "moral treatment" in the nineteenth century illustrates that therapy is only likely to occur within narrow cultural distances. In the first decades of the nineteenth century, small therapeutic institutions were created in the United States to care for the mentally ill (Dain, 1964; Bockoven, 1972; Grob, 1973). Each patient had a private room, there was a small doctor-patient ratio, and daily contact went on between doctors and patients. The patients were drawn from the same native-born, Protestant, higher status groups as the therapeutic personnel that staffed the institutions. The provision of therapy was maximized within these facilities. However, the ethnic and social class composition of patients changed over the course of the century to reflect a patient population more culturally distant from the staff. Because of these changes,

> as a group, psychiatrists—native-born, Protestant, and middle class in origin—could not free themselves from their prejudices about the poor, especially the immigrant Catholic poor, whom they neither knew nor understood. It was difficult to achieve the warm, close relationship, based on mutual respect between physician and patient, that effective moral treatment required [Dain, 1964:126].

As more and more immigrants entered mental hospitals, treatment became less cooperative and more coercive or purely custodial. Grob's (1973) summary of these changes reflects the general proposition regarding therapy and cultural distance:

> The growing heterogeneity of patients in public mental hospitals that began to become evident by the 1840's was a factor of major importance: it contributed to the decline of the therapeutic institution, which assumed a harmonious and trusting relationship between a doctor and patient, and helped to hasten its transformation into a custodial institution. So long as psychiatrists treated patients who came from a background similar to their own and who shared a common religion, values, and culture, no conflict ensued. But when these psychiatrists began to deal with patients—especially impoverished immigrants—whose customs, language, culture, traditions, and values seemed to diverge sharply from their own, they found themselves unable to communicate in the familiar manner to which they had grown accustomed. Even those psychiatrists who genuinely sympathized with the plight of less fortunate individuals found themselves in a difficult situation, for they recognized their inability to create the type of therapeutic relationship that was essential to success [234–235].

As the cultural distance between therapist and patient grew, the mental hospital was transformed into a purely custodial and coercive institution that housed the immigrant poor.

While European immigrants were treated badly in these mental hospitals, blacks, the group at the greatest cultural distance from treatment personnel, received the least treatment. If blacks were admitted into mental institutions at all, they were housed in separate units or facilities. Within these segregated units, conditions were the harshest. Officials at the New York City Almshouse described the building set aside for black inmates in the following terms: "In the building assigned to colored subjects, was an exhibition of squalid misery and its concomitants, never witnessed by your Commissioners in any public receptacle, for even the most abandoned dregs of human society [quoted in Grob, 1973:244]." While conditions are no longer so extreme in mental institutions, blacks are still considerably more likely than whites to be treated in large custodial facilities and considerably less likely to receive psychotherapy (Singer, 1967; Fisher, 1969; Kramer, 1977). In part, this reflects the great cultural distance between psychiatrists and their black patients.

When psychiatric professionals are of high social class position, a corollary of the proposition regarding cultural distance is that:

*The application of psychotherapy varies inversely with the social class of the patient.*

Cooperative relationships between patient and therapist are more likely to develop among higher social class individuals while coercive relationships, or no relationships at all, become more likely as the social class of patients declines.

The most complete study of the kinds of psychiatric treatment provided to persons of different social class status was conducted by Hollingshead and Redlich in New Haven, Connecticut, in the early 1950s. They found that among neurotics members of the two highest social classes were nearly 10 times as likely as members of the lower and working classes and over twice as likely as members of the middle class to receive analytic forms of psychotherapies. In contrast, members of the two lowest social classes were far more likely to receive organic therapies, such as shock treatment, drugs, or lobotomies, or only custodial care (Hollingshead and Redlich, 1958:267). Similar patterns held for patients with all diagnoses and for private therapists, public clinics, and mental hospitals. Numerous studies in the United States, mainly conducted in the 1950s and early 1960s, also show that upper-class persons were more likely than lower-class ones to seek therapy, to be accepted into therapy if they do seek entry, to receive therapy from more experienced and more prestigious therapists, to remain in therapy for longer periods of time, and to obtain the most highly valued types of therapies (Schaffer and Myers, 1954; Imber *et al.*, 1955; Hollingshead and Redlich, 1958; Brill and Stornow, 1960).

Evidence from other settings also provides support for the proposition. For example, in Greece, as well as in the United States, therapy is differentially distributed among social classes. Among Greek males who sought therapy at one psychiatric clinic, 80% of white-collar applicants compared to 30% of blue-collar applicants were offered therapy. Among women, 76% of white-collar but only 33% of blue-collar applicants were provided treatment (Safilios-Rothschild, 1969). In addition, among persons accepted for treatment, white-collar applicants received therapy from higher ranking therapists than did blue-collar applicants.

The provision of psychotherapy in modern Western societies reflects the belief of therapists that they are better able to understand and to explore the personalities of their higher-class patients. While therapists feel their upper- and middle-class patients are oriented to language systems that describe their inner life, unique experiences, and private self, they believe that lower- and working-class patients orient themselves to symbolic systems that emphasize unambiguous authority relationships, action and not thought, and group rather than individual allegiances (Bernstein, 1964). In consequence, only patients from the higher social classes are felt to be capable of exploring their personalities:

> Since [lower-class patients] are not accustomed to using language to describe their inner life, they do not derive any sense of accomplishment or progress from gaining "insights," that is, verbalizations of their feelings or conceptualizations of their problems. In short, they do not share the belief in the healing power of self-knowledge which is basic to psychotherapies devised by educated, middle-class professionals who value it highly [Frank, 1973:182].

In light of these beliefs, the findings that lower- and working-class patients receive directive types of treatment, medication, and organic treatment, while upper status persons receive permissive and cooperative forms of treatment that stress insight, are understandable (Hollingshead and Redlich, 1958:267–270).

The greater focus on treating the personalities of higher status persons is not new but is of ancient origin. The Greek philosopher Plato recognized that higher ranking persons received psychotherapies that focused on the unique nature of their problems and on their individual personalities, while the therapies provided for members of the lower classes tended to focus on objective techniques that operated on the physical organism. In *The Laws*, he compared the treatment provided by physicians of freemen and of slaves:

> The slave (doctor) . . . never talk(s) to (his) patients individually, or let(s) them talk about their own individual complaints; (he merely) prescribes what mere experience suggests, as if he had exact knowledge. . . . But the other doctor, who is a freeman. . . . carried his enquiries far back, and goes into the nature of the disorder; he enters into discourse with the patient and with his friends, and is at once getting information from the sick and also instructing him as far as he is able, and he will not prescribe for him until he has first convinced him; at last, when he has brought the patient more and more under his persuasive influences, and set him on the road to health, he attempts to effect a cure [*Laws*, 720, as quoted in Simon, 1978:226].

In contrast is the treatment to be given a slave:

> If one of those empirical physicians (i.e., slaves) . . . were to come upon the gentleman physician talking to his gentleman patient, and using the language almost of philosophy, . . . he would say, . . . 'Foolish fellow, . . . you are not healing the sick man, you are educating him; and he does not want to be made a doctor, but to get well' [Laws, 857, as quoted in Simon, 1978:226].

Plato believed that physicians of upper-class patients should make detailed inquiries into the nature of the illness, educate the patient about the problem, and only attempt a cure after persuading the patient that the cure was a proper one. On the other hand, the doctor who treated slaves did not persuade or explore the nature of the problem in depth but only took direct action to affect a cure.

The differential provision of psychiatric treatment to persons of different social class status thus has a long history. In ancient Rome,

> relatively few people . . . could afford the [extensive psychotherapeutic and somatic type of] treatment of mania described by Soranus. Patients who could belonged to the upper levels of ancient society. The best kind of care for mental illness required time and favourable circumstances, but very few could afford to submit to medical care under these conditions. Those who had to work for their livelihood required a different kind of treatment; they needed a remedy or a cure that was quick and relatively inexpensive—a drug, a spell, a visit to a religious shrine. This principle, the differential provision of medical care by social class, is to be found in all periods of Greco-Roman civilization, whether in the fifth century B.C. or the second century A.D. It is no surprise therefore to find it present also in the care of the mentally ill [Rosen, 1968:135].

The history of American psychiatry also reflects the social class of the patients who underwent therapy. Upper-class patients were provided with long, intensive, and expensive types of therapy. In the nineteenth century,

> nevertheless, to the majority of superintendents there seemed clear and compelling reasons for differential care. Isaac Ray for one felt that patients from the "poor and laboring" class required less attention than those from "educated and affluent" backgrounds. The former were used to working and were content with simple pleasures such as a walk in the country or performing small tasks. The latter, on the other hand, could only "be satisfied by long and repeated interviews with the superintendent." Each class, therefore, required different forms of therapy [Grob, 1973:227].

Commenting on the provision of moral treatment to middle- and upper-class patients in the nineteenth century, Dain (1964) notes that the superintendents of asylums would visit each patient every day and "gave attention to the specialized needs of each patient and to the nature of his psychosis. . . . The superintendent sought to understand each patient's character and personality in order to treat his particular illness more effectively [116]." In contrast to the long and extensive treatment provided the wealthy, was the neglect of the poor who filled the asylums:

> Many superintendents concluded that patients in the public hospitals were untreatable and incurable; although they should not be treated cruelly, perhaps they did not deserve moral therapy. The result was that custodial institutions became filled with apparently incurable masses of insane inmates who came there to sit and eventually to die, forgotten [Dain, 1964:205].

When therapists are themselves of higher-class status, therapy tends to be reserved only for those patients of similar class standing.

The treatment of the mentally ill in Europe in the nineteenth century also illustrates how persuasive techniques were more likely to be used for higher ranking persons while more authoritarian treatments were reserved for lower-class individuals. Hypnosis was the major form of psychotherapy during the first half of the nineteenth century and was a highly directive technique:

> Hypnosis has been defined as the quintessence of the relation of the dependency of one individual upon another. It is a surrender of one's will to the will of another and is more likely to occur when there is a considerable psychological distance between two individuals, the one endowed with power and prestige, the other passive and submissive. [Ellenberger, 1970: 190. This quotation and following quotations from Ellenberger (1970) are from *The Discovery of the Unconscious* by Henri F. Ellenberger. © 1970 by Henri F. Ellenberger. Published by Basic Books, Inc., New York.]

Because of its authoritarian nature, hypnosis was believed to be most effective in the treatment of persons such as laborers or soldiers, from the lowest social ranks. It was mainly used by persons of higher-class status operating upon those of lower status. One physician wrote in 1818:

> "It is always landlords who operate upon their subalterns, never the latter upon their superiors; it would seem that magnetism always works downward, never upward. The officers who so eagerly magnetized in their garrisons no doubt accomplished marvels upon poor soldiers who felt much honoured that marqueses, counts, knights would be willing to gesticulate over them [quoted in Ellenberger, 1970:190]."

The development of the authoritarian structure of hypnosis from a more patient-directed, bargaining method found in the earlier treatment of magnetism also corresponded to a change in the social class of patients from the aristocracy to the laboring and peasant classes (Ellenberger, 1970:191-192).

The upper classes seemed in need of a less directive method of therapy than hypnosis, as recognized by a Dutch psychiatrist in 1895:

> Van Eeden recognized that hypnosis and suggestion worked only with patients of the lower classes; "it is inadmissible that a therapy be fit only for hospital patients," he added. One had to find a psychotherapy for educated people; it would be a non-authoritarian method, which would keep personal liberty intact, explain to the patient what is going on in his mind, and guarantee "that all the methods employed act only through his own psyche." [Ellenberger, 1970:321].

In order to treat higher class individuals, it was necessary for psychiatrists to develop more cooperative therapies oriented at changing the personality.

An American psychiatrist, Jerome Frank (1973) expresses the contemporary counterpart to the beliefs of the ancient Greeks and Romans and nineteenth century American and European psychiatrists:

> Lower-class patients, who view treatment as something the doctor does to one, are more likely to receive directive treatment, often accompanied by medication. Middle and upper-class patients, who put a high value on self-knowledge and self-direction, are more likely to receive permissive forms of treatment stressing insight [11-12].

The principle that psychotherapy will be more persuasive when it moves within social ranks and more authoritarian when it moves from a higher ranking therapist to a lower ranking patient has wide applicability. In this regard, it reflects a more general principle of social interaction: Interaction that occurs among equals is likely to be cooperative while that occurring between a superior and a subordinate is likely to be coercive and authoritarian (Henley, 1977).

As the class and cultural differences between therapists and patients decline, class differences in the amount of therapy provided should also decrease. Hence if the social background of therapists becomes more congruent with that of a cross section of patients, the provision of psychotherapy to patients of different social class status should become more equal. One recent study supports this expectation (Stern, 1977). In 40 community mental health centers in North Carolina that were largely staffed by semiprofessionals and nonprofessionals, there were few social class differences in acceptance into treatment, the type of treatment offered, and the number of psychiatric interviews provided. This finding indicates that equalizing the amount of therapy provided to the various social classes may stem from an increase in the number of therapists who are members of the working and lower classes.

The close fit between the social and cultural characteristics of the providers and clients of psychotherapy stems from the nature of the therapeutic relationship. Unlike medicine, which involves the manipulation of the body, or coercive social control, which is imposed upon individuals against their will, psychotherapy involves the use of symbolic systems to change the personality. Only when patients and therapists share a common universe of meaning can therapeutic relationships be established. To an even greater extent than other relationships between professionals and clients, psychotherapy tends to occur within a narrow cultural space.

Because the providers of psychotherapy in contemporary American society stem from a narrow cultural and social class base, psychotherapeutic relationships are likely to form with only a small proportion of individuals who have similar backgrounds as therapists. The majority of individuals who do not share the culture of psychiatric professionals are likely to seek help for emotional problems from nonpsychiatric healers who are at a smaller cultural distance from them than are psychiatrists. In the contemporary United States, this means that most people first seek help for emotional problems from clergy or from family physicians. In one nationwide study conducted in 1956, 42% of respondents said they would take a personal problem first to a clergyman and 29% to a general medical practitioner (Gurin *et al.*, 1960:307). Only 12% would first visit a psychiatrist or a psychologist, and those were mostly individuals with high incomes and considerable education. Another study of help-seeking among a cross section of the population in Manhattan found that individuals were most likely to visit a personal physician as a source of help for emotional problems; the second most popular response was visits to clergy (Elinson, 1967). Similarly, compared to middle and upper status individuals, members of the working and lower classes are more likely to seek help from a lay network of friends and relatives, and when they seek professional help it is often from indigenous healers, such as faith healers, fortune-tellers, or mediums (Friedson, 1970:Ch. 13). Ethnic group members who are at a great cultural distance from psychiatric professionals, such as blacks, Puerto Ricans, or Mexican-Americans, also are likely to seek help from indigenous healers rather than from psychiatric professionals (Torrey, 1972).

A wide range of cross-cultural data also indicates that most individuals who develop emotional problems avoid seeking "modern" psychiatric care and instead utilize indigenous native healers for therapeutic help. For example, a group of Puerto Rican schizophrenics who had avoided seeking professional psychiatric care had actively sought help from spiritualist mediums:

> Spiritualism is the most prevalent form of social organization outside the family which helps the schizophrenic person cope with his illness. Viewed more broadly, spiritualism is the one institution to which the people turn for help in their hours of need. They know it will have an answer to their plaintive questions. The medium understands their subculture; she knows how to placate the troubled by plausible interpretations of their troubles. She provides social support to an emotionally disturbed person [Rogler and Hollingshead, 1965:260].

Similarly, in Brazil, two-thirds of a sample of mental patients in Rio de Janeiro had sought the aid of spiritualist mediums before coming to the attention of conventional psychiatrists (Brody, 1973).

Findings from other nations indicate the same phenomenon. One psychiatrist who has practiced in India notes: "The great majority of my village patients regarded their malaise as having a spiritual origin and consulted the priest of a healing shrine rather than a medical man in order to seek their remedy [Carstairs, 1969:406]." Another study of the use of psychiatric facilities in Egypt found that 10% of upper-class patients, 25% of middle-class patients, and 50% of lower-class patients had consulted a native healer before seeking psychiatric treatment (El-Islam and El-Deeb, 1969:305). In Israel, 52% of Moroccan and Yemenite Jews compared to 12% of Polish Jews consulted native healers before entering mental hospitals (Hes, 1966-1967). That individuals seek therapy from persons at a close cultural distance to themselves follows from the nature of the therapeutic process. Only healers who share the same symbolic universe are viewed as competent to understand and to treat emotional problems. Because of this, the appeal of modern psychiatric professionals in modernizing societies is limited to a small group of Westernized individuals who share a common culture with these professionals.

## Mental Illness and Therapeutic Social Control

Psychotherapeutic relationships are only likely to emerge when therapists and patients share a common cultural space. And, when therapists are of higher social class standing, therapy is only likely to occur among higher social status individuals. In addition to relating to the patient's social class and the cultural distance between the patient and the therapist, the perceived severity of patients' mental illnesses also corresponds to whether or not therapeutic control is used.

## 6. The Nature of Therapeutic Social Control

Psychotherapy requires that the providers and receivers of therapy share a common symbolic universe. Persons who appear to be severely mentally ill are those whose actions are incomprehensible to others and who do not share the symbolic system of other members of the society. Because therapeutic relationships require the sharing of a common symbolic universe, they are incapable of bridging wide differences in symbolic meaning systems. It is precisely these differences that distinguish the appearance of severe mental disorders. Hence, it is expectable that not psychotherapy, but some more coercive means of control, will commonly be used to control the most severe cases of mental illness. This indicates the proposition that:

> *The application of psychotherapy is inversely related to the perceived severity of mental illness.*

Psychotherapy is likely to be used only for the seemingly less severely disturbed; as the perceived severity of psychiatric symptoms increases, the use of psychotherapy declines.

The distribution of psychiatric resources in the United States reflects the inverse relationship between therapy and the severity of mental illness. In 1971, 14% of total psychiatric hours were spent in state mental hospitals, which house the patients who are judged to have the most severe and chronic illnesses (Torrey, 1974:59–60). An additional 7% of hours were spent in community mental health centers and 13% in private and general hospitals. Psychiatrists spent the bulk of hours, 41%, in private practice, with the type of patients who are least disturbed. Torrey (1974) aptly notes: "Another peculiarity of psychiatrists as 'doctors' is that they avoid the really 'sick patients.' Instead, they spend the vast majority of their time with those 'patients' who are least 'sick.' This is certainly a curious way to practice medicine [58]." Those psychiatrists who do work in public mental hospitals with the most severely impaired patients, relative to other practitioners, generally have less experience, are graduates of less prestigious medical schools, and are foreign born.

Schofield (1964) calls the type of clients most preferred by psychiatrists "YAVIS"—young, attractive, verbal, intelligent, and successful. Obviously, these persons have the least apparent need for psychotherapy. A study of over 25,000 patients in the New York state hospital system also shows that the youngest, most competent and communicative, and most motivated patients are, in fact, the most likely patients to receive psychotherapy (Link and Milcarek, 1980). In addition, as observed above, the types of persons who are most likely to seek psychiatric treatment and to be provided with more of this treatment are highly educated, upper status individuals. Epidemiological surveys reveal that these types of persons have the mildest types of psychiatric symptoms (Dohrenwend et al., 1980). In contrast, lower-class individuals who appear to be the most severely impaired receive the least amount of therapy.

That psychotherapy only occurs within small cultural spaces has two sorts of consequences for the types of conditions that psychiatric professionals will encounter. First, only highly educated, higher status individuals typically will enter psychotherapy in the first place. Because these persons usually have only mild disturbances, psychiatrists will rarely deal with severe disorders in their day-to-day practices. Yet it is not only selection bias that accounts for the inverse relationship between the application of therapy and the severity of mental illness. The second consequence of the fact that therapy functions only when there is a common symbolic universe between patient and therapist is that the severely mentally ill are precluded from a psychotherapeutic relationship. Because their behaviors cannot be comprehended within the symbolic universe of the culture, it is difficult or impossible for therapists to establish a relationship with them. This fact is commonly known to the practitioners of therapy, who have long proclaimed that psychotherapy is unlikely to be an effective response to psychotics (e.g. Freud, 1924/1960). Because individuals who seem to be severely mentally ill do not share a common universe of meaning with therapists, it is perhaps inevitable that the provision of psychotherapy will be inversely related to the apparent degree of mental illness.

## Conclusion

Whenever there is a divergence in the value systems of therapist and patient, it is unlikely that a therapeutic relationship can be established. This divergence can result when the therapist and patient are culturally distant from one another, when the therapist is of superior and the patient of inferior social status, or when the patient seems severely disordered. Grob (1973) in summarizing the treatment of the mentally ill in nineteenth century American mental hospitals, states:

> The pattern of differential care that ultimately prevailed at mental hospitals was not a simple phenomenon, for the influences of class, ethnic, and racial factors were not equal, nor did they operate independently of each other. It is possible, however, to spell out with some degree of precision the relationships between class, ethnicity, and race on the one hand and the quality of care and treatment on the other hand. In general, the best care was given native-born paying pa-

tients. On a descending scale, they were followed by native poor, and indigent patients, and below them were poor and indigent immigrants. At the bottom were blacks, who received the lowest quality of care [222–223].

Grob's generalization holds not only for the treatment of the mentally ill in the nineteenth century in the United States, but also for the provision of therapeutic control in general. As cultural distance from the therapist grows and social rank declines, individuals are less likely to seek therapy voluntarily, to be provided with therapy if they do seek it, and to receive long-term therapy from a prestigious therapist. Culturally distant and low ranking individuals are more likely to receive coercive control or to be neglected completely. In contrast, higher ranking individuals and those who share the culture of the therapist are more likely to become involved in a long-term cooperative relationship oriented toward changing the personality that is the essence of psychotherapy.

In part, the application of psychotherapy reflects the use of other forms of social control. Whenever social control moves between persons of different social rank, it is likely to be coercive; when it moves among persons of similar rank it is likely to be persuasive (Black, 1976:30). Coercive means of control typically arise when there is a wide social distance between deviants and controllers, where controllers are superiors and deviants inferiors. Similarly, when the mentally ill are culturally distant from controllers or of low social rank, their treatment reflects that of other lower status deviants. They are typically dealt with in a coercive manner and placed in large, custodially oriented mental hospitals where the amount of therapy provided them is small or nil (e.g., Goffman, 1961; Perrucci, 1974). Therapeutic control is likely to arise only when patients and therapists share cultural characteristics and so can develop intimate relationships based on empathy and trust. The most powerful and prestigious members of society receive the most valued forms of psychiatric treatment while the least powerful and least prestigious members obtain the most coercive or neglectful responses. In this respect, psychotherapy is a valued social good that is differentially provided to persons who have the greatest amount of social resources.

Yet the distinctive qualities of therapy compared to medical treatment or other forms of social control should not be overlooked. Physicians control medical problems by acting upon the body. While symbolic systems are not irrelevant to the healing of the body (Frank, 1973), it is not necessary for physicians to share common symbolic systems with patients, for patients to believe in medical treatments, or for them to trust physicians. Medicine can be effective regardless of the cultural characteristics and social rank of patients and physicians. Similarly, coercive control that aims to change behavior does not have to rely on symbolic means or on cooperation between deviants and controllers. In contrast to both medical control that strives to change the physical organism and coercive control that aims to change behavior, therapeutic control requires the voluntary manipulation of a shared symbolic universe between patients and therapists.

The discussion of therapy in this chapter has certain implications for social policy. One development over the past decade has been the increasing use of community members as therapists within treatment settings such as community mental health centers and self-help groups. These developments result in a smaller cultural distance between therapists and their clients and should, if properly administered, enhance the effectiveness of therapy with a wider variety of clients (see Hurvitz, 1974; Albrecht, 1974; Torrey, 1974). On the other hand, trends toward increasing professionalization among psychotherapists and the stricter licensing of psychotherapists should increase the cultural distance between therapists and patients and may hamper the effective provision of psychotherapy. The types of skills that mark an effective psychotherapeutic relationship, such as the ability to generate intimacy, empathy, and trust are not ones that can be produced by professional training but are personality traits that can be cultivated within any social group. If the cultural distance between therapists and patients can be minimized, the effectiveness of psychotherapy should be enhanced.

# 7

## Communal Styles of Therapeutic Social Control

Psychotherapy involves a cooperative relationship between a patient and a therapist in which the therapist uses persuasive means to change the personality of the patient. Through the manipulation of symbols, the therapist induces the patient to believe in the change effort and to achieve a desirable state of mind. The previous chapter examined some of the conditions under which this type of relationship between the patient and therapist tends to develop. The therapeutic relationship is most likely to be cooperative and oriented toward changing the personality when cultural distance is small and the patient's social rank high and most likely to be coercive and directed at the control of behavior when distance is great and the patient's rank low. The provision of psychotherapy is differentially distributed in social space depending on the social location of patient and therapist.

This chapter is concerned with predicting a different aspect of therapeutic social control: the *style* of this control. Therapeutic control involves the manipulation of symbols to change the personality. The style of therapeutic control refers to the content of the symbolic systems used to achieve personality changes. Different types of symbolic systems emerge from different forms of social organization. Here, I use characteristics of social and cultural systems to predict the major styles of therapeutic control.

Only a limited range of therapies, generally called "psychotherapies" are considered in this chapter. The discussion is restricted to situations that involve a cooperative relationship between patient and therapist and that use symbols to change the personality. I will not, then, consider various styles of coercive treatment of the mentally ill nor styles of therapy directed at changing behavior. It is possible that some of these styles are less directly influenced than psychotherapy by the nature of social organization. Drug therapy, for example, is a technology that has been used in a wide variety of social and cultural settings and that may have a relative independence from the nature of the social structure. In contrast, the symbolic systems of psychotherapy more directly reflect the cultural and social systems in which they are located.

The central thesis of this chapter is that the different symbolic systems of psychotherapy reflect different forms of social organization. Variations in social structure and culture are used to predict differences in the symbolic systems used to diagnose, interpret, and treat mental illness. Like other types of social control, the social control of mental illness reflects the nature of the social and cultural setting within which it occurs.

The viewpoint adopted here contrasts with that found in traditional histories of psychiatry. As Chapter 5 indicated, these histories generally adopt a "progressive" or "evolutionary" view of therapeutic social control (e.g., Zilboorg, 1941; Ackerknecht, 1959; Alexander and Selesnick,1966). In the progressive view, the treatment of the mentally ill has evolved from the superstitious and demonological views that prevailed in earlier times to the scientific forms of psychiatry that have developed over the past hundred years. The major breakthrough in psychiatric evolution is seen as the realization that the mentally ill suffer from an illness and are not to blame for their conditions. Usually, Freud is credited as the major figure in introducing "a sound and scientific kind of psychological reasoning that did not appear to threaten medicine with relapse into its magical and animistic origins [Alexander and Selesnick, 1966:23]." Therapeutic systems prior to modern therapies are generally viewed either as precursors of modern therapy or as irrational and unenlightened. In the evolutionary view, modern techniques of therapy that locate the cause of personality problems within past individual experience represent scientific advances over previous styles of therapy that relied on religious, magical, or moral styles of explanation.

Most sociologists have accepted the distinction between modern scientific therapies and alternative therapeutic styles. This is most clear in the literature on social class and psychotherapy (e.g. Hollingshead and Redlich, 1958; Suchman, 1965). Lower- and working-class individuals are viewed as relying on superstitions or physical explanations of personality problems and rejecting insight-oriented therapies. Because of the inferior knowledge of these social classes, "the obvious, but difficult answer to the problem lies in the development of a greater congruence between modern scientific medical and public health practice and the needs of a still largely popular or folk-oriented public [Suchman, 1965:14]." By contrast, the upper and middle classes have more scientific and sophisticated views of mental illness and are better able to "correctly identify" the causes and nature of personality problems because of their knowledge and value systems (Hollingshead and Redlich, 1958:177).

With few differences, sociologists' portrayal of the values of the working and lower classes reflect the views of medical historians regarding pre-twentieth century therapies while the attributed values of the middle and upper classes correspond to modern scientific therapies. Both bodies of literature accept modern systems of psychotherapy as more scientific and "better" than prior systems of therapy or folk belief systems. Neither considers that both modern and folk styles of therapy may represent alternative forms of therapeutic styles that reflect different underlying forms of social experience.

A different approach from the evolutionary view of psychotherapy is the relativist position. The central premise of this position is that systems of psychotherapy are virtually the same in all cultures. Therapists everywhere rely on the same sort of techniques, so modern psychiatrists are essentially no different from witch doctors, religious healers, faith healers, and so forth, who all rely on similar techniques (see especially Torrey, 1972; Frank, 1973). Indeed, "there is no technique used in Western therapy that is not also found in other cultures [Torrey, 1972:56]." The aim of these researchers is to search for the similarities in all therapeutic systems, regardless of time and place, and to identify the common conditions of effectiveness that inhere in all psychotherapeutic systems. The effectiveness of various therapies stems not from their scientific status but in their ability to arouse the expectation of help (Frank, 1973). Because these conditions are the same everywhere, therapeutic systems have not evolved from an inferior to a superior status but every system has the same basic elements as any other.

The viewpoint adopted here differs from both the evolutionary and relativist positions. The various styles of therapy are viewed as reflecting the social organization and culture of different societies. Unlike the evolutionary view, I believe modern "scientific" therapy emerges from a particular social context to the same extent as tribal or religious therapies stem from their social settings. In contrast to the relativist view, the position taken here does not search for the universal features common to all methods of therapy but instead looks for how differences in social organization produce differences in therapeutic styles. The aim is not to judge one therapeutic system as either better than or no different from another system, but to use certain characteristics of the social structure and culture to predict variations in the control of mental illness.

## Types of Societies and Types of Therapies

If the whole gamut of therapeutic styles and social systems were to be considered, the mass of detail would overwhelm any attempt at generalization. Considerable oversimplification of both therapeutic styles and social structures is necessary if one is to be associated with the other. At the cost of eliminating the particulars of each social setting, two ideal types of societies are used that reflect the most general differences in social life. The first type is societies that grip members in a tight network of social relationships and bind them to community purposes. These are societies organized around *communal* principles. The second type is societies based on the individual that place their highest value on the autonomy of each person. These are *individualist* societies. Chapter 5 considered how communal groups are likely to include the mentally ill within the community while individualistic groups tend to exclude them. This chapter concerns the various symbolic means of change incorporated in the psychotherapies in each of these two types of society.

There is both a structural and a cultural distinction between communal and individualist societies. Structure refers to the patterned network of social relationships between people, while culture refers to the systems of meaning and symbols that interpret experience and guide social action (Geertz, 1973:144–45).

In the social structure of the communal group, every member of the group knows the others so that interaction occurs within the same interlocking network of relationships (Bott, 1957). Relationships tend to be multiplex, with persons bound together in a number of different ways, rather than for only a single purpose (Gluckman, 1967:19–20). Geographic and social mobility is low and individuals are likely to spend their entire lives among the same interlocking group of kin, friends, and neighbors. The cultural system of communal groups emphasizes standardized and formal modes of expression that are used by all members of the group with little variation in individual meaning (Douglas, 1973). Group cohesion is high and the subordination of individuals to the demands of the group is stressed. Communal groups have been by far the most common form of social experience in human history, the only major

146

exception being modern Western societies and their immediate precursors.

The individualistic group features fewer ties between its members than does the communal group. Each individual interacts with many different people, most of whom do not know the others. Relationships are typically uniplex, serving one particular interest, and individuals have few encompassing relationships with other people (Gluckman, 1967: 19–20). Geographic and social mobility is high, serving to break established group ties and to make most relationships transitory rather than permanent. Individuals and nuclear families become detached from broader structural ties and become relatively separate and autonomous (Bott, 1957). Society is viewed as an aggregate of separate individuals, each of whom pursues his or her particular interests. The individual stands at the center of group life with individualism as the reigning cultural principle. Symbolic systems emphasize the expression of individual meaning and denigrate the use of standardized expression (Douglas, 1973). The structure and culture of the group reflect a form of social experience stemming from the association of separate individuals. These distinctions suggest the central thesis of this chapter:

*The style of therapeutic control found in a group*
*reflects the major form of social solidarity.*

When the social group grips its members in tight communal bonds, therapeutic control serves to submerge the individual personality into the group. By contrast, when the grip of the social group is relaxed, therapeutic control serves to enhance the autonomy of the personality. Each major style of therapy naturally emerges out of the nature of social relationships in the particular society.

Within communal social groups, the style of therapeutic control tends to absorb the individual into the collective life. The personality is viewed within standardized categories rather than as reflective of the uniqueness of the individual. Therapeutic social control serves to turn the individual away from private experience toward participation in the group. The stress in all aspects of therapy is on the similarities, rather than the differences, between the individual undergoing treatment and others in the group. There is a strong emphasis on the promotion of social conformity in the treatment process. Treatment typically features a high degree of group participation, in addition to only the patient and the therapist, further emphasizing collective solidarity within communal groups.

When the group is individualistic, the therapeutic process reflects a different pattern of social relationships. Personality problems are viewed as reflective of the unique experiences of the individual and the therapeutic process centers on the exploration of the inner experience of the patient. The goal of therapy is the enhancement of personal autonomy and of self-awareness. The symbolic interpretation of problems focuses on either the private history or the current experiences of the individual. The structure of therapy features a private relationship solely between patient and therapist. As the individual becomes the principal focus of social organization, the therapeutic process reflects an individualistic cultural and structural system.

A test of the thesis that the style of therapy reflects the major types of social solidarity requires viewing the therapeutic process in a wide variety of cultural and historical settings. First, I survey therapy in small tribal societies and generalize the basic elements of the psychotherapeutic process found in these groups to a number of diverse communal settings. Following this, in Chapter 8, I examine the emergence of individualistic styles of psychotherapy and the rise of new styles of therapy within contemporary American society. While much of the argument of these chapters is speculative, the evidence suggests that the major styles of therapeutic control reflect the major types of social solidarity.

## Therapeutic Social Control in Tribal Groups

Tribal societies provide the prototype of communal social groups. While there are many differences between different tribal groups, in contrast to modern individualistic societies, the similarities among them are far greater. Individuals are typically bound to a small number of kinsmen and tribesmen with whom they spend their entire lives. Relationships endure throughout the life of the individual and the supreme values are the kinship and tribal groups. When problems arise in such settings, they are not only problems of the individual but also radiate throughout the interlocking network of relationships. In such settings, the social control of the personality serves to turn individuals away from their private preoccupations toward the communal life of the group.

Despite differences in particulars, there are a number of similarities in the style of therapeutic control found in tribal groups. First, problems are interpreted through a small number of ritualized categories. The public nature of these categories allows the individual, family, and community to connect the problematic experiences to the communal symbolism of the group. Second, therapeutic control emphasizes the likeness of the individual to others in the group and stresses the need for conformity to group norms. The therapeutic process reaffirms the normative order of the group for both the sufferer and other group members. Third, both therapeutic symbolism and the structure of the healing process integrate the patient into the group by affirming the values of the collectivity and devaluing the unique aspects of the self. The therapeutic process in tribal groups is an encapsulating one that combats individuality and stresses commonality. After describing the nature of the most common explanations of mental illness found in tribal groups, I then turn to the question of how these explanations reflect the nature of social relationships within these groups.

## DIAGNOSIS AND ETIOLOGY

All groups have therapeutic systems that include a diagnostic system that indicates the kind of problem mental illness is thought to represent and an explanatory system that describes the reasons mental illness occurs. In a worldwide survey of the ethnographic literature Clements (1932) found that tribal groups have only a few basic categories of disease causation. The most common explanations involve the departure of the soul from the body, the breach of a taboo, witchcraft, and the intrusion of some foreign object or spirit into the body. In some cases, all of these explanations may be found in the same tribe; in other cases, a tribe may emphasize one explanation to the exclusion of the others. Subsequent research has affirmed Clements' categories, which are the most commonly used ones in anthropological research (e.g., Kiev, 1964; Murphy and Leighton, 1965; Ellenberger, 1970:Ch. 1).

### Soul Loss

A mental illness viewed as stemming from "soul loss," occurs after the soul of the patient has left his or her body, usually because it has been stolen by evil spirits. The job of the healer is to search for the lost soul and restore it to the body. For example, the St. Lawrence Eskimos believe that illness occurs when one's soul wanders during the night or leaves the body when the person sneezes or is suddenly frightened (Murphy, 1964). A soul leaving the body in this way is believed to be at the mercy of disease-producing spirits who abound in the universe. Unless it can be induced to return to the body, it too will become diseased. Treatment occurs through the struggle between the evil spirits who want to keep the patient's soul and the therapist who wishes to release it. The shaman, or therapist, must track the soul into the world of the spirits and fight with

149

the demons who possess it before the cure can be achieved. Whenever soul loss is viewed as the basis of mental illness, the therapeutic process involves tracking down, bringing back, and restoring the lost soul to the body it has left. In Siberia, for example, shamans track the soul of the patient into the underworld of the spirits, bargain with the spirits who have stolen the soul, and offer gifts to the spirits. If propitiation fails, the shaman must fight with the spirit. After these struggles, the shaman brings the soul back to the body, and a cure results (Ksenofontov, 1955, in Ellenberger, 1970:7).

The belief that mental illness results from the departure of the soul from the body provides a culturally conventional and ritualized expression for experiences that would otherwise remain idiosyncratic. When therapists tell their clients that their souls have been away from their bodies they provide them with a comprehensive and adequate explanation of the experience they have undergone that is accepted by both the sufferer and the other members of the social groups. In addition, patients must entrust the return of normality to the efforts of therapists who act as the representatives of the social group. In these ways, explanation and subsequent cure anchors individual experience in the communal symbolism of the group.

### Spirit or Object Intrusion

A second explanation of mental illness among tribal peoples finds its source in the presence in the body of some harmful foreign object or, more commonly, of evil spirits who have taken possession of the patient's body. Usually, the person who is possessed speaks in the voice of the intruding spirit. Often these spirits are those of dead ancestors. The most common treatment for spirit intrusion is exorcism, in which healing procedures are used to drive the possessing spirit out of the patient's body. Among the Shona of Zimbabwe, for example, exorcism takes place through transferring the spirit from the patient to an animal such as a sheep or a fowl, which is then driven into the woods, taking the curse with it (Gelfand, 1964). More commonly, the spirit is driven out through psychic means. Among the zar cults of the Sudan and Ethiopia, mediums bargain with the possessing spirit by offering a ritual ceremony in exchange for the removal of the illness (Constantinides, 1977). In traditional Japan, patients sometimes became possessed by animals. In one such case, a young woman was possessed by a fox, who, speaking through the voice of the patient, declared that he would leave if provided with a rich meal. Subsequently,

on a certain day at 4 o'clock someone had to go to a Fox Temple, about 12 kilo-
meters away, and bring two pots of rice prepared in a certain way, roasted bean-
cakes, many roasted mice and raw vegetables, that is, all the favorite dishes of
supernatural foxes. Then the fox would leave the patient at exactly the same
time. And so it happened. Exactly at 4 o'clock, at the moment when the dishes
were placed out in the remote temple, the young woman breathed deeply and
said: "He has gone." The possession was cured [Von Baelz, 1906, as quoted in
Ellenberger, 1970:15].

The belief in demonic possession allows patients to translate their individual experiences into a idiom that they and the rest of the culture
believe in. The etiology of the illness can then be easily grasped and the
means for curing it indicated (Obeysekere, 1970). The personal experience of the individual is related to the public belief system of the
community, which can then take the appropriate steps to initiate cure.

### Breach of Taboo

A third typical explanation of mental illness in tribal societies stems
from the breach of a norm or taboo. The patient has become ill because
he or she has engaged in some action that is forbidden by the social
group. The St. Lawrence Eskimos, for example, believe that disease
occurs after a violation of a group norm, such as incest, sexual perver-
sion, or masturbation (Murphy, 1964:63). Because such breaches affect
the well-being of the group as well as of the individual, cure must come
through an elaborate ritual of public confession and acts of expiation.
Sometimes it is not the sick individual's action but those of kin members
that lead to the illness. In Tunisia, for example, people are thought to
become ill after close kin members or other associates have broken social
norms. In such cases,

real recovery can come only when the person who is responsible for the anger or
excessive worry comes to beg forgiveness, make amends and acknowledge
customary duties to the invalid. If these acts are refused, the illness may persist
and visitors to the sickbed, who according to custom must come to wish the invalid well and demonstrate their goodwill toward him, are told the story of how
he has been wronged and who has "sickened" him. Thus, behavior during illness
is associated with social disruption and in order to be complete, therefore, the
cure must include a reordering of human relationships and a redress of the in-
jured feelings [Teitelbaum, 1976:21–22].

The function of such a response to the illness is to reinforce the solidarity
and norms of the group by emphasizing the wrongs of the individual who
has violated the taboo.

The most common cure for mental illness that stems from the breach of a taboo is confession of one's sins. Confession in tribal settings does not involve a detailed inquiry into the patient's background and early experiences, but is a ritualized mechanism used to promote conformity to group norms. LaBarre (1964) reports that confession is widespread throughout American native Indian tribes. For example, the Aqurohuaca Indians of Columbia believe that all sicknesses are inflicted as a punishment for sin. Native healers refuse to treat patients until they have confessed their sins. After confession, the sins can be transferred onto objects such as shells or stones, exposed to the sun, and expiated. Among the Chol Maya, in the sixteenth and seventeenth centuries, individuals

> were in the habit of confessing to their caciques (native chiefs) when sickness afflicted a member of the family, holding the belief that the sickness would end in death unless confession were made by son, father, or husband, etc. Should the whole community be suffering from plague or sickness, the confession of a serious sin would lead to the shooting of the sinner with bow and arrows [Thompson, 1936, as quoted in LaBarre, 1964:37].

Similarly, among the Incas, fathers would confess to the priests when their children became sick and husbands when their wives fell ill (Ellenberger, 1970:24). Such rituals serve to reinforce the norms of the community after illness threatens to disrupt the traditional patterns of social life.

### Witchcraft

The final explanation of mental illness typically found in tribal groups is witchcraft. The illness is said to result from a spell cast by someone recognized as a witch. Sometimes the witch who causes the illness may be the patient; sometimes it is another person. An illustration of the first situation is found among the Temne of Sierra Leone (Dawson, 1964). If one of their young children die, Temne women commonly become violent and hysterical. The native healers then accuse them of witchcraft and tell the women they must confess their deviant activities. In a stereotyped confession common to all women so inflicted, the individual admits her involvement in witchcraft, after which the healer performs rites that reintegrate the woman into the group. In this way, the sins of the individual are cleansed and the norms of the group reaffirmed.

A more common situation is when the witch who is responsible for the illness is not the afflicted individual but is another member of the village. Turner (1964) provides a detailed analysis of one such case involving a member of the Ndembu tribe of Zambia. This man had a number of psychogenic symptoms and had withdrawn from village affairs and shut himself up in his hut. The native healer suggested that the patient's wife, who was having an affair with a neighbor, and his mother-in-law, were responsible for his symptoms. The healing ritual involved addressing the various interpersonal tensions in the village, including those among the patient and his kin, between the patient, his wife, and her family, and within the village as a whole. The result is that "the Ndembu 'doctor' sees his task less as curing an individual patient than as remedying the ills of a corporate group. The sickness of a patient is mainly a sign that 'something is rotten' in the corporate body [Turner, 1964:262]." The witchcraft is seen as a sign of disturbance in social relationships and the therapeutic process serves to heal not only the disorder of the afflicted individual but also that of the social group.

## THE STYLE OF TRIBAL THERAPY

Both the symbolic and structural elements of therapy in tribal societies reflect the communal nature of tribal life. The basic aspect of tribal explanations of mental illness is that they reflect what Bernstein (1964) calls a "restricted code." Restricted codes involve the use of condensed symbols that do not

> facilitate the verbal elaboration of meaning; it is a code which sensitizes the user to a particular form of social relationship which is unambiguous, where the authority is clear cut and serves as a guide for action. It is a code which helps to sustain solidarity with the group at the cost of verbal signalling of the unique differences of its members [Bernstein, 1964:56].

Restrictive linguistic codes serve to limit the signaling of differences between persons and the expression of unique individual experiences (see Douglas, 1973).

The restricted nature of the symbolism that interprets mental illness in tribal groups is evident. Someone who has violated a taboo, is possessed by a demon, has lost his or her soul, or has been bewitched does not have a unique problem but a problem that is articulated with the common symbolic system of the group. If a person violates a taboo, for example, the idea of sin involves a very specific, formal act of wrongdoing. It is the specific external action that is responsible for the illness, not the internal state of mind in which the action was performed. Or, when the illnesses of Taiwanese are explained by the statement "your soul has been away from the body and has not returned yet [Tseng, 1976:166]," the ill person's experiences are anchored in the communal symbolism of the group and not in the idiosyncratic experiences of per-

153

sonal life. All Taiwanese so inflicted will be given the same explanation, regardless of the details of their illnesses. Each of the common explanations of illness ties the patient's experience to the shared idiom of the group. Obeysekere (1970), after presenting a case of demonic possession in Ceylon, notes that

> the existence of a culturally constituted public idiom for the expression of psychological illness is a fact of major importance. In the non-Western world and probably among Fundamentalist sects in the West, illness is often interpreted in religious terms, as in demonic possession or attack. Such theories of illness are derived from the total religious system of the group and are part of a publicly intelligible religious idiom. It should be apparent that when illness is defined in religious terms, it ceases to be something clinically isolable and separate from the totality of the patient's experiences and those of his group. The patient's experience of illness—whether mental or physical—is articulated through concepts such as sin, sorcery, and taboo violation, with the rest of his experience as a human being and that of his fellows [105–106].

In such explanations, there is no room for the unique aspects of the patient's personality to come under scrutiny because the explanation involves a ritualized symbolic system common to all sick members of the group.

In contrast to the practice in many Western psychotherapies, in tribal group treatments of mental illness the inner motivation and unique experiences of the ill individuals are ignored (Murphy, 1964:79; Kaplan and Johnson, 1964:227; Prince, 1964:115). Unlike the language of modern psychological symbolism, such as "repression," "low self-esteem," "ambivalence," or "insight," which refer to elements within the personality of the individual, tribal explanations relate the experience of symptoms to the broader cultural system of the group (Obeysekere, 1970:104). Mental symptoms are divorced from the character and uniqueness of the individual and are transformed into elements of a social category rather than of a personal state. Whatever idiosyncratic aspects of the illness that are present are forced into the standardized categories of group expression.

While certain therapeutic techniques in tribal groups are sometimes viewed as precursors of modern psychotherapies (e.g., Ellenberger, 1970:Ch. 1; Frank, 1973), most of the similarities are superficial. For example, the common practice of confessing sins among tribal peoples has a surface similarity to the recounting of early experiences found in psychoanalytic therapy. However, the confessions that occur in tribal groups are of a ritualized, rather than a personal nature. For example, among the Temne of Sierra Leone, cures for mental illness are obtained after the afflicted individual confesses that she is a witch and recounts her sins. Their ethnographer reports that in the course of his work,

> four cases were encountered in which the patients had had precisely the same type of dream. . . . After the accusation of witchcraft made by the native doctor, there followed the confession, which is also culturally stereotyped, always following an accepted pattern with only slight individual variations. Only by making this cathartic confession can the symptoms be relieved and the person cleansed and consequently reintegrated into society [Dawson, 1964:321–322].

In this manner, the private experiences of individuals become accessible to the community through interpretation within the standardized cultural patterns of expression.

Not only the symbolism but also the structure of therapy in tribal groups reinforces the merging of individual experience into the shared beliefs of the group. One important factor that serves to integrate the patient into the group is the mobilization of the community in the actual therapeutic process. Therapy in tribal groups virtually always is carried out in the presence of family and community members. For example, when confession is used as a treatment for illness, it usually occurs within a public setting when other members of the community are present (LaBarre, 1964). Sometimes, confession takes place at periods of especially intense collective activity, such as hunts, festivals, and before warfare, heightening the merging of individual experience with the collective representations of the group. Cures commonly occur in settings that involve the collective activities of the group, such as feasts and dancing, during which the individual is placed at the center of group attention (Whisson, 1964:303; Kaplan and Johnson, 1964:228; Turner, 1964: 258–259; Prince, 1964:107; Lambo, 1964:448; Murphy, 1964:80; Frank, 1973:58–66; Geertz, 1974:104–105).

Different groups use different mechanisms of collective participation. Sometimes an afflicted individual is inducted into a healing society made up of other persons who have been sick at some time in the past. In Ethiopia, the Sudan, and Egypt, women who become psychologically disturbed are commonly diagnosed as being possessed with a zar spirit (Messing, 1959; Constantinides, 1977). This spirit is feasted in a collective ceremony and the patient is inducted into membership in the zar cult group composed of women who have previously been afflicted by this spirit. Similarly, members of the Mende tribe in Sierra Leone who become ill are inducted into healing societies where they are treated by others of their group who have undergone the same kind of experience (Dawson, 1964).

The Pueblo Indians of North America sometimes respond to illness by ritually adopting the sufferer into a new clan group (J. R. Fox, 1964). Among the Plains Indians of North America, a disturbed individual takes peyote within a collective setting, confesses his sins, and is integrated into the group through collective discussion (Kiev, 1972:112). Group participation in healing ceremonies among the Navaho is involved to the extent that "when hot pokers were applied to the patient's body, the others would receive the same treatment [Kiev, 1964:25-26]." The healing process in tribal groups is one in which kin and tribe are intensely involved. The involvement of a broad social network in therapy further serves to draw individuals away from unique experience toward a commitment to the values of the group.

The treatment of the mentally ill in tribal groups not only serves to heal the patient but also to reaffirm the norms of the entire group. In rural Ceylon, for example, in a typical treatment of mental illness

> an all-night *bali* ceremony was held and was explained by the family as serving to remove the bad influence of the planets from the patient. This dancing and chanting ceremony brought together more than fifty of the family's neighbors, including many children. The gathering functioned also to integrate the patient back into the community, to publicly define him as now "well" and, finally, to reconfirm the values and norms for proper behavior of the whole village [Waxler, 1976:236-237; see also Obeysekere, 1970].

Because mental illness often involves a disruption of interpersonal relationships, tribal healers must discover the source of the disruption and then reestablish social harmony. Among the Ndembu of Zambia:

> The patient will not get better until all the tensions and aggressions in the group's interrelations have been brought to light and exposed to ritual treatment . . . The doctor's task is to tap the various streams of affect associated with these conflicts and with the social and interpersonal disputes in which they are manifested— and to channel them in a socially positive direction. The raw energies of conflict are thus domesticated in the service of the traditional social order. . . . The sick individual, exposed to this process, is reintegrated into his group as, step by step, its members are reconciled with one another in emotionally charged circumstances [Turner, 1964:262].

The collective treatment of illness radiates beyond the particular problems of the afflicted individual and into the broader network of interpersonal relationships, serving to reestablish social harmony and to reinforce the values of the group.

An additional way that the therapeutic process integrates the afflicted person into the social group is through the widespread belief that the cure for mental illness lies in conforming to social norms. There is a strong normative dimension in tribal healing processes whereby the sick individual can only become well by abiding by the values of the group. For example, among the Luo of Kenya, hysteria is a common form of mental disturbance that typically develops after a woman leaves her own clan and finds herself among strangers in the clan of her husband. An elaborate ritual dance is performed to cure the illness, during which the patient is "told by the expert that she must always obey her husband, be respectful and obedient to the older people in the home, and obey the rules of *juogi*—her spirits [Whisson, 1964:300]." Lambo (1964) reports that Africans in general believe that the best protection from disease is found in "peaceful living with neighbors, abstention from adultery, and keeping the laws of gods and men [446]." Taiwanese folk healers often prescribe as the remedy for mental illness observance of the duties and obligations of kinship (Li, 1976). Among the aboriginal tribes of Australia, native therapists use illness as "an inducement to the patient and to others to conform and integrate themselves to society. Illnesses are thus closely linked with social exchanges and with the laws; the doctor operates within this framework [Cawte, 1974:37]." The therapeutic process in tribal groups provides an occasion for reaffirming group norms and emphasizing the solidarity of all group members.

Both the symbolic and structural aspects of therapy in tribal groups promote the reintegration of the individual into the group and reinforce the solidarity of the communal body. The interpretation of personal problems through standardized ritual categories ties the experiences of the individual to the common categories of the group. The healing ritual itself occurs within a highly charged emotional context, with the patient placed at the center of group attention. Within these ceremonies, both the individual and other kin and community members learn that the cure for illness lies in obedience to group demands.

In closely knit groups such as tribal societies, social dissension or withdrawal presents a threat to the solidarity of the entire group. Any individual problem has ramifications for the group as a whole and conformity must quickly be achieved. Therapeutic social control responds to the threat to social solidarity by affirming the bonds between the afflicted individuals and the group and reintegrating them into the collectivity. All aspects of the therapeutic process stress the similarity of the individual to the group, the values of the collectivity, and the promotion of conformity to group norms. Not superstition or ignorance, but the demands of group solidarity shape the nature of therapeutic control in these groups.

Modern psychiatrists who have studied tribal healing practices are often ambivalent about these techniques. For example, the authors of a study of Malaysian folk healers conclude with the statement that

> certain problems with the approach of the native healer must be mentioned. It is rare for any of them to engage the patient in private consultation outside the group and to encourage the patient to state personally how he sees his problems. In this sense it has strengthened denial, repression, and rationalization. Our own experience with many patients in the same cultures indicate that many feel extremely relieved to be able to discuss personally and privately their own problems. In many of the native therapies, the diagnosis is entirely a work of magical, religious speculation and has nothing to do with the patient's own interpretations of the difficulty. It is extremely rare to go into the depths of the personality of the patient, and the interpersonal and intrapsychic stresses that he may be feeling [Kinzie *et al.*, 1976:143–144].

While these researchers accurately characterize the nature of therapy in tribal groups, they do not associate the nature of this healing with the dynamics of tribal social systems. According to the view presented in this chapter, what is characterized as "magical, religious speculation" is one style of symbolic interpretation that emerges when persons are tightly bound together in communal groups. On the other hand, symbolic interpretations such as "denial, repression, and rationalization," only emerge within societies in which individuals have been freed from encompassing group ties. Just as the exploration of the inner feelings of individuals emerges within a particular type of social system based on the principles of individualism, the "denial" of these feelings through symbols that merge the self with the collectivity is also the product of a particular type of social life.

If the thesis presented here is correct, there is nothing "primitive" about therapy in tribal societies. Rather, certain similarities in the style of therapy should emerge whenever a communal form of social solidarity exists. In communal groups, the symbolic and structural aspects of therapeutic control should devalue the unique aspects of the individual and promote conformity to group norms. A test of this thesis requires the examination of therapeutic control in communal settings in widely varied cultural and historical contexts.

## Therapeutic Social Control in Other Communal Groups

My thesis is that the nature of therapeutic control reflects the nature of social solidarity. If so, groups that feature strong social ties between members and a strong collective value system should develop similar styles of responding to the mentally ill. The nature of therapy in communal groups subjects the individual to collective interests. This is done in several ways. First, the interpretation of the problem takes a *ritualistic* form, focusing on concrete and formal sources with little variation by individual. Intrapsychic factors and individual motivation are irrelevant in the interpretation of the problem. Second, therapeutic control has a strongly *normative* component, so that personality problems are seen as stemming from deviations from group norms. Cures arise when conformity to norms is achieved. Third, treatment should take a *collective* form, usually involving the patient's significant others and community members. The therapeutic process heightens the integration of the patient into the group and reaffirms the normative order. In each of these ways, therapeutic control both reflects the communal nature of social relationships and reinforces these tightly knit bonds between people. If this thesis is true, there should be similar elements in therapeutic control in communal groups in widely divergent cultural and historical settings.

One setting reflecting a communal form of social solidarity is the People's Republic of China under the leadership of Mao Zedong. In the 1950s there was a deliberate attempt to implement a communal value system based on the ideology of Mao Zedong. One way the Chinese accomplished this was to create encapsulating groups of between 8 to 15 members called *hsiao-tsu* (Whyte, 1974). These groups carried out activities such as work, military training, and academic study and met on a regular basis to engage in political study. Their major function was "the encapsulation of individuals in all walks of life into *hsiao-tsu*, and then the manipulation of interactions and emotions within these groups through political study and mutual criticism [Whyte, 1974:230]." The dominant goal of these groups was to promote group solidarity and conformity to the dominant ideology.

The social control of mental illness in China during this period reflected the collective organization of the group. The same ideology of Mao Zedong that these groups were organized to transmit was also used to interpret the private problems of individuals. The aim of therapeutic control was to subject the individual to the authority of the group through a ritualistic interpretation of the problem common to all persons so inflicted. In one case, the person reported:

My trouble was that I had subjective thinking which was not objectively correct. My wife had not written letters wanting to divorce me; my wife actually loves me. My subjective thinking was divorced from the practical condition and my disease was caused by my method of thinking. I was concerned with the individual person; I was self-interested. I haven't put revolutionary interests in the first place but if I can put the public interest first and my own interest second I can solve the contradictions and my mind will be in the correct way. From now on I will study Chairman Mao and apply his writings [Sidel, 1975:128].

In this case, the problem of the individual, who had been diagnosed as a paranoid schizophrenic, is viewed as an excessive degree of self-absorption. The cure is found through tying him to the symbolic system of the group. The self is to be submerged into the ritualized symbolism of the collectivity. As another patient states: "Now whenever I have hallucinations, I study the works of Chairman Mao and attract my mind and my heart so I will get rid of my trouble [Sidel, 1975:128]."

The symbolic interpretations of mental problems in Chinese psychiatry are far removed from explanations involving witchcraft, soul loss, or spirit possession. Yet while grounded in a thoroughly secular political ideology, their ritualized nature is similar and all problems are interpreted in like manner. Their function is the same as in tribal groups: to direct attention away from self-exploration and to subordinate individual interests to the common goals of the culture. One student of Chinese psychiatry notes:

> Instead of supporting the patient's efforts to achieve private ambition and promote personal growth as American therapists might do, Chinese doctors discourage private ambition and desire for personal gain, while urging identification with the collectivity and its common goals [Lu, 1978:10].

The structure of Chinese psychiatry also takes a collective emphasis. Within the hospital, therapy focuses on the intensive study of Mao Zedong's writings in group sessions (Sidel, 1975). Heavy reliance is also placed on mobilizing the patient's significant others to deal with all areas of the problem (Lu, 1978:10). Both the symbolic and structural nature of Maoist psychiatry serve to denigrate individuality and reinforce ties to the communal group.

Students of Chinese psychiatry have explained this style of therapy as emergent from the particular value system of this society. Lu (1978), for example, speaks of "the Chinese experiment in the collective approach to the treatment of mental illness [12]." Yet the stress on a formal, ritualistic interpretation of the problem, the cure through identification with the group and through conformity to group norms, and the mobilization of the group to deal with personality problems all mirror the formal elements of therapy in tribal groups. In the Chinese case, the society is deliberately organized to implement a secular ideology rather than to transmit religious or "superstitious" customs that have persisted for centuries. Nevertheless, both settings involve a communal type of social solidarity that emphasizes the collectivity and devalues the individual personality in the interest of group solidarity. The style of Chinese psychiatry is predictable from the more general proposition that communal therapies emerge whenever group ties are strong.

The Soviet Union is another modern, secular society with a collectivist orientation. While Soviet social structure is not as tightly knit as the Chinese structure, the value system is one in which individual interests are subordinated to those of the group. Soviet psychiatry, like Chinese psychiatry, reflects the communal nature of the society. In the Soviet Union, psychiatry is marked by a "violent rejection" of Freud because of his stress on the exploration of the inner self of individuals (M. G. Field, 1960:290). Instead, problems are interpreted within a purely mechanistic framework that suppresses any unique aspects of the individual and provides similar explanations of the problems of all individuals regardless of their particular situations. Treatment, in addition to physiological therapies, focuses on reeducating patients to conform to the dominant ideology, not on the exploration of personal factors underlying problems. As in other communal settings,

> personal mental adjustment is to be found in the submerging of one's wishes and desires to the needs of the group or society, in the assumption that society has rights against the individual and not vice-versa. . . . It is stressed to the patient that he must "give to others and not be concerned with himself," that he must not isolate himself from others. Even if his family rejects him, his fellow citizens are ready to welcome him "with open arms [M. G. Field, 1960:294]."

To implement these goals, most treatment occurs within the community and often involves the participation of family members as well as patients (M. G. Field, 1960). In providing standardized interpretations of problems, denying the relevance of individual factors, and treating mental illness through promoting conformity to social norms, Soviet psychiatry reflects the nature of collectivist societies.

Both China and the Soviet Union are modern societies organized to implement a secular, communist ideology. It is not this ideology, however, that is responsible for the style of therapy but the more general communal nature of these societies. For example, modern Japan emphasizes a totally different value system than either China or the Soviet Union. Japanese culture is a traditional one where individual deference to the kin and communal group is extremely strong. It is not surprising that, as Doi (1976) explains, "psychoanalytic therapy has never caught the fancy of Japanese people [276]," because their orientation to communal living makes them uncomfortable about searching within the individual to find the source of personality problems. Instead, "the emphasis in Japanese psychotherapies is not so much upon seeking a hidden secret as upon rescuing the person entrapped in his hiding place and bringing him back to communal living [Doi, 1976:275]." As in other communal groups, therapy turns patients away from their selves toward participation in group life and culture.

The "cure of souls" in religious groups also illustrates the principle that communal therapies emerge within social groups that denigrate the individual and emphasize conformity to the group. McNeil's (1951) summary of the history of religious healing in both Western and non-Western societies reflects the central thesis of this chapter:

> Both aims and methods in the cure of souls have varied with the flow of history. They have reflected the changing philosophies of the relation of the individual to the group (or church). Where high interpretations of group authority prevail, the individual who breaks the pattern is subjected to an authoritative corrective discipline. The object sought is the subjection of the individual, and concern for the group interest rather than the interior recovery of the personality becomes the determining factor. Close attention is paid to specific acts, and there is a corresponding neglect of the more fundamental concept of personal character as a whole, of which acts are but symptoms and indices. "Sins" become more important than "sin," legal restraint than inner motivation [viii–ix].

For example, between the second and sixth centuries, Christianity was mainly confined to a few zealous and selective communities marked by a strong interdependence among members. At this time, all sins had to be confessed in public and each member had the obligation of frequently repeating acts of confession and penance (McNeil, 1951:Ch. V). Penance resulted not through a change in motivation or heart but through the performance of ritualized, formal exercises in public (Tentler, 1977:25). Healing occurred through ritualistic acts with no emphasis on inner motivation. As Christianity spread beyond small communities of believers to become the established church in Western societies, confession and penance gradually became private matters between the priest and the penitent, and inner motivation as well as formal, external penance became important in the "cure of souls" (Tentler, 1977).

No direct evidence exists regarding the actual amount of healing of the mentally ill that was carried out by religious healers in Western societies during this period. Yet it is likely, given the value orientation of the culture, that the emotionally troubled would have turned to the church for cure (McNeil, 1951). If so, the healing of personality problems would have stressed the formal ritual acts of penance that are emphasized in the confessional. Cure would come from the external action of the priest, carried out in the proper ritualist manner. This is, however, speculation that assumes the healing of the mentally ill reflected the reigning religious values of the time.

The denigration of the personality in the service of the group is also found in more contemporary religious sects that are marked by tight bonds between their members. In some religious communes in nineteenth-century United States, "excessive introspection was considered a sin" and confession of sins was commonly used to obtain conformity (Kanter, 1972:16; see also Zablocki, 1971). Hasidic Jewish groups also forbid excessive introspection and believe that therapeutic cures arise "not through insight but through 'exsight,' not by being preoccupied with one's own problems but by being involved with the others to whom one is responsible [Rotenberg, 1978:154]." In such groups, the treatment of the mentally ill often involves the participation of the collectivity, as in the "powwowing" ceremonies among the Pennsylvania German religious sects in which the entire group lays its hands on the patient while repeating prayers and incantations (Guthrie and Noll, 1966). In these kinds of groups, the cure for mental illness is not found within self-exploration but through reliance on the collective ideology and on other members of the group.

If the thesis that the style of therapeutic control reflects the form of social solidarity is correct, then those individuals in contemporary American society who are bound within communal groups should deal with mental illness through communal rather than individualistic therapies. When people are tied to tightly knit social groups, they should deemphasize the importance of inner life and seek cure through formal and ritualized means. If so, the common reasons cited for the rejection of insight-oriented therapies by members of groups distant from the culture of psychiatrists (such as those who lack education or are members of the working class) may reflect, in part, the nature of social relationships among these people. Conversely, the "greater knowledge" presumably possessed by more educated members of society may reflect the more individualistic nature of the social life in which they participate. There is some evidence from studies of communal groups in modern societies that the values and attitudes toward psychotherapy of various "folk" and working-class groups does reflect a particular form of social solidarity.

A study of therapy among the Hutterites, an Anabaptist group who live in self-contained tightly knit communities in the Upper Midwest and Southern Canada supports the central thesis:

Hutterite "psychiatry" emphasizes the importance of the patient's social and value milieu in treatment, with little consideration of the specific and unique psychic problems of the individual. It contrasts sharply with much of modern psychiatry, which is much more psychologically oriented and is focused on the patient [Eaton and Weil, 1955:176].

Treatment among the Hutterites does not encourage thought about past events or introspection; healing is thought to arise from faith in the religious beliefs of the group. While Eaton and Weil (1955) believe that "much more could be done for Hutterite patients if their problems were viewed in more intrapersonal or psychological terms [177]," the system of therapeutic healing they describe is one perfectly suited to the communal character of Hutterite life. The denigration of individual motivation, emphasis on conformity to group norms, and public involvement in treatment reflect the healing processes of mental illness within tightly knit communities in general.

A very different form of communal social solidarity is found among some urban ethnic communities in the United States. For example, in an Italian neighborhood in Boston marked by tightly interlocking kinship and friendship groups, psychosomatic and mental symptoms were viewed as deviations from group norms and interpreted as moral rather than as pathological problems (Gans, 1962:138–139). Treatment consisted of attempts to integrate the individual into the group and, integration failing, through punishment of the deviant. Personality problems were regarded not only as problems of the individual but also as problems that threatened to disrupt the solidarity of the group (Gans, 1962:266). While Gans attributes the style of interpretation and the response to mental illness to "working-class culture," the similarity of "therapy" within this Italian community to other communal groups with widely differing cultures indicates that their response to mental illness may not reflect working-class culture but rather the nature of the group life and type of social relationships within this community.

Another ethnic group in the United States that is oriented to close and interdependent familial relationships is the Mexican-Americans. The explanation for the development of mental illness among Mexican-Americans commonly is found in the violation of their moral and ethical codes; the illness is viewed as a punishment for sins (Madsen, 1964). They believe cure often is achieved after the confession of sins. As in many communal groups, the healing ceremony takes place within a collective setting:

> The family of the patient is present throughout the curing session and becomes intimately involved. They may be specifically told how to help the patient, or to make votive offerings. This enables the *curandero* to make extensive use of family and social manipulation if he wishes. Thus, treatment is not merely the result of the doctor-patient relationship but is instead a form of social reintegration through socially reorganized methods [Torrey, 1972:121].

In their interpretation and treatment of emotional problems, Mexican-Americans are similar to other groups with communal forms of social solidarity. Individual symptoms are interpreted and treated not as intrapsychic problems but as deviations from interpersonal and community norms.

Small towns are another contemporary setting that somewhat approximate a communal social structure. In many of these towns, everybody knows everybody else, community members are tightly connected with each other, and there is a high degree of community-mindedness and identification. The suppression of the individual personality in these towns has long been a theme in American literature (e.g., Lewis, 1920) and it may also occur in the response to the mentally ill. While there seems to be no direct ethnographic evidence on the response to mental illness in these settings, Vidich and Bensman's (1960) study of a small town in upstate New York illustrates some of the same processes found in other communal settings. The authors emphasize the lack of introspection and self-reflection and the loss of the individual self in participation in the objective, external, and ritual ceremonies of the community (Vidich and Bensman, 1960:Ch. 11). When a community member becomes ill, the community mobilizes to draw the individual out of isolation and toward social involvement:

> The activities of externalization must continuously be repeated and reinforced with little surcease. This is why illness, retirement and other unusual circumstances which make for prospects of "time on your hands" are dreaded and why social activities are organized to prevent social isolation on such occasions. The organized "visitations" of the ill and the "sunshine" committees of almost all organizations help to keep the bedridden and the incapacitated involved [Vidich and Bensman, 1960:317].

The individual is not allowed to establish differences or separation from others but is encapsulated within the group. While Vidich and Bensman's study does not deal directly with the response to mental illness, it is expectable that psychotherapeutic control in such settings would denigrate individuality and reinforce the ties between the individual and the group.

## Conclusion

The notion of a "communal" social group is a considerable oversimplification and masks many important differences in the therapy that emerges in these groups. This chapter has overlooked these differences in order to focus on certain central similarities in therapeutic styles within groups. In these groups, the diagnosis and etiology of mental problems are of a *ritualistic* nature. Standardized categories that do not vary according to the characteristics of individuals provide the explanation of symptoms. The interpretation and treatment of problems have a strongly *normative* component, with the difficulties often viewed as stemming from a deviation from group norms and the cure as arising from conformity to these norms. The treatment process reaffirms the normative order of the group for both the patient and other members of the group. Finally, treatment is of a *collective* nature and usually involves other members of the collectivity aside from the patient and the therapist. This community involvement serves to heighten the integration of the patient into the group and the reaffirmation of group norms. The entire therapeutic process subordinates the individual to the authority of the group, emphasizing the power of the collectivity over that of the individual.

As significant as the various elements present in communal therapy are those that are absent. There is little or no exploration of intrapsychic processes; individual motivation remains unexplored. The therapeutic process does not strive to increase self-awareness or individual autonomy but to suppress these factors. Finally, the one-to-one relationship between therapists and patients characteristic of modern therapies is rarely found in communal settings. In these respects, communal therapies reverse the elements of modern individualistic therapies.

The kinds of explanations and treatment of mental illness found in communal therapies do not represent "superstitious," "magical," "demonological," "religious," or "primitive" responses to mental illness. Rather, they naturally arise whenever a particular form of social solidarity characterizes a social group. The types of therapy that are found among tribal and other communal groups are as expectable within these settings as are the supposedly more "scientific" psychotherapies that emerge in individualistic societies. An adequate test of this thesis also requires an examination of the conditions under which individualistic psychotherapies arise and the individuals to whom they appeal.

# 8

## Individualistic Styles of Therapeutic Social Control

The form of social solidarity in communal groups promotes the welfare of the group over that of the individual and submerges individual identity into the collectivity. Therefore, communal groups produce therapeutic styles that are oriented to ritualistic expression, social conformity, and collective participation. When the form of social solidarity becomes individualistic, the style of therapeutic control should correspondingly change. Individualistic groups do not have the same requirements for group orientation and social conformity as communal groups. With the development of individualism, therapeutic social control comes to emphasize the individual elaboration of meaning, the promotion of autonomy, and a privatized therapeutic relationship.

Groups that feature an individualistic form of social solidarity are rare. Dumont (1976) has stated: "Among the great civilizations the world has known, the holistic type of society has been overwhelmingly predominant: indeed, it looks as if it has been the rule, the only exception being our modern civilization and its individualistic type of society [4]." Because of this, it is not possible to make broad cross-cultural and historical comparisons among individualistic groups. Individualistic styles of therapy are virtually unique to modern Western societies.

Beginning at about the end of the eighteenth century and continuing throughout the nineteenth and twentieth centuries, Western societies have been marked by increasing individualization. Industrialization and the accompanying division of labor broke down the tightly knit communal groups that had predominated in previous eras. Large scale movements from rural to urban areas created a great amount of geographic and social mobility, further breaking down ties to kin and community groups. Political and cultural values became oriented to the sovereignty of the autonomous individual, and the individual, rather than the group, became the bearer of rights and duties (Unger, 1975). Because of these structural and cultural changes, individuals in modern Western societies are far more autonomous than ever before. Freed of binding group ties, the individual has become the center of group life and culture.

Only in the last two hundred years or so, and only in the West, has individualism become the predominant structural and ideological order of entire societies. Consequently, in the modern world, the notion that mental illness is a problem rooted in the personality of individuals is a fairly recent conception. Foucault (1976) locates this shift as occurring in the latter part of the eighteenth century in Europe when madness became: "inscribed within the dimension of interiority; and by that fact, for the first time in the modern world, madness was to receive psychological status, structure, and signification [72]." The notion of therapeutic control as involving the comprehension of the private states of individuals, now taken for granted in psychotherapy, is a more or less new development. Modern individualistic styles of therapy have developed within the context of social and cultural changes that are a unique feature of modern Western societies.

## The Development of Individualistic Psychotherapy

Sigmund Freud's system of psychoanalysis is the paradigmatic form of an individualistic psychotherapeutic technique. Most of the elements of psychoanalysis had been proposed in one form or another before Freud developed his system. In particular, magnetism, developed toward the end of the eighteenth century by Franz Anton Mesmer, emphasized the psychological aspects of the mind, the unconscious, and an intense individualized relationship between patient and therapist that are also the focus of psychoanalysis (see Ellenberger, 1970). Freud, however, represents a turning point in the history of psychotherapy as the first practitioner of individualistic psychotherapy to develop a comprehensive theory and technique of therapy. Despite its recent decline in popularity, psychoanalysis remains the paradigmatic form of individualistic psychotherapy.

## 8. Individualistic Styles of Therapeutic Social Control

Before reviewing the major elements of psychoanalysis as a system of psychotherapy, it is useful to mention the social context in which psychoanalysis developed. Psychoanalysis emerged in Vienna, an urban center of European culture at the turn of the twentieth century, and possibly the most cosmopolitan city of the time (Janik and Toulmin, 1973). It was a place of "cultural concentration where the level of education was extremely high. Numerous artists, musicians, poets, writers, and playwrights, as well as scientists of the highest distinction lived there [Ellenberger, 1970:260]." Vienna was the capital of the Hapsburg monarchy, which ruled over a conglomeration of many different ethnic minorities. One of these minorities was the Jews. While some Jews retained the strong ties to the community typical of traditional Jewish culture, many others had become assimilated into the wider cosmopolitan culture of Vienna. Freud's father was a freethinker who raised his children in a secular atmosphere. As Rieff (1961) points out, Freud's religion was "not of the Jew integrated into his own community but of the 'infidel Jew' standing on the edge of an alien culture and perpetually arrayed against it [283]."

Both the social context within which psychoanalysis was developed and its originator were thus prototypes of the emergent individualistic culture. The city of Vienna was an urban, cosmopolitan center of culture. Freud was an urban intellectual alienated from the culture of his forefathers and a member of a marginal ethnic group. It is fitting that the foremost developer of individualistic psychotherapy was someone who, in his own life, had none of the long-standing bonds characteristic of communal social groups.

While the psychoanalytic system of psychotherapy Freud developed is only one of innumerable individualistic therapies that have arisen over the past century, it is of much greater importance than the number of its practitioners or clients indicates. It has become the prototype of twentieth century Western psychotherapy and has had a tremendous influence on the intellectual life of the century. Even now, after it has been widely rejected as a viable therapeutic system, it retains an influential position among psychiatrists and intellectuals. Therefore, I will explore its nature in some depth in order to capture the basic elements of individualistic styles of psychotherapy.

Individualistic societies require styles of psychotherapy that are radically different from those found in communal groups. Psychoanalysis is one psychotherapeutic style perfectly suited to the social setting of Freud's time. Each element of psychoanalytic therapy *inverts* the essential aspects of communal therapies (see Levi-Strauss, 1964). Symbols drawn from self-experience, not ritualized and communal symbols that do not correspond to a personal state of mind, are used to interpret personality problems. Cure occurs through self-exploration and consequent self-awareness, not through conformity to the normative order of the group. The individual personality is not denigrated by the therapeutic process, as in communal therapy, but becomes of paramount concern in therapy. Finally, the therapeutic process itself becomes a private relationship between the patient and the therapist that is an oasis from the social world, rather than a communal affair mobilizing the energies of the community. In each of these aspects, psychoanalytic therapy reflects the development of an individualistic society and the liberation of the individual from the ties of the communal group.

The symbolic system of psychoanalysis reverses that found in communal styles of therapy. Communal therapy uses a small number of restricted symbols that provide standardized interpretations of problems without individual variations in meaning. In contrast, individualistic therapies use what Bernstein (1971) calls an *elaborated* symbolic system. Elaborated speech systems are based on the communication of individualized variations in meaning, a wide range of alternative constructions of meaning, and an emphasis on the subjective intent of the speaker. Associated with the development of elaborated speech systems is the rejection of ritual:

> The confirmed anti-ritualist mistrusts external expression. He values a man's inner convictions. Spontaneous speech that flows straight from the heart, unpremeditated, irregular in form, even somewhat incoherent, is good because it bears witness to the speaker's real intentions [Douglas, 1973:74].

Douglas' portrayal of the antiritualist fits the major symbolic and structural elements of Freudian therapy.

In psychoanalysis, external actions and speech presumably hide the true inner meaning of symptoms. Cure arises through the use of the technique of free association, the opposite of any ritualized speech system. True meaning is hidden from the conscious mind and knowledge is acquired only by the exploration of the private and obscure layers of the self that lead to the unconscious. Public communication is mistrusted and the real self is only found after the social self is stripped away in therapy. In contrast to communal therapies, psychoanalysis renounces what is public and strives to uncover the self through an exploration of private meaning.

While communal therapies interpret private experience through the categories of the social world, analytic therapy turns the patient away from the public area to examine the self and personal emotions. Private experiences do not acquire meaning in communal symbols; even the public spheres of politics, religion, and culture are interpreted in terms of inner psychological dynamics and early family experience (Freud, 1928, 1930/1962). The Freudian view of the individual is not of one who is intrinsically tied to a network of encompassing social and cultural ties, but of a person who is constantly in conflict with social and cultural demands. Human nature is inherently and permanently unsocial (Rieff, 1961). The embattled ego faces the repressive social demands transmitted by the superego and the natural drives unconsciously urged by the id. In communal therapy, the individual is brought in harmony with the environment and social integration represents the fulfillment of the individual. In contrast, for Freud, acquiescence to the demands of society represents the sacrifice of individuality.

The goal of psychoanalysis is to emancipate individuals from social repression, not to further the integration of the individual into the group. The achievement of this goal requires an intensive analysis of the inner self and of past individual experiences. One psychiatric text summarizes the aims of psychoanalysis as follows:

> It allows the individual to pay attention to the interconnections of his internal and private sensations and feelings. With the support of the analyst, the patient can update his earlier and private modes of experience and see himself and others with some new perspective [Redlich and Freedman, 1966:277].

The source of current emotional difficulties is presumed to lie in repressed unconscious wishes and motives that publicly appear in disguised and distorted forms such as dreams, slips of the tongue, or forgetting (Freud, 1924/1960). In the therapeutic process, patients learn to overcome the various defense mechanisms and resistances that they use to avoid understanding the true motivations that lie behind their symptoms. The sources of these motivations are assumed to lie in forgotten experiences of childhood and especially in childhood sexuality. Cure is achieved only after these private memories and resistances are uncovered and resolved. This sort of exploration of the inner self is neglected in communal therapies.

Communal therapies are oriented to a normative view of the personality whereby the source of problems often lies in a violation of social norms and the cure for problems is in conformity to the normative order of the group. Analytic therapy also reverses this aspect of the therapeutic process. For Freud, the traditional moral codes are a major cause of mental symptoms, not the source of their cure. The repression of instinctual desires because of social demands leads to guilt and to the emergence of

171

symptoms as an unsuccessful attempt to resolve the conflict between physical instinct and social repression. Cure is effected through the person's coming to understand the nature of these repressions and making a conscious choice of whether or not to conform to social norms. Fromm-Reichmann (1949) states:

> The aim of psychoanalytic therapy is to bring these rejected drives and wishes, together with the patient's individual and environmental moral standards, which are the instruments for his rejections, into consciousness and in this way place them at his free disposal. In doing this the conscious self becomes strengthened, since it is no longer involved in the continuous job of repressing mental content from his own awareness. The patient can then decide independently which desires he wants to accept and which he wishes to reject, his personality no longer being warped or dominated by uncontrollable drives and moral standards. This process permits growth and maturation [122–123].

This view of the goals of therapy is far removed from the goals of communal styles of therapy. Cure is achieved through emancipation from, not conformity to, the demands of the social order.

Just as the interpretations of personality problems in individualistic styles of therapy are found in private experience, so do the techniques of therapy become privatized. The primary technique of analysis is introspection: "Psychoanalysis is learnt first of all on oneself through the study of one's own personality [Freud, 1924/1960:23]." Therapeutic techniques turn individuals inward to gain insight into how their past experiences have led to their current problems. The success of psychoanalytic therapy

> depends not on the physician's technically successful influence on a sick organism but on the course of the sick person's self-reflection. And the latter proceeds only as long as analytic knowledge is impelled onward against motivational resistances by the interest in self-knowledge [Habermas, 1971:235].

The major goal of the therapeutic process is the growth of self-awareness and self-knowledge, not the enhanced integration of the patient into the community.

Not only the interpretation of problems and the technique of analysis, but also the style of the individualistic therapeutic relationship inverts the structure of communal therapy. Psychoanalysis occurs within a private dialogue between the patient and the therapist with no participation by outside family or community members:

> The dialogue which constitutes the analysis will admit of no audience. . . . For these communications relate to all his most private thoughts and feelings, all that

which as a socially independent person he must hide from others, all that which, being foreign to his own conception of himself, he tries to conceal even from himself [Freud, 1924/1960:22].

The therapist no longer represents the values of the community but is a stranger who stands outside of social conventions. Within the private therapeutic process, the usual punishments for revealing tabooed material are lifted and the patient can report all thoughts and feelings without restriction or censorship. The psychoanalytic relationship reflects an intensifying of an individualistic society to the extent that the patient hides nothing from a total stranger.

The role of the individualistic therapist diverges from the position of the therapist in communal therapy. The individualistic therapist does not represent the community, but is a stranger upon whom an earlier private relationship is projected. Especially in his later writings, Freud believed that the cure for symptoms mainly lay in the transference relationship that developed between patients and their therapists (Freud, 1924/1960). The therapist represents the parent and the therapeutic relationship recapitulates the central aspects of patients' earlier relationships with their parents. The neurosis of the patient collapses into the transference relationship and, once worked through, the individual can be freed of earlier attachments and can become autonomous. The therapist no longer symbolizes the collective representations of the community, but the private relationship between patients and their parents.

In all of its elements, analytic therapy represents a drastic change from communal therapy. The therapeutic process, which does not tie individuals to the community, but rather frees them from it, "emancipate[s] man's I from the communal we [Rieff, 1961:362]." The goal of analytic therapy is to achieve autonomy for patients and to allow them to regulate their lives by norms of their own choosing. In dramatic contrast with communal therapy, analytic therapy affirms no values beyond the self, but only the value of personal independence. Its aim of freeing the individual from the burdens of group and communal life reflects the changes in the underlying social structure that make autonomous individuals the major components of social organization.

Unlike communal therapy, analytic therapy does not tell individuals what goals they should pursue but provides them with the option to choose their own goals. Because an individualistic society does not have strong shared objective values, the therapist cannot represent a consensual normative order. The communal therapist attaches the suffering of the patient to the collective representations of the society and prescribes ritual penance. The analytic therapist is unable to do this because these external sources of security no longer exist. The therapist can only try to free the self from binding attachments to the group. The source of the cure lies within the individual, not in conformity to the objective values of a homogeneous society. As Rieff (1961) notes, Freudianism inculcates: "skepticism about all ideologies except those of private life [278]." The self-absorption found at the heart of analytic therapy reflects the self-absorption an individualistic society creates.

The essential transformation in analytic therapy is not from a religious to a scientific point of view but from attachments to communal symbols to belief in nothing but the individual self. Freud is the spokesman for the modern individual who is differentiated from all communal ties:

> The essentially secular aim of Freudian spiritual guidance is to wean away the ego from either a heroic or a compliant attitude to the community. Here Freud differed not only from the physicians of established faiths—Catholic or other— but also from the propagandists of secular faiths, those socialists and other radicals still essentially engaged in absorbing the individual into the community. He was not impressed by the clerical strategy of confirming faith by strengthening the individual's identification with the community. . . . What is needed is to free men from their sick communities [Rieff, 1961:361–362].

Indeed, while a religious world view is usually the mainstay of communal therapies, for Freud, religion itself was a sickness (Freud, 1928). All authoritarian belief systems, including religion, represented a regression to the infantile need for a parent and an abdication of the self and of individual responsibility. In communal groups, therapy embodies a picture of the patient as one link in a chain extending backward to ancestors and forward to descendants (Reiff, 1961). Analytic therapy attempts to break this chain by freeing the individual from past social relationships and from communal ideologies.

Each aspect of analytic therapy reflects a type of social solidarity that has freed individuals from binding social attachments to an extent unprecedented in human history. Therapeutic symbolism stems from the interior life of the patient, not from the communal life outside. Explanations of problems do not reinforce the similarities of the individual to other communal members but elaborate individual differences. Therapy does not attach individuals to the normative order but allows them to live separate from each other without encapsulating social ties or ideologies. Insight and self-awareness, not belief in any system beyond the individual, bring about cure in an individualistic society. Left with no one but their therapists, analytic patients explore the nature of their selves to the end of living free from binding social ties and beliefs. In these respects, psychoanalysis is as suited for its social context as communal therapy is for the settings in which it develops. Just as communal therapies emanate from and reinforce a form of social solidarity in which individuals are tightly bound together, analytic therapy reflects a society made up of separate individuals.

The particular elements of an individualistic society that psycho-analysis represents also explain the nature of its development and appeal. Psychoanalysis emerged in one of the cosmopolitan centers of its time, Vienna, and its founder and most of his disciples were members of a cosmopolitan Jewish ethnic group. In both Europe and the United States psychoanalysis gained its greatest acceptance within artistic and intellec-tual circles, among persons who were least tied to traditional cultural bonds and social relationships (see Ellenberger, 1970; Hale, 1971). In ad-dition, psychoanalysis attained its greatest popularity and influence in the United States, the country where individualism has flourished to the greatest extent. While psychoanalysis has lost much of its popularity and influence in contemporary society, its primary practitioners and users are still cosmopolitan intellectuals alienated from conventional culture and society (see Chapter 4). The development, diffusion, and current location of analytic therapy all stem from a form of social life in which individuals have a heightened sense of self but no strong social bonds or traditional belief system that provide them with a sense of meaning. While immer-sion in traditional cultures and strong social groups turns individuals away from the exploration of their selves, the breakdown of communal culture and society turns them inward to the depths of their personalities.

Psychoanalysis emerged and flourished with the breakdown of com-munal culture and society. While it was the major therapeutic technique in the first half of the twentieth century, its current influence is con-siderably reduced and it is now only one of many individualistic therapies. If the thesis presented here is correct, the decline in the popu-larity of analysis and the emergence of other styles of individualistic therapies should also reflect a transformation in the underlying social structure. Because all psychotherapies attain their healing power through their congruence with social reality, a change in the nature of the society that analytic therapy represents would render this therapy obsolete. The plethora of therapies that have emerged in recent years may reflect a new form of social structure unimagined in Freud's time. In this sense, psychoanalysis may represent more the end point of one era of Western society than the beginning of another era.

## Psychotherapy after Psychoanalysis

While psychoanalysis was the first widely institutionalized form of individualistic therapy in the modern West, and still stands as its paradigmatic case, in recent decades it has declined in popularity. On the one hand, among many psychiatric professionals, drug-oriented therapies and behavior modification have enjoyed growing popularity (Murray, 1979). These therapies are primarily directed toward changing the physical organism or outward behavior and are little concerned with the symbolic aspects of the personality. Hence, they do not fit our definition of psychotherapy and will not be considered here. On the other hand, especially during the late 1960s and early 1970s, a tremendous number and variety of alternative psychotherapeutic approaches arose. Largely emergent outside of the psychiatric profession, existential therapy, Gestalt therapy, self-actualization, client-centered therapy, and many others became popular.

The proponents of most of these newer styles of therapy view them as a reaction against Freudian theory and techniques (e.g., Rogers, 1951; Laing, 1967; Bart, 1974). From a broader sociological point of view, however, they reflect an *intensification* of the individualistic nature of therapy as compared to psychoanalysis. The emphasis on the individual self and the denigration of social convention found in the newer psychotherapies is unprecedented in the history of psychotherapy.

What unites the practitioners of the multitude of contemporary individualistic therapies in their rejection of psychoanalysis is their belief that psychoanalysis, because of its mechanistic nature, does not do enough justice to the uniqueness of the individual personality. Instead, these advocates believe that more attention should be paid to individuals' internal subjective experiences. For example, Carl Rogers (1951) claims that psychoanalysis constructs barriers to seeing the uniqueness of patients, overestimates the importance of past experiences and consequently underestimates the importance of the immediate moment, and prevents clients from total "self-actualization." Similarly, the Gestalt therapy developed by Fritz Perls (1964) rejects any study of personal history, or even any intellectualization of problems, because this impedes a focus on the unique present moment. The encounter group movement also strove to liberate people from their past by utilizing immediate contacts with others in the present moment (Back, 1973).

The various therapies that emerged in the 1960s emphasized the unique, creative, and spontaneous aspect of individual experience, freed of any form of commitment apart from the satisfaction of individual desires. The unplanned and spontaneous act, unconstrained by social roles, was viewed as the only place where genuine authenticity could be found. For example, a therapist at the Esalen Institute, one of the centers of the humanistic movement, stated:

> I guess largely I feel that most people in our culture tend to carry around a lot of chronic tension, and that they tend to respond largely on the basis of *habit* behavior and often goal-motivated behavior. And what I call sensory awakening is a method to get people to quiet their verbal activity, to let go their tension, and focus their awareness on various parts of their body or various activities or feelings in their body. And of experiencing the *moment*, experiencing what it is they are actually doing as opposed to any kind of concept or conditioned kind of habit behavior [quoted in Back, 1973:81].

Here, even talk is viewed as a social convention to be overcome in the search for pure individual uniqueness, freed from all past "habits." The ideal is an individual who is liberated from all social categories and oppression: "The structure of society, with its emphasis on role-appropriate behavior in interaction, is considered a barrier to full humanness [Bart, 1974:33]."

In contrast to communal therapies, which rely on strict rituals, and even to psychoanalysis, which utilizes specific therapeutic techniques, there is no formal agenda in the variety of contemporary psychotherapies. Instead, treatment occurs through a constant analysis of the feelings and dynamics that occur within relationships formed in the present situation (see Back, 1973). Self-expression rather than social norms, nonverbal exploration of feelings and senses instead of language, and immediacy and not habit are the central dynamics in these therapies. The cure for problems lies in a celebration of the unique aspects of the self and the exploration of one's self free from all preconceived social categories. Unlike psychoanalysis, contemporary psychotherapies reject the examination of personal history, enduring social structures, or even the symbolization of experience. Instead, they discard the "language of symbols in favor of direct experience and action [Back, 1973:79]."

Unlike psychoanalysis, but like most communal therapies, contemporary psychotherapies are often conducted within groups. However, these group settings have nothing in common with the group character of communal therapies. The group members are not people with whom the patient has kin or community ties but of strangers with whom the person has no ties aside from membership in the therapy group itself. The group has neither history nor future; it functions totally in the immediate situation, and its members are totally interchangeable. The "community" found in these therapeutic groups is a community of strangers whose bonds disintegrate after the therapeutic session.

Communal therapy heals by drawing patients into the store of the community's collective representations; psychoanalysis heals by creating strong and autonomous individuals who can withstand the demands of the social world. In contrast, the aim of contemporary psychotherapies is to create individuals who can freely and indiscriminately relate to interchangeable others with warmth, spontaneity, and openness. Carl Rogers (1968), a leading proponent of these therapies, states: "Temporary relationships will be able to achieve the richness and meaning which heretofore have been associated only with lifelong attachments [269]." The participant in a modern therapy group is not tied to a strong community but to a multitude of fleeting relationships with strangers.

Because participants in these therapy groups are encouraged to display their "real" feelings and to keep nothing hidden, their operation is sometimes compared to confessionals within religious and other communal groups (e.g., Ruitenbeek, 1970). In fact, however, there is little in common between contemporary psychotherapies and religious confessionals. Sin, a deviation from the normative order of the group, is the essence of the religious confessional. In contemporary psychotherapies, however, sin cannot exist because social norms have no credence. In the new individualistic therapies, there is no notion of good and evil aside from what satisfies the immediate needs of the individual. In contrast to communal groups where the individual is tied to a presence beyond the self, experience in encounter groups leads the individual to "be in better touch with one's real self." Not commitment to group norms but only "self-actualization" in the present moment is the aim of these contemporary therapies.

Even those contemporary therapies that are usually considered to be "radical" are thoroughly individualistic. Perhaps the most well-known radical therapist is R. D. Laing. Laingian "therapy" involves a voyage to the most interior parts of the self, allowing one to explore private symbolism freed of all social constraints (Laing, 1967). Radical therapists commonly view the social structure as "sick" and find "sanity" in the inner depths of individual psyches (Scheff, 1975:19). In their rejection of society, radical therapists often fall back on the exploration of the inner self and their therapies become thoroughly individualistic.

Just as the development and diffusion of psychoanalysis reflected the changes that occurred in Western societies in the late nineteenth and early twentieth centuries, the development of the new individualistic therapies reflect new forms of social existence. These therapies have only had appeal in the United States, and only among a particular segment of the American population. Their participants are typically mobile, affluent, and white members of the upper middle class (Back, 1973). Moving from one relationship to another, these individuals in their own lives are differentiated from binding group ties. In addition, they feel no commitment to any strong belief system. While Freud and his followers were still burdened by a cultural heritage they sought to overcome, the clients of the modern therapies, who often have grown up in suburbia, have never suffered from the same type of oppressive social and cultural restraints.

Because of the changing nature of society, the problems faced by clients of the newer therapies have drastically altered since Freud's time. Psychoanalytic patients usually had well-defined symptoms that Freud felt were produced by social and psychic repressions in childhood. Freud's patients suffered from conscious or unconscious guilt feelings because they still had to reckon with powerful social norms, especially in the area of sexuality. The clients of the newer therapies, however, were usually socialized in a far less repressive atmosphere and are less likely to suffer from the sorts of sexual repressions that presumably created the problems of Freud's patients.

The clients of modern therapies do not confront a society that restrains their instincts or that requires a strong and autonomous self. Instead, their existence does not allow for the creation of binding social or cultural ties and their lives are lived in the "here and now." The recent emergence of narcissism as the archetypal pathology of our era (e.g., Sennett, 1978; Lasch, 1978) reflects this form of social existence. Narcissism is marked by a feeling of perpetual emptiness, an inability to relate to goals or people outside the self, a lost identity, and an isolation from others (Beldoch, 1975). These problems reflect the social situation of individuals who have never been constrained by binding social or cultural ties.

The sort of "therapeutic" experience found in the modern therapies fits the social reality of their users. The atomization of social reality requires that individuals be able to adapt flexibly to a multitude of situations and strangers. In this sense, the therapy group becomes a microcosm of daily existence. At the extreme, as at the Esalen Institute, clients enjoy casual sex with one another, a "treatment" suited to a society marked by casual and transitory sexual relationships (Bart, 1974).

Psychoanalysis developed in a society where social conventions repressed instinctual desires. Because of this, analytic patients felt they did not know their real wants and desires. To find their "true selves" they had to explore the depths of their psyches and eliminate the layers of social repression that disguised their needs. Now, however, with less social repression and with instinctual desires more freely gratified, individuals have little need to explore past history or the depths of their

**179**

selves. Instead, people live their lives on the surface, in the immediate moment (Lasch, 1978). The newer forms of therapeutic control reflect this transitory style of social existence that emerged among a portion of the upper middle class in the United States of the 1960s and 1970s.

## Modern Communal Therapies

The conditions of social existence in modern Western societies do not readily lend themselves to the development of communal styles of therapy. Most "therapeutic communities" that develop are collections of strangers with no bonds outside of the therapy group and with no communal symbols to which members can tie their experiences. Not surprisingly, the goals of these groups involve the promotion of individual growth and self-awareness, rather than integration into the community (Marx and Seldin, 1973). Most modern group therapies reflect an individualistic form of social solidarity in which individuals explore the nature of the self in the company of a fleeting group of strangers.

Some forms of modern group therapies, however, do bear some resemblances to communal therapies. Because these therapies have emerged within individualistic societies, it is useful to explore their nature. Two of the most well-known examples of modern communal therapy are the Alcoholics Anonymous and Synanon programs.

Therapy in the Alcoholics Anonymous (AA) program occurs within group sessions, all members at some time having been alcoholic. Each member, without exception, proceeds through the same "12-step" formula of treatment. The problem of the alcoholic is interpreted through a purely standardized explanation and the AA member learns to tie his or her drinking problem to a "Power greater than the self and to transfer his worries and the direction of his will to that Power [Bales, 1962:573]." Alcoholism is viewed as an "allergy" and participants learn that they are not different from any other alcoholic.

For my purposes, what is important about the Alcoholics Anonymous program is that the ritualized style of explanation of problems it provides is accompanied by the creation of a communal-like social structure. The AA program involves an enveloping round of group activities (see Lofland, 1969:Ch. 11). Group meetings take place every night of the week, special activities are held on weekends and holidays, and members are encouraged to have only other AA members as friends. Spouses and children of AA members also often become involved in the therapy process through adjunct programs such as Al-Anon and Al-Ateen. While hardly comparable to a tribal setting, membership in AA

180

becomes as encompassing as possible for a middle-class person in American society. Without the creation of a communal-like social setting, it is doubtful that AA could effectively utilize a communal style of therapy.

Another example of a therapeutic community that utilized a communal style of therapy was the Synanon program for drug addicts, as this program operated during the 1960s (Johnson and Cressey, 1963). The Synanon program stressed the likeness of each individual addict to all other addicts and interpreted the problems of all drug addicts in similar ways. Therapy involved making each member as dependent as possible on the group. The structure of the program featured continuous mutual activity between members, and through a number of control mechanisms such as cutting off one's hair, severing past family and friendship ties, and not entering dyadic friendships (which are forbidden), the individual was assimilated into the group (Johnson and Cressey, 1963). Graduates of Synanon rarely left the program but instead remained working within one of the various Synanon organizations. The communal nature of the therapy in Synanon could only be maintained through the encapsulating structure within which the therapy occurred.

In both the Alcoholics Anonymous and Synanon programs, it is more accurate to say that the form of social solidarity reproduces the form of therapeutic control than the opposite. These therapeutic programs were constructed on the basis of the therapeutic ideologies. Yet both programs illustrate the principle that if individuals can tie their personalities to communal types of symbolic systems, the symbolism must be grounded in an interlocking network of social relationships. Communal styles of therapy can only be maintained within tightly binding social structures. Similarly, contemporary religious sects such as the Hari Krishnas or Children of God couple a ritualistic set of beliefs with an encapsulating communal group structure. Given the conditions of modern social existence, if any group wishes to promote a ritualistic form of expression, it must also create the type of group solidarity that can maintain this symbolic style.

What programs such as Alcoholics Anonymous or Synanon have in common with tribal societies, the People's Republic of China, or religious sects is that in them the unique qualities of individuals and their unique motivations become irrelevant to the interpretations and control of personality problems. The view of alcoholism as an "allergy," for example, is similar in form to the view of personality problems as instances of "sin," "demonic possession," or "ideological deviation." In each interpretation, the experience of the individual is grounded in the collective representations of the group. Through the uses of standardized interpretations, the individual is turned away from the self and outward toward the group. Such interpretations, however, can only be sustained when they are grounded in a form of social solidarity that envelops individuals and commits them to the common life of the group. When individuals can align their experiences to strong and binding groups and symbolic systems, the explanation and control of personality problems is not likely to be found within individual selves. Individualistic interpretations and treatments of personality problems only emerge when people cannot turn to broader social groups or cultural values for solace and healing.

## Conclusion

The primary task of psychotherapy is to provide sufferers and those around them with the means to grasp the nature of their distress. This involves incorporating the experiences of the patient within a culturally shared universe of meaning. Therapists occupy strategic social control roles in society because they must enforce whatever is considered to be the standard of meaningful reality in the group. Each system of psychotherapy is more or less adequate, not according to the universal canons of science, but according to its fit with the symbolic universe of the particular social context. Cure occurs only if patients believe the particular interpretative scheme therapists provide. Because therapeutic social control operates through the use of symbolic systems of meaning, it is intrinsically linked to the social context within which it operates.

The last two chapters have examined therapeutic control within two ideal types of social settings, communal and individualistic settings. Communal groups are marked by many interlocking ties between members, strong group cohesion, and an emphasis on group rather than on individual welfare. The therapeutic systems that arise in communal groups reflect this form of social solidarity. Therapeutic symbolism takes a ritualistic form, and the diagnosis and explanation of problems incorporate individual experience into standardized categories. Therapy is strongly normative and treatment involves promoting conformity to group norms as a means of cure. The therapeutic process commonly calls for the presence of other group members besides the patient and therapist, reinforcing the ties of the individual to the group.

When the social structure becomes individualistic, as in modern Western societies, the nature of therapeutic social control correspondingly changes. Therapeutic symbolism becomes interior and emphasizes intrapsychic processes and individual motivation. The goal of therapy ceases to be social conformity but involves the promotion of self-awareness and individual autonomy. Finally, the therapeutic process becomes one solely between the patient and the therapist. The emergence of a highly mobile, affluent upper middle class in the United States in the 1960s produced a further intensification of the individualistic nature of psychotherapy. As befits a social existence marked by numerous and interchangeable, but superficial, social relationships, psychotherapy came to emphasize immediate experience rather than deep intrapsychic processes. In each case, the nature of psychotherapy reflected the social context in which it emerged.

The view of psychotherapy taken here contrasts with the typical position of its practitioners that characterizes the various forms of communal therapies as "demonological," "magical," or "superstitious," and modern therapies as more "scientific" or "rational." This chapter has developed the view that each style of therapy reflects a particular form of social solidarity. When the group grips its members in tight communal bonds, the treatment of personality problems stresses ritualized explanations of problems, the likeness of the patient to others in the group, and social integration. The view that personality problems stem from the nature of individual experience only develops when the form of social existence becomes an individualistic one.

Like all styles of social control, therapeutic control deals with deviation from normative standards, in this case standards of "healthy" and "unhealthy" personalities. Those standards of mental health that contemporary psychiatric professionals take for granted—self-fulfillment, spontaneity, freedom, autonomy, and so on—are premised on a notion of an individuated personality that is virtually unique in history. Even within contemporary Western societies, individualistic therapies have had little appeal beyond highly educated members of the upper middle class. By contrast, standards of mental health traditionally have been found through conforming to the demands of the group and suppressing individuality in the service of the collectivity. The obsession with the self found among contemporary educated people is as predictable from their form of social experience as is the use of ritual among tribal peoples. Because therapeutic symbolism gains meaning only within a particular social context, the psychoanalysis of a Haitian peasant, for example, would be as senseless a therapeutic process as the exorcism of a demon from a New York intellectual (Berger and Luckmann, 1967). Each style of symbolizing and controlling personality problems corresponds to the ties that bind individuals to one another in that society.

The styles of psychotherapy explored in this chapter are only one aspect of the social control of mental illness. Indeed, psychotherapy is not likely to be used at all with individuals who appear to be severely mentally ill. Persons who behave in incomprehensible ways do not generally share with therapists the symbolic systems that are a prerequisite of effective psychotherapy. Hence, psychotherapy is most likely to be a control mechanism for persons with mild forms of psychic distress, not for those who seem severely mentally ill.

Up to the present, individualistic forms of social solidarity and therapy have been limited to a narrow segment of the population in modern Western societies. However, many social indicators point to a continual expansion and flourishing of individualistic styles of psychotherapy. For example, Black (1976) describes the movement of modern social structures as follows:

> Traditional ties have been loosening, even falling apart altogether. The community is weaker than ever before, and so is the neighborhood and family. The life span of relationships grows shorter and shorter. Increasingly, marriage does not last, for instance, and friends fluctuate from month to month, if not from week to week or day to day. Encounters replace the social structures of the past, and people increasingly have closeness without permanence, depth without commitment [135].

Black sees these trends leading to a decline of law and to an emergence of an anarchic style of social control. If these trends continue they will also be consistent with an expansion of individalistic styles of therapeutic control. Individuals cut adrift from encompassing belief systems and social groups will turn increasingly to therapeutic control to find some meaning in their lives.

One possible outcome of these trends would be that the therapeutic experience will replace the loss of stable commitments and permanent relationships. This is the belief of Carl Rogers, one of the leading proponents of "humanistic" forms of individualistic therapies. Rogers (1968) feels that in therapeutic groups

> There will be possibilities for the rapid development of closeness between and among persons, a closeness which is not artificial, but is real and deep, and which will be well suited to our increasing mobility of living. Temporary relationships will be able to achieve the richness and meaning which heretofore have been associated only with lifelong attachments [268–269].

If so, the newer forms of individualistic therapies will be ideal treatments for the personality problems of individuals who have been freed from long-standing commitments.

On the other hand, if the central thesis of Emile Durkheim's work (e.g., 1893/1964; 1897/1951) is correct—that the meaning of life is found in strong group attachments—the continuing individuation of society will make meaningful social existence less possible. People who are freed of group ties and symbolic commitments should eagerly seek individualistic therapies to resolve their problems, yet the emphasis in these therapies on unique experience, self-awareness, and autonomy may only reinforce the conditions that led them to seek therapy in the first place. The aphorism of the Viennese satirist Karl Kraus: "Psychoanalysis is the disease of which it pretends to be the cure," may aptly apply to all styles of individualistic therapies (Kraus, 1977:227). Yet structural individuation and the breakdown of communal belief systems have undermined the possibilities for communal therapies. Perhaps only the emergence of new forms of social existence can turn modern individuals away from the focus on the self that they now experience in psychotherapy toward some new, as yet unknown, style of therapeutic social control.

# References

Ackerknecht, Erwin H.
1959    A Short History of Psychiatry. New York: Hafner.
Albrecht, Gary L.
1974    "The indigenous mental health worker: The cure-all for what ailment?" Pp.
        235–253 in P. Roman and H. M. Trice (eds.), The Sociology of Psychotherapy.
        New York: Jason Aronson.
Alexander, Franz, and Sheldon Selesnick
1966    The History of Psychiatry. New York: Harper.
Al-Issa, Ihsan and Birgitta Al-Issa
1969–1970    "Psychiatric problems in a developing country: Iraq." International Jour-
        nal of Social Psychiatry 16:15–22.
Angrist, Shirley, Mark Lefton, Simon Dinitz, and Benjamin Pasamanick
1968    Women after Treatment: A Study of Former Mental Patients and Their Normal
        Neighbors. New York: Appleton.
Aubert, Vilhelm, and Sheldon L. Messinger
1958    "The criminal and the sick." Inquiry 1:137–160.
Ausebel, David P.
1961    "Personality disorder is disease." American Psychologist 16:69–74.
Aviram, Uri, and Steven Segal
1973    "Exclusion of the mentally ill: Reflection on an old problem in a new context."
        Archives of General Psychiatry 29:126–131.
Back, Kurt W.
1973    Beyond Words: The Story of Sensitivity Training and the Encounter Movement.
        New York: Penguin
Bakwin, Ruth Morris
1963    "Attitudes of parents of mentally ill children." Journal of the American Medical
        Women's Association 18:305–318.

Baldwin, Beverley Ann, H. Hugh Floyd, Jr., and Dennis R. McSeveney
　1975　"Status inconsistency and psychiatric diagnosis: A structural approach to label-
　　　ing theory." Journal of Health and Social Behavior 16:257–267.
Bales, Robert F.
　1962　"The therapeutic role of Alcoholics Anonymous as seen by a sociologist." Pp.
　　　572–585 in D. J. Pittman and C. R. Snyder (eds.), Society, Culture and Drink-
　　　ing Patterns. Carbondale: Southern Illinois University Press.
Bart, Pauline B.
　1968　"Social structure and vocabularies of discomfort: What happened to female
　　　hysteria?" Journal of Health and Social Behavior 9:188–193.
　1974　"Ideologies and utopias of psychotherapy." Pp. 9–57 in P. Roman and H. M.
　　　Trice (eds.), The Sociology of Psychotherapy. New York: Jason Aronson.
Beldoch, Michael
　1975　"The therapeutic as narcissist." Pp. 105–123 in R. Boyers (ed.), Psychological
　　　Man. New York: Harper.
Benedict, Ruth
　1934　Anthropology and the abnormal. Journal of General Psychology 10:59–80.
Berger, Peter L., and Thomas Luckmann
　1966　The Social Construction of Reality. Garden City, New York: Doubleday.
Berndt, Catherine H.
　1964　"The role of native doctors in Aboriginal Australia." Pp. 264–282 in Ari Kiev
　　　(ed.), Magic, Faith and Healing. New York: Free Press.
Bernstein, Basil
　1964　"Social class, speech systems, and psycho-therapy." British Journal of Sociology
　　　15:54–64.
　1971　Class, Codes and Control: Volume I. Theoretical Studies Towards a Sociology
　　　of Language. London: Routledge & Kegan.
Bittner, Egon
　1967　"Police discretion in apprehending the mentally ill." Social Problems
　　　14:278–292.
Black, Donald
　1976　The Behavior of Law. New York: Academic Press.
　1979　"Comment: Common sense in the sociology of law." American Sociological Re-
　　　view 44:18–27.
　1980　The Manners and Customs of the Police. New York: American Press.
Black, Donald, and Maureen Mileski (eds.)
　1973　The Social Organization of Law. New York: Seminar Press.
Blum, Alan, and Peter McHugh
　1971　"The social ascription of motives." American Sociological Review 36:98–109.
Bockoven, J. Sanbourne
　1972　Moral Treatment in Community Mental Health. New York: Springer Publ.
Bott, Elizabeth
　1957　Family and Social Network. London: Tavistock.
Brill, Norman Q., and Hugh A. Stornow
　1960　"Social class and psychiatric treatment." Archives of General Psychiatry 3:340–
　　　344.
Brodbeck, May
　1968　"General Introduction." Pp. 1–11 in M. Brodbeck (ed.), Readings in the Phil-
　　　osophy of the Social Sciences. New York: Macmillan.

**188**

# References

Brody, Eugene B.
1973   The Lost Ones: Social Forces and Mental Illness in Rio De Janeiro. New York: International Universities Press.

Brody, Eugene, Robert Derbyshire, and Carl Schliefer
1967   "How the young adult Baltimore Negro male becomes a Maryland mental health statistic." Psychiatric Epidemiology and Mental Health Planning, Report No. 22. Washington, D.C.: American Psychiatric Association.

Carstairs, Morris G.
1969   "Changing perception of neurotic illness." Pp. 405–414 in W. Caudill and T.-Y. Lin (eds.), Mental Health Research in Asia and the Pacific. Honolulu, Hawaii: East-West Center Press.

Cawte, John
1974   Medicine Is the Law: Studies in Psychiatric Anthropology of Australian Tribal Societies. Honolulu: Univ. Press of Hawaii.

Chambliss, William, and Robert Seidman
1971   Law, Order, and Power. Reading, Massachusetts: Addison-Wesley.

Chesler, Phyllis
1972   Women and Madness. New York: Avon.

Clark, Alexander and Jack Gibbs
1965   "Social control: A reformulation." Social Problems 12:398–415.

Clarke, Basil
1975   Mental Disorder in Earlier Britain. Cardiff: Univ. of Wales Press.

Clausen, John A., and Marian Radke Yarrow (eds.)
1955   "The impact of mental illness on the family." The Journal of Social Issues 11, entire issue.

Cleary, Paul D.
1980   "The determinants of psychotropic drug prescribing." Unpublished doctoral dissertation, Department of Sociology, University of Wisconsin, Madison.

Clements, Forrest E.
1932   Primitive Concepts of Disease. University of California Publications in American Archaeology and Ethnology 32: 185–252.

Cohen, F.
1966   "The function of the attorney and the commitment of the mentally ill." Texas Law Review 44: 424–469.

Conrad, Peter, and Joseph W. Schneider
1980   Deviance and Medicalization: From Badness to Sickness. St. Louis, Missouri: Mosby.

Constantinides, Pamela
1977   "Ill at ease and sick at heart: Symbolic behaviour in a Sudanese healing cult." Pp. 61–84 in I. Lewis (ed.), Symbols and Sentiments. New York: Academic Press.

Cooley, Charles Horton
1909   Social Organization. New York: Scribner.

Coulter, Jeff
1973   Approaches to Insanity: A Philosophical and Sociological Study. New York: Wiley.

Crocetti, Guido M., Herzl R. Spiro, and Iradj Siassi
1974   Contemporary Attitudes toward Mental Illness. Pittsburgh, Pennsylvania: Univ. of Pittsburgh Press.

Cumming, Elaine, and John Cumming
    1957    Closed Ranks: An Experiment in Mental Health Education. Cambridge, Massa-
            chusetts: Harvard Univ. Press.
Dain, Norman
    1964    Concepts of Insanity in the United States, 1789–1865. New Brunswick, New
            Jersey: Rutgers Univ. Press.
Daniels, Arlene K.
    1972    "Military psychiatry: The emergence of a subspecialty." Pp. 145–162 in E.
            Freidson and J. Lorber (eds.), Medical Men and Their Work. Chicago, Illinois:
            Aldine-Atherton.
D'Arcy, Carl, and Joan Brockman
    1976    "Changing public recognition of psychiatric symptoms? Blackfoot revisited."
            Journal of Health and Social Behavior 17:302–310.
Davis, Kingsley
    1938    "Mental hygiene and the class structure." Psychiatry 1: 55–65.
Dawson, John
    1964    "Urbanization and mental health in a West African community." Pp. 305–342
            in A. Kiev (ed.), Magic, Faith, and Healing. New York: Free Press.
Deutsch, Albert
    1949    The Mentally Ill in America: A History of Their Care and Treatment from Co-
            lonial Times, 2nd ed. New York: Columbia University Press.
Dinitz, Simon, Mark Lefton, Shirley Angrist, and Benjamin Pasamanick
    1961    "Psychiatric and social attributes as predictors of case outcome in mental
            hospitalization." Social Problems 8:322–328.
Dohrenwend, Bruce P., and Edwin Chin-Shong
    1967    "Social status and attitudes toward psychological disorder: The problem of
            tolerance of deviance." American Sociological Review 38:327–339.
Dohrenwend, Bruce P., and Barbara Snell Dohrenwend
    1969    Social Status and Psychological Disorder: A Causal Inquiry. New York: Wiley
            (Interscience).
Dohrenwend, Bruce P., Barbara Snell Dohrenwend, Madelyn Schwartz Gould, Bruce Link,
Richard Neugebauer, and Robin Wunsch-Hitzig
    1980    Mental Illness in the United States: Epidemiological Estimates. New York:
            Praeger.
Doi, L. Takeo
    1976    "Psychotherapy as 'hide and seek.' " Pp. 273–277 in W. Lebra (ed.), Culture-
            Bound Syndromes, Ethnopsychiatry, and Alternate Therapies. Honolulu: Univ.
            Press of Hawaii.
Douglas, Mary
    1973    Natural Symbols: Explorations in Cosmology. New York: Vintage.
Dumont, Louis
    1976    From Mandeville to Marx. Chicago, Illinois: Univ. of Chicago Press.
Durkheim, Emile
    [1893]  The Division of Labor in Society. New York: Free Press.
    1964
    [1897]  Suicide: A Study in Sociology. New York: Free Press.
    1951
Eaton, Joseph W., and Robert J. Weil
    1955    Culture and Mental Disorders. Gelencoe, Illinois: Free Press.

# References

Edgerton, Robert B.
1966    "Conceptions of psychosis in four East African societies." American Anthropologist 68:408–425.
1969    "On the 'recognition' of mental illness." Pp. 49–72 in S. C. Plog and R. B. Edgerton (eds.), Changing Perspectives in Mental Illness. New York: Holt.

Elinson, Jack, Elena Padilla, and Marvin E. Perkins
1967    Public Image of Mental Health Services. New York: Mental Health Materials Center.

El-Islam, M. Fakhr, and Henda El-Deeb
1969    "The educational and occupational correlates of psychiatric disorder: A study at an Arab psychiatric clinic." The International Journal of Social Psychiatry 15:288–293.

Ellenberger, Henri F.
1970    The Discovery of the Unconscious: The History and Evolution of Dynamic Psychiatry. New York: Basic Books.

Entralgo, Pedro Lain
1970    The Therapy of the Word in Classical Antiquity. New Haven, Connecticut: Yale Univ. Press.

Feinberg, Joel
1970    "What is so special about mental illness?" Pp. 272–292 in Doing and Deserving. Princeton, New Jersey: Princeton Univ. Press.

Felstiner, William L. F.
1975    "Influences of social organization on dispute processing." Law and Society Review 9:63–94.

Field, M. J.
1960    Search for Security: An Ethno-Psychiatric Study of Rural Ghana. New York: Norton.

Field, Mark G.
1957    Doctor and Patient in Soviet Russia. Cambridge, Massachusetts: Harvard Univ. Press.
1960    "Approaches to mental illness in Soviet society: Some comparisons and conjectures." Social Problems 7:277–297.

Fisher, Joel
1969    "Negroes and whites and rates of mental illness: Reconsideration of a myth." Psychiatry 32:428–446.

Flew, Antony
1973    Crime or Disease? New York: Harper.

Foucault, Michel
1965    Madness and Civilization: A History of Insanity in the Age of Reason. New York: Pantheon.
1976    Mental Illness and Psychology. New York: Harper.

Fox, J. Robin
1964    Witchcraft and clanship in Cochiti therapy. Pp. 174–202 in A. Kiev (ed.), Magic, Faith, and Healing. New York: Free Press.

Fox, Richard W.
1978    So Far Disordered in Mind: Insanity in California 1870–1930. Berkeley: Univ. of California Press.

Frank, Jerome D.
1973    Persuasion and Healing, 2nd ed. Baltimore, Maryland: Johns Hopkins Press.

Freeman, Howard E., and Ozzie G. Simmons
1963    The Mental Patient Comes Home. New York: Wiley.
Freidson, Eliot
1970    Profession of Medicine: A Study of the Sociology of Applied Knowledge. New York: Harper.
Freud, Sigmund
[1924]  A General Introduction to Psychoanalysis. New York: Washington Square
1960    Press.
1928    The Future of an Illusion. New York: Liveright.
[1930]  Civilization and Its Discontents. New York: Norton.
1962
Fried, Marc
1964    "Effects of social change on mental health." American Journal of Orthopsychiatry 34:3–28.
Fromm-Reichmann, Frieda
1949    "Recent advances in psychoanalytic therapy." Pp. 122–129 in P. Mullahy (ed.), A Study of Interpersonal Relations. New York: Hermitage Press.
Gans, Herbert J.
1962    The Urban Villagers: Group and Class in the Life of Italian-Americans. New York: Free Press.
Geertz, Clifford
1973    The Interpretation of Cultures. New York: Basic Books.
Gelfand, Michael
1964    "Psychiatric disorders as recognized by the Shona." Pp. 156–173 in A. Kiev (ed.), Magic, Faith, and Healing. New York: Free Press.
Gibbs, Jack P.
1962    "Rates of mental hospitalization: A study of societal reaction to deviant behavior." American Sociological Review 27:782–792.
1972a   Social Control. Warner Modular Publications, Module 1:1–17.
1972b   "Issues in defining deviant behavior." Pp. 39–68 in R. A. Scott and J. D. Douglas (eds.), Theoretical Perspectives on Deviance. New York: Basic Books.
1977    "Social control, deterrence, and perspectives on social order." Social Forces 56:408–423.
Gillis, L. S., and M. Keet
1965    "Factors underlying the retention in the community of chronic unhospitalized schizophrenics." British Journal of Psychiatry 111:1057–1067.
Gluckman, Max
1967    The Judicial Process among the Barotse of Northern Rhodesia, 2nd ed. Manchester: Manchester Univ. Press.
Goffman, Erving
1961    Asylums: Essays on the Social Situation of Mental Patients and Other Inmates. Garden City, New York: Doubleday.
1971    Relations in Public: Microstudies of the Public Order. New York: Harper.
Gove, Walter R.
1970    "Societal reaction as an explanation of mental illness: An evaluation." American Sociological Review 35:873–884.
1972    "The relationship between sex roles, marital roles, and mental illness." Social Forces 51:34–44.
1975    "Labelling and mental illness: A critique." Pp. 35–81 in W. R. Gove (ed.), The Labelling of Deviance: Evaluating a Perspective. New York: Halsted Press.

# References

Gove, Walter R., and Patrick Howell
    1974    "Individual resources and mental hospitalization: A comparison and evaluation of the societal reaction and psychiatric perspectives." American Sociological Review 39:86–100.
Gove, Walter R., and Jeanette Tudor
    1973    "Adult sex roles and mental illness." American Journal of Sociology 78:812–835.
Grad, Jacqueline, and Peter Sainsbury
    1963    Mental illness and the family. Lancet 7280 (March 9):544–547.
Greenley, James R.
    1972    "The psychiatric patient's family and length of hospitalization." Journal of Health and Social Behavior 13:25–37.
Greenley, James R., and David Mechanic
    1976    "Social selection seeking help for psychological problems." Journal of Health and Social Behavior 17:249–262.
Grob, Gerald N.
    1973    Mental Institutions in America: Social Policy to 1875. New York: Free Press.
    1977    "Rediscovering asylums: The unhistorical history of the mental hospital." Hastings Center Report 7:33–41.
Gurin, Gerald, Joseph Veroff, and Sheila Feld
    1960    Americans View Their Mental Health. New York: Basic Books.
Guthrie, G., and G. Noll
    1966    "Powwow in Pennsylvania." Pennsylvania Medicine 69:37–40.
Habermas, Jurgen
    1971    Knowledge and Human Interests. Boston: Beacon Press.
Hale, Nathan G., Jr.
    1971    Freud and the Americans: The Beginnings of Psychoanalysis in the United States, 1876–1917. London and New York: Oxford Univ. Press.
Halleck, Seymour L.
    1971    The Politics of Therapy. New York: Science House.
Hammer, Muriel
    1963–1964    "Influence of small social networks as factors in mental hospital admission." Human Organization 22:243–251.
Haney, C. Allen and Robert Michielutte
    1968    "Selective factors operating in the adjudication of incompetency." Journal of Health and Social Behavior 9: 233–242.
Henley, Nancy
    1977    Body Politics: Power, Sex, and Nonverbal Communication. Englewood Cliffs, New Jersey: Prentice-Hall.
Hes, Jozef, Ph.
    1966–1967    "From native healer to modern psychiatrists: Afro-Asian immigrants to Israel and their attitudes towards psychiatric facilities." International Journal of Social Psychiatry 8:21–27.
Hollingshead, August B., and Frederick C. Redlich
    1958    Social Class and Mental Illness. New York: Wiley.
Horwitz, Allan
    1973    "Social organization and mental disorder: A Jamaican case study." Paper presented at the meeting of the American Sociological Association, New York, August 1973.
    1977a    "Social networks and pathways into psychiatric treatment." Social Forces 56: 86–106.

1977b    "The pathways into psychiatric treatment: Some differences between men and women." Journal of Health and Social Behavior 18:169-178.

1978    "Family, kin, and friend networks in psychiatric help-seeking." Social Science and Medicine 12:297-304.

Hurvitz, Nathan
1974    "Peer self-help psychotherapy groups: Psychotherapy without psychotherapists." Pp. 84-138 in P. Roman and H. M. Trice (eds.), The Sociology of Psychotherapy. New York: Jason Aronson.

Imber, Stanley D., Earl H. Nash, Jr., and Anthony R. Stone
1955    "Social class and duration of psychotherapy." Journal of Clinical Psychology 11:218-284.

Janik, Allan, and Stephen Toulmin
1973    Wittgenstein's Vienna. New York: Simon & Schuster.

Jayasundera, M. G.
1969    "Mental health surveys in Ceylon." Pp. 54-65 in W. Caudill and T.-Y. Lin (eds.), Mental Health Research in Asia and the Pacific. Honolulu, Hawaii: East-West Center Press.

Jewell, Donald P.
1952    "A case of a 'psychotic' Navaho Indian male." Human Organization 11:32-36.

Johnson, Rita Volkman, and Donald Cressey
1963    "Differential association and the rehabilitation of drug addicts." American Journal of Sociology 69:129-142.

Joint Commission on Mental Illness and Health
1961    Action for Mental Health. New York: Science Editions.

Kadushin, Charles
1958    "Individual decisions to undertake psychotherapy." Administrative Science Quarterly 3:379-411.

1969    Why People Go to Psychiatrists. New York: Atherton.

Kahne, Merton J., and Charlotte Green Schwartz
1978    "Negotiating trouble: The social construction and management of trouble in a college psychiatric context." Social Problems 25:461-475.

Kanter, Rosabeth Moss
1972    Commitment and Community: Communes and Utopias in Sociological Perspective. Cambridge, Massachusetts: Harvard Univ. Press.

Kaplan, Bert, and Dale Johnson
1964    "The social meaning of Navaho psychopathology and psychotherapy." Pp. 203-230 in A. Kiev (ed.), Magic, Faith, and Healing. New York: Free Press.

Kessler, Ronald C., Roger L. Brown, and Clifford L. Broman
1981    "Sex differences in psychiatric help-seeking: Evidence from four large-scale surveys." Journal of Health and Social Behavior 22: 49-64.

Kessler, Ronald C., and Paul D. Cleary
1980    "Social class and psychological distress." American Sociological Review 45: 463-478.

Kiev, Ari
1964    "The study of folk psychiatry." Pp. 3-35 in A. Kiev (ed.), Magic, Faith, and Healing. New York: Free Press.

1972    Transcultural Psychiatry. New York: Free Press.

Kinzie, David, Jin-Inn Teoh, and Eng-Seong Tan
1976    "Native healers in Malaysia." Pp. 130-146 in W. Lebra (ed.), Culture-Bound Syndromes, Ethnopsychiatry, and Alternate Therapies. Honolulu: Univ. Press of Hawaii.

# References

Kitano, Harry H. L.
1969    "Japanese-American mental illness." Pp. 257–284 in S. C. Plog and R. B. Edgerton (eds.), Changing Perspectives in Mental Illness. New York: Holt.

Kittrie, Nicholas
1971    The Right to Be Different: Deviance and Enforced Therapy. Baltimore, Maryland: Johns Hopkins Press.

Kohn, Melvin L.
1959    "Social class and parental values." American Journal of Sociology 64:337–351.

Kramer, Morton
1977    Psychiatric Services and the Changing Institutional Scene, 1950–1985. Washington, D.C.: National Institute of Mental Health.

Kraus, Karl
1977    No Compromise: Selected Writings of Karl Kraus. Frederick Ungar (ed.). New York: Frederick Ungar.

Krohn, Marvin D. and Ronald L. Akers
1977    "An alternative view of the labelling versus psychiatric perspectives on societal reaction to mental illness." Social Forces 56:341–361.

Kulka, Richard A., Joseph Veroff, and Elizabeth Douvan
1979    "Social class and the use of professional help for personal problems: 1957 and 1976." Journal of Health and Social Behavior 20:2–17.

Kutner, Luis
1962    "The illusion of due process in commitment proceedings." Northwestern University Law Review 57:383–399.

LaBarre, Weston
1964    "Confession as cathartic therapy in American Indian tribes." Pp. 36–49 in A. Kiev (ed.), Magic, Faith, and Healing. New York: Free Press.

Ladurie, LeRoy E.
1978    Montaillou. New York: Braziller.

Laing, Ronald D.
1967    The Politics of Experience. New York: Pantheon.

Lamb, H. Richard, and Victor Goertzel
1971    "Discharged mental patients—Are they really in the community?" Archives of General Psychiatry 24:29–34.

Lambo, T. Adeoye
1964    "Patterns of psychiatric care in developing African countries." Pp. 443–453 in A. Kiev (ed.), Magic, Faith, and Healing. New York: Free Press.

Langner, Thomas S.
1962    "A twenty-two item screening score of psychiatric symptoms indicating impairment." Journal of Health and Human Behavior 3:269–276.

LaPiere, Richard T.
1954    A Theory of Social Control. New York: McGraw-Hill.

Lasch, Christopher
1978    The Culture of Narcissism: American Life in an Age of Diminishing Expectations. New York: Norton.

Leifer, Ronald
1969    In the Name of Mental Health: The Social Functions of Psychiatry. New York: Science House.

Leighton, Alexander H.
1959    My Name is Legion. New York: Basic Books.
1969    "Cultural relativity and the identification of psychiatric disorders." Pp. 448–

462 in W. Caudill and T.-Y. Lin (eds.), Mental Health Research in Asia and the Pacific. Honolulu, Hawaii: East-West Center Press.

Leighton, Alexander H., T. Adeoye Lambo, Charles C. Hughes, Dorothea C. Leighton, Jane M. Murphy, and David B. Macklin
  1963    Psychiatric Disorder among the Yoruba. Ithaca, New York: Cornell Univ. Press.

Leighton, Dorothea C., John S. Harding, David B. Macklin, Allister M. Macmillan, and Alexander H. Leighton
  1963    The Character of Danger: Psychiatric Symptoms in Selected Communities. New York: Basic Books.

Lemert, Edwin M.
  1946    "Legal commitment and social control." Sociology and Social Research 30: 370–378.
  1962    "Paranoia and the dynamics of exclusion." Sociometry 25:2–20.

Lemkau, Paul V., and Guido M. Crocetti
  1962    "An urban population's opinions and knowledge about mental illness." American Journal of Psychiatry 118:692–700.

Lemkau, Paul V., and Carlo de Santis
  1950    "A survey of Italian psychiatry, 1949." American Journal of Psychiatry 107: 401–408.

Levi-Strauss, Claude
  1964    "The effectiveness of symbols." Pp. 181–201 in Structural Anthropology. Garden City, New York: Doubleday Anchor.

Levy, Leo, and Louis Rowitz
  1973    The Ecology of Mental Disorder. New York: Behavioral Publications.

Lewis, Sinclair
  1920    Main Street. New York: Harcourt.

Li, Yih-Yuan
  1976    "Shamanism in Taiwan: An anthropological inquiry." Pp. 179–188 in W. Lebra (ed.), Culture-Bound Syndromes, Ethnopsychiatry, and Alternate Therapies. Honolulu: Univ. Press of Hawaii.

Link, Bruce, and Barry Milcarek
  1980    "Selection factors in the dispensation of therapy: The Matthew effect in the allocation of mental health resources." Journal of Health and Social Behavior 21:279–290.

Linn, Erwin
  1961    "Agents, timing, and events leading to mental hospitalization." Human Organization 20:92–98.

Linn, Lawrence S.
  1967    "Social characteristics and social interaction in the utilization of a psychiatric outpatient clinic." Journal of Health and Social Behavior 8:3–14.

Linsky, Arnold S.
  1970a    "Community homogeneity and exclusion of the mentally ill: Reaction and consensus about deviance." Journal of Health and Social Behavior 11:304–311.
  1970b    "Who shall be excluded: The influence of personal attributes in community reaction to the mentally ill." Social Psychiatry 5:166–171.

Lofland, John (with the assistance of Lyn H. Lofland)
  1969    Deviance and Identity. Englewood Cliffs, New Jersey: Prentice-Hall.

# References

Lowenthal, Marjorie Fiske
    1964    Lives in Distress: The Paths of the Elderly to the Psychiatric Ward. New York: Basic Books.

Lu, Yi-Chuang
    1978    "The collective approach to psychiatric practice in the People's Republic of China." Social Problems 26:2–15.

Macaulay, Stewart
    1963    "Non-contractual relations in business: A preliminary study." American Sociological Review 28:55–67.

McHugh, Peter
    1970    "A common sense conception of deviance." Pp. 61–88 in J. D. Douglas (ed.), Deviance and Respectability: The Social Construction of Moral Meanings. New York: Basic Books.

McNeil, John T.
    1951    A History of the Cure of Souls. New York: Harper.

Madsen, William
    1964    "Value conflicts and folk psychotherapy in South Texas." Pp. 420–440 in A. Kiev (ed.), Magic, Faith, and Healing. New York: Free Press.

Maine, Henry Sumner
    [1861]    Ancient Law: Its Connection with the Early History of Society and Its Relation
    1963    to Modern Ideas. Boston: Beacon Press.

Maisel, Robert
    1970    "Decision-making in a commitment court." Psychiatry 33:352–361.

Marmor, Judd
    1975    Psychiatrists and Their Patients: A National Study of Private Office Practice. Washington, D.C.: American Psychiatric Association.

Marx, John H., and Joseph E. Seldin
    1973    "Crossroads of crisis: I. Therapeutic sources and quasi-therapeutic functions of post-industrial communes." Journal of Health and Social Behavior 14:39–50.

Marx, John H., and S. Lee Spray
    1969    "Religious biographies and professional characteristics of psychotherapists." Journal of Health and Social Behavior 10:275–288.
    1972    "Psychotherapeutic 'birds of a feather': social class status and religio-cultural value homophily in the mental health field." Journal of Health and Social Behavior 13:413–428.

Mechanic, David
    1962    "Some factors in identifying and defining mental illness." Mental Hygiene 46:66–74.
    1978    Medical Sociology, 2nd ed. New York: Free Press.
    1980    Mental Health and Social Policy, 2nd ed. Englewood Cliffs, New Jersey: Prentice-Hall.

Medvedev, Zhores and Roy Medvedev
    1971    A Question of Madness. New York: Macmillan

Mehryar, Amir, and Farrokh Khyjavi
    1974–1975    "Some implications of a community mental health model for developing countries." International Journal of Social Psychiatry 21:45–52.

Mendel, Werner, and Samuel Rapport
    1969    "Determinants of the decision for psychiatric hospitalization." Archives of General Psychiatry 20:321–328.

**197**

Menninger, Karl
  1963   The Vital Balance: The Life Process in Mental Health and Illness. New York: Viking Press.
Messing, Simon D.
  1959   "Group therapy and social status in the Zar cult of Ethiopia." Pp. 319–332 in M. Opler (ed.), Culture and Mental Health. New York: Macmillan.
Michael, S. T.
  1967   "The family with problems, social class, and the psychiatrist." The International Journal of Social Psychiatry 8:93–100.
Milazzo-Sayre, Laura
  1978   "Statistical note 145." Washington, D.C.: National Institute of Mental Health.
Miller, Dorothy, and Michael Schwartz
  1966   "County lunacy commission hearings: Some observations of commitments to a state mental hospital." Social Problems 14:26–35.
Mills, C. Wright
  1942   "The professional ideology of social pathologists." American Journal of Sociology 49:165–180.
Mishler, Elliott, and Nancy Waxler
  1963   "Decision processes in psychiatric hospitalization." American Sociological Review 28:576–587.
Murphy, Jane M.
  1964   "Psychotherapeutic aspects of shamanism on St. Lawrence Island, Alaska." Pp. 53–83 in A. Kiev (ed.), Magic, Faith, and Healing. New York: Free Press.
  1976   "Psychiatric labeling in cross-cultural perspectives." Science 191:1019–1028.
Murphy, Jane M., and Alexander H. Leighton (eds.)
  1965   Approaches to Cross Cultural Psychiatry. Ithaca, New York: Cornell Univ. Press.
Murray, Robin M.
  1979   "A reappraisal of American psychiatry." Lancet 8110 (February 3):255–258.
Myers, Jerome K., and Bertram H. Roberts
  1959   Family and Class Dynamics in Mental Illness. New York: Wiley.
Myers, Jerome K., Jacob J. Lindenthal, and Max Pepper
  1971   "Life events and psychiatric impairment." Journal of Nervous and Mental Disease 152:149–157.
Nader, Laura
  1969   "Styles of court procedure: To make the balance." Pp. 69–91 in L. Nader (ed.), Law in Culture and Society. Chicago: Aldine.
Newman, Philip
  1964   " 'Wild man' behavior in a New Guinea highlands community." American Anthropologist 66:1–19.
Nunnally, Jum C., Jr.
  1961   Popular Conceptions of Mental Health. New York: Holt.
Obeysekere, Gananath
  1970   "The idiom of demonic possession: A case study." Social Science and Medicine 4:97–111.
Osborne, Oliver H.
  1969   "The Yoruba village as a therapeutic community." Journal of Health and Social Behavior 10:187–200.
Parsons, Talcott
  1942   "Propaganda and social control." Psychiatry 25:551–572.

# References

1951    The Social System. New York: Free Press.
1977    The Evolution of Societies (edited by Jackson Toby). Englewood Cliffs, New Jersey: Prentice-Hall.

Pearlin, Leonard I., and Joyce S. Johnson
1977    "Marital status, life-strains, and depression." American Sociological Review 42:704–715.

Perls, Fritz
1964    Ego Hunger and Aggression. New York: Random House.

Perrucci, Robert
1974    Circle of Madness: On Being Insane and Institutionalized in America. Englewood Cliffs, New Jersey: Prentice-Hall.

Phillips, Derek
1964    "Rejection of the mentally ill: The influence of behavior and sex." American Sociological Review 29:679–687.
1967    "Education, psychiatric sophistication, and the rejection of mentally ill help-seekers." Sociological Quarterly 8:122–132.

Prince, Raymond
1964    "Indigenous Yoruba psychiatry." Pp. 84–120 in A. Kiev (ed.), Magic, Faith, and Healing. New York: Free Press.

Rabkin, Judith
1974    "Public attitudes toward mental illness: A review of the literature." Schizophrenia Bulletin 10:9–32.

Redfield, Robert
1947    "The folk society." American Journal of Sociology 52:293–308.

Redlich, Frederick C., and Daniel X. Freedman
1966    The Theory and Practice of Psychiatry. New York: Basic Books.

Rieff, Philip
1961    Freud: The Mind of the Moralist. Garden City, New York: Doubleday Anchor.
1966    The Triumph of the Therapeutic. New York: Harper.

Rogers, Carl R.
1951    Client-Centered Therapy. Boston: Houghton.
1968    "Interpersonal relationships U.S.A. 2000." Journal of Applied Behavioral Science 4:208–269.

Rogler, Lloyd H., and August B. Hollingshead
1965    Trapped: Families and Schizophrenia. New York: Wiley.

Rogow, Arnold A.
1970    The Psychiatrists. New York: Putnam.

Rose, Charles L.
1959    "Relatives' attitudes and mental hospitalization." Mental Hygiene 43:194–203.

Rosen, George
1968    Madness in Society. New York: Harper.
1970    "Mental disorder, social deviance and culture pattern: Some methodological issues in the historical study of mental illness." Pp. 172–194 in G. Mora and J. L. Brand (eds.), Psychiatry and Its History: Methodological Problems in Research. Springfield, Illinois: Thomas.

Rosenhan, D. L.
1973    "On being sane in insane places." Science 179:250–258.

Ross, Edward Alsworth
1901    Social Control: A Survey of the Foundations of Order. New York: Macmillan.

Rotenberg, Mordechai
1978    Damnation and Deviance: The Protestant Ethic and the Spirit of Failure. New York: Free Press.
Rothman, David J.
1971    The Discovery of the Asylum: Social Order and Disorder in the New Republic. Boston: Little, Brown.
Ruitenbeek, Heinrich M.
1970    The New Group Therapies. New York: Avon.
Rushing, William A.
1971    "Individual resources, societal reaction, and hospital commitment." American Journal of Sociology 77:511–526.
1978    "Status resources, societal reactions, and type of hospital admission." American Sociological Review 43:521–533.
1979    "The functional importance of sex roles and sex-related behavior in societal reactions to residual deviants." Journal of Health and Social Behavior 20: 208–217.
Rushing, William A., and Jack Esco
1977    "Status resources and behavioral deviance as contingencies of societal reaction." Social Forces 56:132–147.
Safilios-Rothschild, Constantina
1968    "Deviance and mental illness in the Greek family." Family Process 7:100–117.
1969    "Psychotherapy and patients' characteristics: A cross-cultural examination." International Journal of Social Psychiatry 15:120–128.
Sakamoto, Y.
1969    "A study of the attitude of Japanese families of schizophrenics toward their ill members." Psychotherapy and Psychosomatics 17:365–374.
Sampson, Harold, Sheldon Messinger, and Robert Towne
1964    Schizophrenic Women: Studies in Marital Crisis. New York: Atherton.
Sarbin, Theodore R.
1969    "The scientific status of the mental illness metaphor." Pp. 9–31 in S. C. Plog and R. B. Edgerton (eds.), Changing Perspectives in Mental Illness. New York: Holt.
Schaffer, Leslie, and Jerome K. Myers
1954    "Psychotherapy and social stratification: An empirical study of practice in a psychiatric out-patient clinic." Psychiatry 17:83–93.
Scheff, Thomas J.
1964    "Social conditions for rationality: How urban and rural courts deal with the mentally ill." American Behavioral Scientist 7:21–24.
1966a   Being Mentally Ill: A Sociological Theory. Chicago: Aldine.
1966b   "Users and non-users of a student psychiatric clinic." Journal of Health and Human Behavior 7:114–121.
1974    "The labelling theory of mental illness." American Sociological Review 39: 444–452.
1975    "On reason and sanity: Some political implications of psychiatric thought." Pp. 12–20 in T. J. Scheff (ed.), Labeling Madness. Englewood Cliffs, New Jersey: Prentice-Hall.
Schofield, William
1964    Psychotherapy: The Purchase of Friendship. Englewood Cliffs, New Jersey: Prentice-Hall.

# References

Schwab, John J., and Mary E. Schwab
    1978    Sociocultural Roots of Mental Illness: An Epidemiologic Survey. New York: Plenum.

Schwartz, Charlotte Green
    1957    "Perspectives on deviance—Wives' definitions of their husbands' mental illness." Psychiatry 20:275–291.

Scull, Andrew T.
    1977    "Madness and segregative control: The rise of the insane asylum." Social Problems 24:337–351.
    1979    Museums of Madness: The Social Organization of Insanity in Nineteenth-Century England. New York: St. Martin's Press.

Segal, Stephen P., Jim Baumohl, and Elise Johnson
    1977    "Falling through the cracks: Mental disorder and social margin in a young vagrant population." Social Problems 24:387–400.

Selby, Henry A.
    1974    Zapotec Deviance: The Convergence of Folk and Modern Sociology. Austin: Univ. of Texas Press.

Sennett, Richard
    1978    The Fall of Public Man: On the Social Psychology of Capitalism. New York: Vintage Books.

Sidel, Ruth
    1975    "Mental diseases in China and their treatment." Pp. 119–134 in T. J. Scheff (ed.), Labeling Madness. Englewood Cliffs, New Jersey: Prentice-Hall.

Siegler, Miriam, and Humphrey Osmond
    1974    Models of Madness, Models of Medicine. New York: Harper.

Silver, Archie A.
    1955    "The home management of children with schizophrenia." American Journal of Psychotherapy 9:196–215.

Simon, Bennett
    1978    Mind and Madness in Ancient Greece: The Classical Roots of Modern Psychiatry. Ithaca, New York: Cornell Univ. Press.

Singer, Benjamin D.
    1967    "Some implications of differential psychiatric treatment of Negro and White patients." Social Science and Medicine 1:77–83.

Smith, Dorothy
    1978    " 'K' is mentally ill." Sociology 12:23–54.

Smith, Kathleen, Muriel Pumphrey, and Julian Hall
    1963    "The 'last straw': The decisive incident resulting in the request for hospitalization in 100 schizophrenic patients." American Journal of Psychiatry 119:228–232.

Spiro, Melford E.
    1950    A psychotic personality in the South Seas. Psychiatry 13:189–204.

Spitzer, Robert L.
    1976    "More on pseudoscience in science and the case for psychiatric diagnosis." Archives of General Psychiatry 33:459–470.

Spitzer, Stephen
    1975    "Punishment and social organization: A study of Durkheim's theory of penal evolution." Law and Society Review 9:613–635.

Srole, Leo, Thomas S. Langner, Stanley T. Michael, Marvin K. Opler, and Thomas A. C. Rennie
  1962    Mental Health in the Metropolis: The Midtown Manhattan Study. New York: McGraw-Hill.
Stanton, Alfred H., and Morris S. Schwartz
  1954    The Mental Hospital. New York: Basic Books.
Star, Shirley A.
  1955    The public's ideas about mental illness. Paper presented at the annual meeting of the National Association for Mental Health, Indianapolis, November 1955.
Stern, Maxine Springer
  1977    "Social class and psychiatric treatment of adults in the mental health center." Journal of Health and Social Behavior 18:317–325.
Suchman, Edward A.
  1965    "Social patterns of illness and medical care." Journal of Health and Human Behavior 6:2–16.
Szasz, Thomas S.
  1961    The Myth of Mental Illness. New York: Harper.
  1963    Law, Liberty, and Psychiatry: An Inquiry into the Social Uses of Mental Health Practices. New York: Macmillan.
  1970    Ideology and Insanity: Essays on the Psychiatric Dehumanization of Man. Garden City, New York: Doubleday.
  1979    The Myth of Psychotherapy. Garden City, New York: Doubleday Anchor.
Teitelbaum, Joel M.
  1976    "Humoral theory and therapy in Tunisia." Pp. 19–23 in J. Westermeyer (ed.), Anthropology and Mental Health. The Hague: Mouton.
Temerlin, Maurice K.
  1968    "Suggestion effects in psychiatric diagnosis." Journal of Nervous and Mental Disease 147:349–358.
Tentler, Thomas N.
  1977    Sin and Confession on the Eve of the Reformation. Princeton, New Jersey: Princeton Univ. Press.
Teoh, Jin-Inn, J. D. Kinzie, and Eng-Seong Tan
  1972–1973    "Referrals to a psychiatric clinic in West Malaysia." International Journal of Social Psychiatry 18:301–307.
Thomas, William Isaac
  1923    The Unadjusted Girl: With Cases and Standpoint for Behavior Analysis. Boston: Little, Brown.
Toby, Jackson
  1973    "The socialization and control of deviant motivation." Pp. 85–100 in D. Glaser (ed.), Handbook of Criminology. Chicago: Rand McNally.
Tonnies, Ferdinand
  [1887]    Community and Society. New York: Harper.
  1963
Torrey, E. Fuller
  1972    The Mind Game: Witchdoctors and Psychiatrists. New York: Emerson Hall.
  1974    The Death of Psychiatry. Radnor, Pennsylvania: Chilton.
Townsend, John Marshall
  1978    Cultural Conceptions and Mental Illness: A Comparison of Germany and America. Chicago, Illinois: Univ. of Chicago Press.

# References

Tseng, Wen-Shing
  1976   "Folk psychotherapy in Taiwan." Pp. 164–178 in W. Lebra (ed.), Culture-Bound Syndromes, Ethnopsychiatry, and Alternate Therapies. Honolulu: Univ. Press of Hawaii.
Tudor, William, Jeannette F. Tudor, and Walter R. Gove
  1977   "The effect of sex role differences on the social control of mental illness." Journal of Health and Social Behavior 18:98–112.
Turner, Victor W.
  1964   "An Ndembu doctor in practice." Pp. 230–264 in A. Kiev (ed.), Magic, Faith, and Healing. New York: Free Press.
  1968   The Drums of Affliction: A Study of Religious Processes Among the Ndembu of Zambia. London and New York: Oxford Univ. Press.
Unger, Roberto Mangabeira
  1975   Knowledge and Politics. New York: Free Press.
Velho, Gilberto
  1976   "Accusations, family mobility, and deviant behavior." Social Problems 23: 268–275.
Vidich, Arthur J., and Joseph Bensman
  1960   Small Town in Mass Society. Garden City, New York: Doubleday Anchor.
Wallace, Anthony F. C.
  1972   "Mental illness, biology, and culture." Pp. 363–402 in F. Hsu (ed.), Psychological Anthropology rev. ed. Cambridge, Massachusetts: Schenkman.
Walton, John K.
  1979   "Lunacy in the Industrial Revolution: A study of asylum admissions in Lancashire, 1848–50." Journal of Social History 13:1–22.
Warheit, George J., Charles E. Holzer III, and Sandra A. Arey
  1975   "Race and mental illness: An epidemiologic update." Journal of Health and Social Behavior 16:243–256.
Waxler, Nancy E.
  1974   "Culture and mental illness: a social labeling perspective." Journal of Nervous and Mental Disease 159:379–395.
  1976   "Social change and psychiatric illness in Ceylon: Traditional and modern conceptions of disease and treatment." Pp. 222–240 in W. Lebra (ed.), Culture-Bound Syndromes, Ethnopsychiatry, and Alternate Therapies. Honolulu: Univ. Press of Hawaii.
Weber, Max
  [1922]   The Theory of Social and Economic Organization, edited by T. Parsons. New
  1964   York: Free Press.
  [1925]   Max Weber on Law in Economy and Society, edited by M. Rheinstein. Cam-
  1954   bridge, Massachusetts: Harvard Univ. Press.
Wenger, Denis and C. Richard Fletcher
  1969   "The effect of legal counsel on admissions to a state mental hospital: A confrontation of professions." Journal of Health and Social Behavior 10:66–72.
Whisson, Michael G.
  1964   "Some aspects of functional disorders among the Kenya Luo." Pp. 283–304 in A. Kiev (ed.), Magic, Faith, and Healing. New York: Free Press.
Whyte, Martin King
  1974   Small Groups and Political Rituals in China. Berkeley: Univ. of California Press.

Wilde, William
  1968    "Decision-making in a psychiatric screening agency." Journal of Health and
          Social Behavior 9:215–221.
Wilkinson, Gregg S.
  1975    "Patient-audience social status and the social construction of psychiatric
          disorders: Toward a differential frame of reference hypothesis." Journal of
          Health and Social Behavior 16:27–38.
Wing, John
  1978    Reasoning about Madness. London: Oxford Univ. Press.
Wood, Edwin, C., John M. Rakusin, and Emanuel Morse
  1960    "Interpersonal aspects of psychiatric hospitalization: I. The admission." Ar-
          chives of General Psychiatry 3:632–641.
Yarrow, Marian Radke, Charlotte Green Schwartz, Harriet S. Murphy, and Leila Calhoun
Deasy
  1955    "The psychological meaning of mental illness in the family." The Journal of
          Social Issues 11:12–24.
Zablocki, Benjamin
  1971    The Joyful Community. Baltimore, Maryland: Penguin.
Zilboorg, Gregory
  1941    A History of Medical Psychology. New York: Norton.

# Subject Index

**A**

Aborigines
  perception of mental illness, 15
  reaction to mental illness in, 92
  therapeutic control among, 157
Adjudicatory social control, 124–125
Alcoholics Anonymous (AA), 180–181
Amish, therapeutic control in, 163
Aqurohuaca Indians, confession
    among, 152
Asylums, capitalism and development of,
    101–102, *see also* Institutions
Australian aborigines, *see* Aborigines

**B**

Behavior, incomprehensibility of, 14–21
Behaviorist position, treatment of mental
    illness and, 86, 88
Blacks
  psychiatric treatment of, 130, 131–132
  psychotherapy sought by, 137
Brazil
  psychotherapy sought by, 138
  social class recognition of mental illness
    in, 67

**C**

Capitalism, asylum development and,
    101–102
Ceylon
  normalization of symptoms of mental
    illness and, 94–95
  therapeutic control in, 154, 156
Children
  parents' recognition of mental illness
    in, 38
  recognition of mental illness in parents,
    38–39
Children of God, 181
China
  psychiatry in, 159–161
  reaction to mentally ill in, 97–98
Chol Maya, confession among, 152
Christianity, cure of souls in, 162
Cohesive groups, reaction to mental illness
    and, 90, *see also* Reaction, to
    mental illness
  breakdown of, 100–103
Committment proceedings, psychiatric
    professional's recognition of mental
    illness and, 54

Communal groups, *see also* Psychotherapy;
     specific groups
   modern, 177–178, 179, 180–182
   reaction to mental illness by, 89–90, 91,
     97–99, *see also* Reaction, to mental
     illness
Community, psychotherapy in, 165
Community care, mental illness and,
     107–109
Community integration, 107–109
   social marginality and, 109–112
Conciliatory social control, 123, 124–125
Conduct, social control of, 123–124
Confession
   breach of taboo and, 152
   tribal therapeutic control and, 154–155
Crime, as deviant behavior, 26–27
Cultural distance, *see* Social distance,
     recognition of mental illness and
Cultural relativism, mental illness and,
     21–24

**D**

Developing nations, social class labeling of
     mental illness in, 67–68
Deviance, mental illness as, 26–28
Disease, mental illness as, 25–26
Divorce, exclusion ratio of, 11
Dobuans, mental illness perceived by, 21

**E**

East African tribesmen
   mental illness accepted by family
     members of, 41
   mental illness perceived by, 15, 19,
     22–23
   mental illness recognized by, 31–32
     by children in parents, 39
     by parents in children, 38
     among strangers, 45
Eccentricities, mental illness perceived
     with, 19–20
Education
   institutionalization and, 116
   mental illness labeling and, 70–71, 73,
     74
Egypt
   psychotherapy sought by, 138
   social class recognition of mental illness
     in, 67
   Zar cult in, 150, 155

Encounter groups, 176
Esalen Institute, 177, 179
Eskimos
   breach of taboo in, 151
   mental illness perceived by, 15, 25
   normalization of symptoms of mental
     illness, 95
   soul loss and mental illness in, 149
Ethiopia, Zar cult in, 150, 155
Ethnic groups, *see also* specific groups
   exclusion reaction towards, 112–114
   as labelers of mental illness, 73
   psychotherapy sought by, 137–138
   reaction to mental illness among
     American urban, 98–99
   recognition of mental illness in
     unconventional, 48–49
Europe, medieval, *see* Medieval Europe
Evolutionary view, 144–145
Exclusion–inclusion continuum, reaction to
     mental illness and, 85–86, *see also*
     Exclusion reaction; Inclusion
     reaction
Exclusion reaction
   blacks and, 114
   breakdown of cohesive communities and,
     100–103
   community care and, 107–109
   to ethnic groups, 112–113
   to immigrants, 112
   males and, 117–118
   reaction of family to mental illness
     and, 106
   social marginality and, 109–112
   social power and, 115–117
   unmarrieds and, 116
Exorcism, tribal groups and, 150

**F**

Family
   reaction to mental illness in, 103–107
     breakdown and, 105–106, 107
   recognition of mental illness in, 36–42,
     46–47
     acceptance of, 41–42
     denial of, 40–41
     distant relations and, 42–44
     initial, 40–41
     parents and children, 38–39
     response to affected individuals and,
       39–40

spouses, 36–38, 39–40, 76–77
variation in, 39–40
Friends, recognition of mental illness
among, 43
Freudian theory (psychoanalysis), 168, *see
also* Psychotherapy
aims of, 171–172, 174–175
nature of, 169–175
significance of, 87, 144, 169
social context of development of, 169
style, 172–173
techniques of, 172
therapist–client relationship, 172–174
appeal of, 175
decline of, 175–176

**G**
Gender
labeling mental illness and, 75–78
reaction to mental illness and, 117–118
Gestalt therapy, 176
Greece
ancient
psychotherapy and social class and,
133–134
reaction to mental illness, 100, 104
social marginality and, 110
mental illness perceived in, 19–20
mental illness stereotyped in, 18
psychotherapy and social class in, 132–
133
recognition of mental illness among
family, 37–38.
women as labelers of mental illness in,
77
Group cohesiveness, reaction to mental
illness and, 90, *see also* Reaction, to
mental illness
breakdown of, 100–103
Group therapy, 177–178, 179, 180–182
Gururumba, reaction to mental illness of,
94

**H**
Hari Krishnas, 181
Hasidic Jewish groups, therapeutic cures
of, 163
Hospitalization, breakdown of family
groups and, 105–106, *see also*
Asylums; Institutions

Humanistic approach, Rogers and,
176, 178
Humanistic pursuits, mental illness labeling
and, 71–72, 73
Husbands
recognition of mental illness of wife,
37–38, 39–40
wife's recognition of mental illness of,
36–37, 39–40, 76–77
Hutterites
reaction to mental illness, 98
social control in, 163–164
Hypnosis, social class and application of,
135–136

**I**
Ifaluk, reaction to mental illness in, 93
Immigrants
exclusion reaction to, 112
institutionalization of, 112–113
psychiatric treatment of, 131
recognition of mental illness among,
48–49
Incas, confession among, 152
Inclusion reaction
communal groups, 97–99
family reaction to mental illness,
103–107
social power and, 116–117
tribal societies, 91–97
Income, mental illness labeling and, 70–71
Incomprehensibility, of mental illness,
14–21
India
mental illness labeling in, 81
psychotherapy sought by, 138
social class recognition of mental illness
in, 67
Individualistic groups, reaction to mental
illness and, 89–90, 91, *see also*
Psychotherapy; Reaction, to mental
illness
Indoctrinatory social control, 125–126
In-laws, recognition of mental illness
among, 43
Institutions, *see also* Asylums; Hospitals
blacks in, 114
capitalism and, 115
education and, 116
farm workers, 111
gender and, 117–118

Institutions (*cont.*)
  immigrants committed to, 112–113
  poor lower class and, 115–116
  release from, 108
  social marginality and, 110, 111
  unmarried, 111–112
Intellectuals, mental illness labeling and,
    72, 74
Iran, recognition of mental illness among
    family members in, 38
Israel
  ancient
    social marginality and, 110
    social power and, 115
  psychotherapy sought by, 138
Italian-Americans
  reaction to mental illness, 98
  therapeutic control and, 164
Italians, reaction to mental illness, 98–99

J
Jamaica
  recognition of mental illness among
    strangers, 45
  social class recognition of mental illness
    in, 67
Japan
  exorcism in, 150–151
  parent's recognition of mental illness
    in children, 38
  psychotherapy in, 161–162
Japanese-Americans, reaction to mental
    illness of, 99
Jews
  as clients of psychiatrists, 129
  as labelers of mental illness, 73
  psychiatrists and, 128
  psychotherapy for Moroccan and
    Yemenite, 138

K
Kwakutl, mental illness perceived by, 21

L
Labelers, of mental illness, 61–63, *see also*
    Perception, of mental illness
  culture and, 70–75
    education and, 70–71, 73, 74
    humanistic pursuits and, 71–72, 73
    income and, 70–71

intellectuals and, 72, 74
    psychiatric professionals, 72–73
  direction in social space and, 62
  gender and, 75–78
  social class and, 63–70
    direction in social space, 68–70
    location of social space and, 67–68
    reasons for, 74
  social evolution and, 78–83
    cultural distance and, 78–79, 81–82
    psychiatric professional influence and,
      78–79, 80–81, 82
    social distance and, 78–79, 80, 82
  social location of labelers and range of
      labeling, 61–62
Labeling theory, of mental illness, 5–10
Laingian therapy, 178
Lower class
  institutionalization of, 115–116
  as labelers of mental illness, 64–70, 73,
      74–75
  psychotherapy and, 132–137, 138–140
Luo, therapeutic control among, 157

M
Malaysia
  social class recognition of mental illness
      in, 67
  therapeutic control in, 159
Mao Zedong
  psychiatry and, 159–161
  reaction to mentally ill and, 97–98
Marginality
  exclusion reaction and, 109–112
  social class and, 116
  women and, 118
Medieval England, symptoms of mental
      illness in, 14–15
Medieval Europe
  reaction to mental illness, 100–101
  social marginality and, 110
Men
  exclusion reaction to, 117–118
  single, 112
  as labelers of mental illness, 75–78
Mende, therapeutic control among, 155
Mental illness, *see also* Labelers, of mental
      illness; Perception of mental illness;
      Reaction, to mental illness;
      Recognition of mental illness

labeling perspective, 5–10
psychiatric perspective, 3–5, 6, 7, 8, 9
as residual rule-breaking, 4, 5
Mesmer, Franz Anton, 168
Mexican-Americans
  psychotherapy among, 137, 164–165
  reaction to mental illness, 99
Middle class, as labelers of mental illness, 66
Migrant farm workers, exclusion ratio for, 111
Military psychiatrist, recognition of mental illness by, 56–57
Morality, recognition of mental illness in departure from, 49
Moroccan Jews, psychotherapy sought by, 138

### N
Navaho Indians
  reaction to mental illness, 92
  therapeutic control among, 156
Ndembu
  therapeutic control among, 156
  witchcraft among, 152–153
Normalization, of mental illness symptoms, see Reaction, to mental illness
Nuclear family, see Family

### O
Object intrusion, tribal group psychotherapy and, 150–151

### P
Parents
  children's recognition of mental illness in, 38–39
  recognition of mental illness in children, 38
Pennsylvania German religious sects, therapeutic cures and, 163
Perception of mental illness, 13–14, 28
  as deviance, 26–28
  as disease, 25–26
  incomprehensibility of, 14–21
  relativist view, 21–24
  universal theory, 24
Perls, Fritz, 176
Personality, social control of, 126, see also Psychotherapy

Physical illness
  crime compared with, 26–27
  mental illness compared with, 25–26
Plains Indians, therapeutic control among, 156
Political values, recognition of mental illness in divergent, 50–51
Power, reaction to mental illness and, 115–117
Predictability, mental illness stereotype and, 18–19
Progressive view, treatment to mentally ill and, 87, 88, 144
Protestant ethic, deviance from and recognition of mental illness, 48
Psychiatric professionals, see also Psychotherapy
  culture of, 128
  of patients, 127–128
  labeling of mental illness and, 72–73, 129–130
  cultural distance and, 73
  social evolution and, 78–79, 80–81, 82
  recognition of mental illness and, 52–57
Psychiatry, 3–5, 6, 7, 8, 9
  evolution of, 144–145
Psychoanalysis, see Freudian theory
Psychotherapy, 121
  aim of, 122
  application of, 128
    cultural distance and, 128–138
    perceived severity of mental illness and, 138–140
    social class and, 132–138
    therapeutic relationship, 128–129, 137
  clients, 138–140
  communal style of, 143–146, 158–165, see also specific groups
    modern, 177–178, 179, 180–182
  definition, 124, 126–127
  evolutionary view of, 144–145
  individualistic styles of, 147, 148, 167–185
    development of, 168–175, see also Freudian theory
    group therapy, 177–178, 179, 180–182
    modern therapies, 176–180
  progressive view of, 144
  relativist position, 145
  social solidarity and, 146–148

# Subject Index

Psychotherapy (*cont.*)
  tribal groups and, 148–158, *see also* specific groups
    diagnosis and etiology, 149–153
    therapy style, 153–158
Pueblo Indians, therapeutic control among, 156
Puerto Rico
  perception of mental illness, 17
  psychotherapy sought by, 137–138
  reaction of families to mental illness, 103–104
  recognition of mental illness
    among family members, 38
    in-laws', 43
  wives as labelers of husband's mental illness, 76

## R

Range, labeling practices and, 61–62
Reaction, to mental illness, 85–89
  cohesive groups and, 90
    breakdown of, 100–103, 105–106
  exclusion or inclusion continuum and, 85–86
  individual variation in, 109
    cultural distance, 112–114
    gender and, 117–118
    social integration and, 109–112
    social power and, 115–117
  normalization techniques, 90–91
    psychiatric technologies and, 108–109
    tribal societies and, 94–95
  social variation in, 89–91
    in communal groups, 89–90, 91, 97, 99, *see also* specific groups
    community care and, 107–109
    individualistic group, 89–90, 91
    in interpersonal networks, 103–107
    in tribal societies, 91–97, *see also* specific societies
  treatment, 86–88
Recognition of mental illness, 31–33, *see also* Labelers, of mental illness; Social distance, recognition of mental illness and
  as distinct, 32–34
  initial, 32, 33–34
  parties involved with, 34
  psychiatric professionals and, 52–57

Relational distance, *see* Social distance, recognition of mental illness and
Relativist view
  of mental illness, 21–24
  of psychotherapy, 145
Religions, recognition of mental illness in divergent, 51
Religious healing, cure of souls in, 162–164
Repressive social control, 122–123
Residual rule-breaking, mental illness as, 4, 5
Restitutive social control, 122–123
Restricted codes, 153
Rogers, Carl, 176, 178
Rome, ancient
  acceptance of mental illness among family members and, 42
  psychotherapy and social class and, 134
  social marginality and, 110
Rule-breaking, mental illness as residual, 4, 5

## S

Schizophrenia, relativist view of, 21–22
Self-actualization, modern psychotherapy and, 177, 178
Sex, *see* Gender
Shamans, *see* Tribal groups
Shasta Indians, reaction to mental illness, 96
Shona, exorcism in, 150
Siberia
  reaction to mental illness, 96
  soul loss and mental illness in, 150
Small towns, therapeutic control in, 165
Social class, *see also* Labelers, of mental illness
  exclusion ratio and marrieds and, 116
  psychotherapy and, 132–138, 138–140
  reaction to mental illness, 115–117
  recognition of mental illness among, 39
Social control
  adjudicatory, 124–125
  conciliatory, 124–125
  definition, 1
  indoctrinatory, 125–126
  research on, 2–3
  styles of, 122–124
  theory of, 4–5, 8–9, 11
  therapeutic, *see* Psychotherapy

Social distance, recognition of mental
    illness and, 34
  cultural distance, 47–51, *see also*
    Labelers, of mental illness
    communal group and, 89
    individualistic groups and, 89
    psychiatric professionals and, 72–73
    reaction to mental illness and,
      112–114
    social evolution and mental illness
      labeling and, 78–79, 81–82
    therapeutic relationship and, 128–138
    women as labelers and, 77
  relational distance, 35–36
    definition, 34–35
    among family members, 36–42, 46–47
    among more distant relations, 42–44
    among psychiatrists, 56
    reaction to mental illness and,
      109–112
    social class and, 68–70
    social evolution and mental illness
      labeling and, 78–79, 80, 82
    among strangers, 44–47
Social evolution, *see* Labelers, of mental
    illness
Social integration, reaction to mental
    illness, 109–112
Social interaction, incomprehensibility of
    behavior in, 14–21
Social marginality, *see* Marginality
Social solidarity
  psychotherapy style and, 146–148
    tribal, 157
  therapeutic control in communal groups
    and, 159
Social workers, recognition of mental
    illness and, 56
Socrates, mental illness perceived by, 17
Soul loss, tribal group psychotherapy and,
    149–150
South Africa
  reaction of families to mental illness,
    104–105
  recognition of mental illness among
    family members, 38
Soviet Union, psychiatry in, 161
  recognition of mental illness and, 57
Spirit intrusion, tribal group psychotherapy
    and, 150–151

Spouses, recognition of mental illness of,
    36–38, 39–40, 76–77
Stereotypes, of mental illness, 18–19
Strangers, recognition of mental illness
    among, 44–47
Sudan, Zar cult in, 150, 155
Symbolism, tribal therapy and, 153–154
Synanon program, 181

**T**
Taboo, breach of in tribal societies,
    151–152, 153
Taiwan, therapeutic control in, 153–154,
    157
Talmudic scholars, mental illness perceived
    by, 23
Temne
  confession among, 154–155
  witchcraft among, 152–153
Teutonics, unpredictability of mental
    illness and, 19
Therapeutic social control, *see*
    Psychotherapy
Therapy group, 177–178, 179, 180–182
Treatment, *see* Psychotherapy; Reaction,
    to mental illness; Social control
Tribal societies, reaction to mental illness
    in, 91–97, *see also* Psychotherapy;
    specific societies
Tunisia, breach of taboo in, 151

**U**
Universality, of mental illness labels, 24
Unmarried, exclusion ratio and, 116
Unpredictability, of mentally ill, 18–19
Upper class
  as labelers of mental illness, 70, 73,
    74–75
  psychotherapy and, 132–137, 138–140

**V**
Values
  communal groups, 89
  cultural distance and, *see* Social
    distance, recognition of mental
    illness and
  deviance from and recognition of mental
    illness, 47–51
  individualistic group, 89

## Subject Index

Values (*cont.*)
   relational distance and labeling of
      mental illness and, 69
Violence, mental illness perceived with,
   19

## W

Witchcraft, tribal group psychotherapy
   and, 152–153
Wife
   husband's recognition of mental illness
      of, 37–38, 39–40
   recognition of mental illness of husband,
      36–37, 39–40, 76–77
Women
   exclusion ratio and, 117–118
   as labelers of mental illness, 75–78

Workmates, recognition of mental illness
   and, 44

## Y

Yemenite Jews, psychotherapy sought by,
   138
Yoruba
   in-laws' recognition of mental illness, 43
   as labelers of mental illness, 79–80
   mental illness perceived by, 22
   reaction to mental illness, 92–93

## Z

Zapotec Indians
   mental illness perceived by, 17
   normalization of symptoms of mental
      illness by, 95
Zar cults, 150, 155